US–Japan alliance diplomacy 1945–1990 is a pioneering study of a remarkable postwar relationship. Based upon extensive American primary sources, it traces how the US moved from hostility to close friendship in its relations with Japan over the past forty-five years.

Professor Roger Buckley is concerned with three principal issues: the degree of continuity in American policies towards Japan, the role of personalities and the beneficiary of foreign policy arrangements. He addresses these questions by highlighting the main features of each phase of the changing relationship. The author also stresses both the inequalities of US–Japan ties until the 1970s and the present strains that the two nations face in attempting to come to terms with the twin challenges of shifts in relative economic power and a rapidly evolving international environment. The study concludes with an analysis of the overall character of this extraordinary alliance and demonstrates how strengthening ties are now the key to peace and stability in the entire Asian-Pacific region.

In this book, Roger Buckley presents for the first time the historical background to a relationship that attracts widespread interest not only in the US and Japan, but in the entire Asian-Pacific region and beyond. It will therefore be widely read by students and specialists of Japanese and American history, Asian studies and international relations.

CAMBRIDGE STUDIES IN INTERNATIONAL RELATIONS: 21

US–JAPAN ALLIANCE DIPLOMACY 1945–1990

CAMBRIDGE STUDIES IN INTERNATIONAL RELATIONS

US-JAPAN ALLIANCE DIPLOMACY 1945-1990

ROGER BUCKLEY

*Professor of the History of International
Relations, International Christian
University, Tokyo*

CAMBRIDGE
UNIVERSITY PRESS

Published by the Press Syndicate of the University of Cambridge
The Pitt Building, Trumpington Street, Cambridge CB2 1RP
40 West 20th Street, New York, NY 10011–4211, USA
10 Stamford Road, Oakleigh, Melbourne 3166, Australia

First published 1992
Reprinted 1993

Printed in Great Britain by Antony Rowe Ltd, Chippenham, Wiltshire

A catalogue record for this book is available from the British Library

Library of Congress cataloguing in publication data
Buckley, Roger, 1944–
    US–Japan alliance diplomacy, 1945–1990 / Roger Buckley.
        p.   cm. – (Cambridge studies in international relations; 21)
    Includes bibliographical references and index.
    ISBN 0 521 35141 3
    1. United States – Foreign relations – Japan. 2. Japan – Foreign
relations – United States. I. Title. II. Series.
E183.8.J3B78 1992
327.73052 – dc20   91–27006   CIP
ISBN 0 521 35141 3 hardback

In Memoriam
H. B. and M. F. H. B.

There is no relationship more important to peace and prosperity in the world than that between the US and Japan.

President Reagan, 2 January 1985

Yet in diplomacy nothing lasts, nothing is absolute.

John le Carré, *A Perfect Spy*

CONTENTS

PREFACE

This is an unfashionable survey of a fashionable subject. It is a narrative account of American dealings with post-surrender Japan and is intended to provide a degree of background and reassurance to the somewhat more frantic accounts presently on offer. It is no more than an introductory text that sketches out how the United States has handled its relations with contemporary Japan. Its inadequacies will be obvious, not least in its limited coverage of the Japanese version of events, yet a start deserves to be made to assist those students who wish to learn something of American–Japanese ties but soon discover that the subject is largely restricted to specialist monographs. There ought to be more for the curious than yet another account of US–Japan trade confrontation or predictions on the future role of Japan in international society. What follows is diplomatic history. It attempts to redress slightly the intellectual balance whereby political scientists and economists have long had the field to themselves.

International history rests on chronology and is peopled by people. Those impatient with what the proverbial Foreign Office clerk said to his colleague will prefer the sweep of grand theory, yet for such architecture to prove itself earthquake-proof it is first necessary for the historian to provide some building blocks. This study attempts to draw the outlines of a remarkable postwar alliance. Despite the necessary cautions over gaps in the official record, enough is now known, at least on the American side, to describe the skeleton and offer some tentative analysis of the relationship.

Historians, like journalists, are only as good as their sources. The bulk of this work is based on US policy papers towards Japan from the moment of surrender in August 1945 to the end of the Johnson presidency in January 1969. Since official evidence is rarely available for later American administrations, my remarks on the 1970s and 1980s are speculative. Yet the extent of the secondary sources on offer presently is so enormous that the interested reader could spend his days merely attempting to keep up with a fraction of the reportage and commentary. The sheer volume of press coverage from Tokyo is an accurate reflection of Japan's current importance today. The rest of the world has no choice but to take Japan very seriously indeed, and it is undoubtedly the United States that provides the bulk of what can be valuable source material; until its more recent presidential and governmental archives are opened the unofficial hoardings and recollections of participants will have to do.

I have been particularly fortunate during my years in Japan to have enjoyed the friendship of three senior scholars: Professor Ikeda Kiyoshi, formerly of Tohoku University, Professor Hosoya Chihiro of the International University of Japan, and Professor Saito Makoto of International Christian University. Their patience over my bumblings both on Japan and, even worse, in Japanese is here acknowledged. On the British front, I must thank Professor Ian Nish of the LSE for kindnesses extended over an even longer period, while in the United States I have benefited from conversations with Mr Charles Kades, Professor Robert Ferrell, Dean George Packard and Professor Roger Dingman.

Past and present employers in Japan should also be acknowledged for their assistance : the International University of Japan, The School of International Studies in Tokyo, Keio University, the University of Tokyo, and International Christian University. I am grateful too for funding from both the Truman Presidential Library and the School of International Studies in Tokyo, as well as assistance from the staffs of the Public Record Office, the National Archives, the Japanese Diplomatic Record Office, the International House of Japan, the Foreign Correspondents' Club of Japan, the BBC, the Truman, Eisenhower, Kennedy and Johnson Presidential Libraries and custodians of the MacArthur, Dulles and Mansfield collections. Ms Felicia Caponi and Mr Robert Kwan kindly typed up the manuscript, while the editorial staff of CUP worked wonders on a grossly delayed text.

Lastly, I am particularly grateful to my wife Machiko for help on explaining all things Japanese and encouraging what she knew, but never voiced, to be mission impossible.

Mitaka,
March 1991

Japanese names in the text follow Japanese convention with the family name placed before the given name.

INTRODUCTION

Historians work in the dark. For them the evidence is invariably fragmentary and incomplete; the selection and interpretation necessarily subjective. There is never a complete record or unbiased author. The time is always wrong and the word definitive an impossibility. Potential readers deserve to be cautioned on the limitations of this survey of a highly complex and controversial period of contemporary international history. Yet postwar US–Japan relations warrant attention precisely because of their challenge to the student and their impact on current Asian-Pacific affairs.

The approach followed in this monograph has been to employ American sources as the basis of information and analysis. These bulky records have been supplemented by some Japanese, British and other files in the hope that clarity might emerge. For all the inevitable gaps and contradictions the material available is enormous. Politicians, diplomats, soldiers, economists and journalists have followed events carefully and endeavoured to mould the changing relationship to the liking of their governments and professions. Some of the more distinguished (or more combative) of these figures later wrote up their recollections and defended their actions in front of camera and tape recorder. The documentary outpourings will continue, but the questions asked by succeeding scholars of this treasure trove will presumably change. My search has been for answers to perhaps three principal issues: first, since I came to the subject after looking at the Allied occupation and the San Francisco peace settlements, the degree of continuity in American policies towards Japan in the years from the first, heady moments of the summer of 1945 to more recent challenges and rebuffs from an increasingly assertive and successful Japan; next, the role of personality and its influence on the changing US–Japan relationship and, lastly, the constant, nagging factor of foreign policy analysis and the problem of who is benefiting from these arrangements. The suggestion that this can be adequately resolved by reference to mutual advantage is doubtful.

1

The methodology employed has been to approach these issues within a chronological framework and to stress only the more important subjects in each approximate period. A comprehensive survey of the many diverse elements within the US–Japan relationship has hardly been possible and areas, such as cultural diplomacy, have received much shorter shrift than I would have liked. A comprehensive survey of archival sources in the host of nations that regularly commented on American ties with Japan is not my purpose. Whatever the attractions of such an undertaking, funding and time limitations impose their fiat. It has been necessary to rely heavily on American material and to neglect perhaps the roles of other participants. The reader should also be advised of the lacunae that remain within the record. The records of the American government are only open to 1960, though presidential holdings and the papers of certain other figures are accessible for later years; yet these disadvantages are less than those facing users of Japanese material. There are major omissions to the Japanese side of the story. Successive Japanese governments have been reluctant to release what presumably are sensitive portions of its holdings. Pressures from Japanese and foreign scholars to persuade the ministries involved to relent has been largely unsuccessful and it would be foolhardy to expect any imminent change in present policies.[1] Too many of yesterday's politicians and bureaucrats have remained near the centres of power. The era of open markets is closer than that of open government. It, however, has to be noted that other states have also attempted to guide the researcher's hand by retaining sensitive files from the public domain.[2] No government can be said to be overkeen to have the entrails of its diplomacy dumped unceremoniously on the slab for outsiders to cut up.

There are other handicaps ahead for the prospective researcher, aside from acquiring material that may well embarrass the donor. The diplomat-historian Sir George Sansom suggested in correspondence with his American counterpart Hugh Borton in 1953 that 'the Western student should not as a rule devote himself to the kind of original research that can be most effectively done by native scholars. The proper business of the Western scholar is to survey the results of Japanese scholarship, to analyze, to criticize, to correlate and compare, and thus to endeavour to draw from the material which he studies some conclusions, however tentative, which may also be of use in the general study of human experience.'[3] Sansom's remarks can also be reversed, since much Japanese scholarship on the occupation and peace schemes has drawn heavily on Western sources and ideas.[4] At times there has not been much choice, given the gaps in the

2

Japanese record. Yet national perspectives can not be wished away entirely and cross-fertilization still has some way to go. Issues that excite controversy in Japanese academic circles may appear less than engrossing to non-Japanese. Equally, the curiosity of British students in examining the roles of Allied governments in drafting the San Francisco settlements is hard to sustain in front of Japanese audiences as I have discovered to my cost. A twin-track system of scholarship is likely to live on with each side concentrating on what it can do best.

The Western world has few Japanologists and since I am not a member of this crack unit I have necessarily relied upon the works of others to gain an understanding of events with Japan. The fact that I am not an American historian (though hopefully a student of American history) also has to be declared. But passports can prove to be barriers and it may be that distance contributes to objectivity what it loses to cultural detail. There may be advantages behind the presumptuous undertaking of surveying US–Japan relations from without. The rules of racing require that each horse shall be run on its merits. Attempts at nonpartisanship may be easier by those from Europe whose place in Asian affairs has diminished under the twin blows of decolonization and economic malaise. Its claims to political influence and market shares have been effectively silenced by the strengths of the United States and now a confident Japan. By 1990 the European day was long over, while American hegemony was in some doubt and Japan's future still problematic. It remains now to chart how the two principal antagonists of the Pacific war repaired their differences and set about creating an improbable but yet enduring relationship.

1 ROOTS: THE OCCUPATION YEARS

Japan has conquered in 150 days the white man's Far Eastern structure of 150 years.
Lt. Col. Gerald Wilkinson (UK) to General MacArthur, 9 May 1942

American long-range interests require friendly relations with the Orient based on mutual respect, faith and understanding. In the long run it is of paramount, national importance that Japan harbor no lasting resentment.
Brigadier General Bonner F. Fellers (military secretary) to General MacArthur, 2 October 1945

The freedom and democracy of the post-war era were not things I had fought for and won; they were granted to me by powers beyond my own.
Kurosawa Akira, *Something Like an Autobiography*

The summer of 1985 marked the fortieth anniversary of Japan's defeat by the United States in the Pacific war. The occasion revealed much about the current state of US–Japan relations and indeed of international opinion on the performance of contemporary Japan since its surrender in August 1945. The headlines were instructive; the attention by the world's media evidence aplenty of Japan's achievements. The American press tended to recall events surrounding the formal surrender of Imperial Japan and contrast American hegemony then with the challenge it currently faces from an economically assertive rival. Some American commentators clearly begrudged Japan its present success and took pains to remind their readers of the substantial American contribution to the phoenix-like resurgence of today's Japan. Tokyo had become Number One in too many fields for the Japan-bashers to imagine that this could have been anything but the result of American guidance and assistance combined with underhand collusion between Japan's bureaucrats and industrialists. Those, unfortunately, who protested at this stereotype risked falling into the other trap of uncritically praising what was heralded as 'the risen sun'. Neither view of postwar Japan can be easily recommended.

Japanese behaviour on VJ Anniversary Day was equally instructive. While Vice President Bush led the American ceremonies in San Francisco, Prime Minister Nakasone became the first postwar Japanese premier to attend Yasukuni Shrine in Tokyo in his official capacity. Despite protests from religious and civil groups that claimed such acts were in violation of the 1947 Constitution, Nakasone was determined to be seen as honouring the memory of those who had died in the costliest war in Japan's history. Not surprisingly the Japanese media concentrated on the atomic bombings of Hiroshima and Nagasaki and found less to say over the humiliation of unconditional surrender that followed quickly after the air attacks, the tightening Allied blockade and the Soviet declaration of war. Some editorials drew attention to the role of the United States in Japan's postwar history but the general theme was of the nations's voluntary replacement of militarism by two generations of peace and prosperity. On neither side of the Pacific was 1985 an excuse for detailed examinations of the evolution of the US–Japan relationship. No joint ceremony of reconciliation or presidential visit to Japan took place. Memories on both sides were presumably too diverse and the political failure of Reagan's unfortunate journey to West Germany on the occasion of VE Anniversary Day was hardly a good omen. It must be assumed that no Japanese cabinet would have wanted anything to do with a bilateral gathering. The Pacific war remains too close for too many Japanese families.

Politicians, editors and commentators were inclined to look back to the ending of the war and then press on to either praise or denigrate current US–Japan ties. Between the surrender and the immediacy of the 1980s lies a void.[1]

To account for both the omissions and self-congratulatory rhetoric it is necessary to return to the war years. The defeat of Imperial Japan was the greatest achievement in American military history. The close of the Pacific war left the United States master of the region and predominant power in the forthcoming Allied occupation of Japan. It was President Truman who determined the surrender terms for ending the war and it was at his insistence that General MacArthur gained the post of supreme commander for the Allied powers to oversee the occupation process. The attack on Pearl Harbor and the loss of the Philippines had finally been avenged by the formal signing of the terms of surrender on board the USS Missouri in Tokyo Bay and by the presidential ruling that an American be 'top dog commander over Hirohito'.[2] The Pacific had been transformed through total war into the American lake and the Japanese archipelago was now America's prize.

After three and a half years of bitter fighting Japan had been slowly and at great cost pushed back from an empire that had stretched from the Aleutians to the Coral Sea and from Manchuria to Burma. Even in the summer of 1945 the allied leaders who gathered at Potsdam were informed that Japan's military strength exceeded 4,500,000 men.[3] Japan was eventually defeated but it was a lengthy, difficult task made all the more dangerous by the ominous increase in American casualties as its forces inched nearer to the Japanese homeland. Allied command of the seas and absolute supremacy in the air had dented but not destroyed Japanese morale. Despite the deaths in the Pacific and Asian campaigns, the Imperial forces expected to fight on. Citizens in the urban centres still attempted to work in what was left of the munitions industry, despite the horrific firebombings of the spring of 1945, the inadequate rations and privations of wartime Tokyo and Osaka. Military and civilian resistance during the fierce fighting for Okinawa in the period between April and June could be taken by American commanders only as a portent of what might well follow, despite the logistical failings of the Japanese war effort and the absurdity of committing raw civil defence forces against US marines and armour.[4]

Yet the Japanese government was hopelessly divided over the crucial question of surrender.[5] Its failure to accept military realities without first obtaining assurances over the fate of the Emperor only delayed the inevitable, and multiplied the sufferings of the Japanese people.[6] The protracted, convoluted discussions over surrender terms demonstrated the failing of Japan's leadership and its contempt for the citizenry it was supposedly defending. Eventually a face-saving formula was prepared that was sufficiently elastic to satisfy those Japanese figures who placed the future of the Imperial line above all else and also to permit the American administration to claim that the surrender of Japan remained unconditional.

The Pacific war left the United States eager to assume new responsibilities in the wake of its hard-won victories. It was a challenge that the United States took up with alacrity. There was little hesitation or doubt within the American administration and bureaucracy that Washington should enforce an ambitious series of programmes and controls on occupied Japan. Victory in the Pacific led almost automatically to dominance in post-surrender Japan. The conquerors wasted no time in getting down to business.

After flying five hours from Manila a succession of US transport

6

planes reached the Japanese coast, flew in formation over Kamakura and landed at Atsugi. It was the afternoon of 30 August 1945 and General Eichelberger, the commander of the US Eighth Army, had only an hour and a half to sort out the inevitable chaos before MacArthur arrived in occupied Japan. All too soon MacArthur appeared. Eichelberger saluted as the military band struck up and the camera crews filmed for posterity. MacArthur reportedly announced 'Bob, this is the pay-off', though Eichelberger's version was merely a flat 'How are you, Bob'.[7] The occupation was underway. Through a combination of military efficiency, hasty improvisation and constant publicity, the United States was to run the show for more than half a decade.

Events at Atsugi set the tone for much of what was to follow. The Japanese authorities also moved immediately to cooperate with the American commanders in the hopes that such ploys would ameliorate conditions for their nation and act to accelerate the eventual ending of the humiliation of occupation. On the evening of his first day in Japan Eichelberger wrote to his wife from the Grand Hotel in Yokohama to note both the conditions under which urban life was struggling to exist and the perquisites in store for American officials. Eichelberger's professional eye had noted that the Japanese gendarmerie and soldiers lining the route to Yokohama had been issued with new rifles and he was equally surprised to see that the city trams were running despite the destruction. Food was obviously in short supply (his first hotel meal consisted largely of beer) but Eichelberger could claim the choicest accommodation (with the Japanese government expecting 'to furnish the houseboys and cooks and the yardboys') and an expropriated 1940 model Lincoln Zephyr. The vast gap between victor and vanquished was to persist throughout the occupation and beyond. Indeed, the legacies of this 'occupation mentality' still endure today to muddy the relationship for both sides.

American conduct in occupied Japan rested on a tripod of agreements. The framework for the Allied occupation consisted of a series of international documents, instructions from the United States government to its commanding officer and General MacArthur's own privileged 'back channel' communication with Washington. All three were crucial. Each needs to be examined in turn to place the occupation in perspective.

Allied debates on what to do with post-surrender Japan had been limited before Tokyo's unexpectedly rapid capitulation in August 1945. Even the United States government imagined that it might take eighteen months to two years of arduous combat to flush out all

7

pockets of resistance if landings on the Japanese mainlands were found necessary. The probability of house-to-house fighting and the likelihood of protracted guerilla war made it difficult to imagine the condition of Japan at the moment of surrender, but the United States certainly hoped for considerable military contributions from its Allies and would also have to reckon with the domestic political consequences on its own public. Fortunately, this eventuality was removed by Japan's recognition of defeat and its fears of what might be in store if the Soviet Union were to gain a major role in controlling Japan; fortunately, too, from Japan's point of view, the British war coalition inevitably had more immediate priorities nearer home, the Chinese regime was fighting Imperial Japan and then the Chinese Communist movement and the Soviet Union had remained neutral until August 1945.

The first basic document issued by the principal Allies resulted from the Cairo conference's resolve on 1 December 1943 to prolong the war against Japan until unconditional surrender had been achieved. Once Japan had been defeated its empire would then be divided.[8] Nothing was said on how the victors might carry out their occupation beyond the statement that they were fighting 'to restrain and punish the aggression of Japan'.[9] From this modest exercise in Allied cooperation little else emerged, since the Soviet Union was obliged to remain on the sidelines and the British and American leaders held diametrically opposed views on the value and future status of Chiang Kai-shek's China. President Roosevelt felt it politic to bolster up China since it was fighting Japan, while Churchill's comments were scathing and the Foreign Office planners reckoned that for the postwar world 'China did not really count'.[10]

The Cairo conference proved to be the peak of China's international influence since the United States' eagerness to encourage Chiang decreased as its own forces advanced in both MacArthur's South West Pacific command and Nimitz's Central Pacific theatre. Yet progress was slow and Japanese troops fought to the last man to delay the outcome. The Japanese leadership was not prepared to reckon with surrender until the situation was long past hopeless. The Potsdam Declaration's dire warnings of 26 July 1945 elicited no formal response from Tokyo that would have safely ended the war without Soviet intervention[11] and the dropping of the two atom bombs. The military remained determined to engage the Allies when they launched their attacks on the Japanese coasts. Its leaders appeared unable or unwilling to reckon with a Japanese polity that did not clearly contain a privileged role for the Emperor and the Imperial forces. Their insistence on this stance led ironically to a postwar Japan that requires no more than a highly constricted role for the Emperor and holds widespread misgivings over the constitutionality and function of the Self-Defence Forces.

The Potsdam Declaration was Japan's last chance. The wording was crystal clear as to the consequences of postponement. Tokyo simply had to surrender unconditionally or test whether it could prevent what the Allies warned would be 'prompt and utter destruction'.[12] The Potsdam Declaration was rejected by the Suzuki cabinet; the Japanese government was quoted by the *Asahi Shimbun* as regarding the call to surrender 'a thing of no great value' that 'will only serve to re-enhance the government's resolve to carry the war forward unfalteringly to a successful conclusion'.[13] The war continued. For those, however, attempting to reckon with the Allies' intentions (Moscow associated itself with the message once it had declared war on Japan) the Potsdam Declaration offered important clues. It spoke out primarily against Japan's rulers and attempted to draw a comparison between 'those self-willed militaristic advisers whose unintelligent calculations have brought the Empire of Japan to the threshold of annihilation' and the Japanese people. The distinction contributed nothing to ending the war, but hinted as to Allied thinking over the occupation. The general tone was far from harsh. The militarists would have to go; they would also face punishment. Yet Truman, Attlee and Chiang stated that '[w]e do not intend that the Japanese shall be enslaved as a race or destroyed as a nation'. Freedoms of speech, religion and thought would also be established. Industrial recovery would also be permitted – in part to permit the exaction of reparations to Asia and the West – and '[e]ventual Japanese participation in world trade relations shall be permitted'. To oversee what was defined as 'a new order' there would be an Allied occupation.[14] Point 12 spoke of a definite end to this process when the Japanese state and people had fulfilled their Potsdam obligations and devised 'a peacefully inclined and responsible government'. It was to be MacArthur's contention from the first months of 1947 onwards that this stage already had been reached, though his government was far from ready to accept that international circumstances permitted Washington to grant Japan its freedom.

The Japanese government's eventual surrender was based on its qualified acceptance of the Potsdam Declaration. At issue were the critical questions of the future of the throne and how the occupation might be conducted. The Imperial forces eventually gave way when the Emperor personally intervened on 9 August, after hopeless division within the inner cabinet and the supreme council, to inform the government that in his opinion the war must end. Those who had wanted suicidal resistance on the Japanese mainland and additional clarification to the Potsdam terms were rebuffed.[15] Yet the final outcome depended on the reactions in Washington to Japan's willingness to surrender 'with the understanding that the said declaration does not compromise any demand which prejudices the prerogatives of His Majesty as a sovereign ruler'. The issue was now out of Japan's hands.

American planners had spent a considerable time debating the fate of both the Emperor and the Imperial line during the Pacific war, but the decisions eventually taken by the American administration in August 1945 owed more to the exigencies of domestic politics than long-term strategy for the Pacific. (The United States may well have had firmer ideas about postwar Asia than divided Europe but clearly much was still imprecise and contingent.) Secretary of Navy James Forrestal proposed a *via media* between those in government who were eager for abolishing the position of the Emperor and those in the State Department who had persistently argued that it was essential for the United States to employ the Emperor's person to promote occupation objectives in Japan. After reviewing the government's option, Secretary Byrnes, who had refused the pleas of Joseph Grew and others in favour of retaining the Emperor to refer to the throne in the Potsdam Declaration, drafted the American government's reply that the Emperor's position and indeed the entire governmental structure of Japan would ultimately 'be established by the freely expressed will of the Japanese people'. Byrnes, who had resisted any reference to the Emperor in the Potsdam Declaration because of the risks involved in the (very probable) rejection of that document by Japan and the difficulties this would pose for the United States if the concession was not taken up, now had to face a further conundrum to gain peace. He had to balance domestic pressures to end the war following Japan's qualified acceptance of the Potsdam terms with his government's wish to avoid reneging over unconditional surrender.[16] His formula, after agreement had been gained from London, Chungking and Moscow, was then relayed by the Swiss government to Tokyo.

After further inconclusive debate the Emperor once again was able to assert himself and the belated decision to surrender was adopted on 14 August. The formal instrument of surrender stressed that Japan accepted 'the unconditional surrender to the Allied Powers of the Japanese armed forces and all armed forces under Japanese control wherever situated', while 'the Emperor, the Japanese Government and their successors' would 'carry out the provisions of the Potsdam Declaration in good faith'. Rival interpretations immediately sprang up over the degree to which the Potsdam Declaration limited the Allies' powers over Japan. As early as 6 September 1945 the Joint Chiefs of Staff informed MacArthur that his authority did not rest on a contractual basis, 'but on an unconditional surrender. Since your authority is supreme, you will not entertain any question on the part of the Japanese as to its scope.' Truman had already stated that the unconditional surrender formula had not been dented and MacArthur was instructed to observe the Potsdam terms without regarding them as anything beyond evidence of American 'good faith with relation to Japan' and 'to peace and security in the Far East'.[17]

Consideration of how the United States might further its own interests in Japan was inevitably complicated by the need to recall that the occupation was legally an Allied venture. Japan's formal surrender had been accepted by MacArthur as supreme commander for the Allied powers, while Nimitz had been the signatory at the surrender ceremony as the American representative. Although events later demonstrated the United States' ability to preserve its privileged position in and over Japan it was certain that the other powers would insist on at least a share of responsibility in the forthcoming occupation. Yet the United States had two immense advantages in these international manoeuvrings. It had already installed its forces on the spot and knew what it wanted from the occupation.

The two allied institutions that eventually emerged from discussion among the American, British, Soviet and Chinese governments can all too easily be written off as doomed from their inception. It might be more accurate to note that both the Far Eastern Commission and the Allied Council for Japan were capable on occasion of offering useful advice to the United States and that responsibility for their demise is still contested. The fact remains, however, that it was not until the December 1945 meeting of the Big Three foreign ministers in Moscow that a loose supervisory body (FEC) and an unfortunate group that was expected to meet publicly in Tokyo to proffer advice to General MacArthur on how the occupation ought to be conducted (ACJ) finally appeared.[18] The timing was all wrong for those allied officials who were serious about multilateralism and MacArthur made it apparent from the first meeting of the ACJ what he thought of foreign governments telling him how to do his job.[19]

The powers of the FEC and the ACJ were sufficiently limited to make it unlikely that the United States government or its officials would be seriously embarrassed by outside interference. Certainly

11

neither body proved as challenging as MacArthur had initially feared, though the frequency with which the ACJ, for example, saw the Chinese, British Commonwealth (represented by Australia) and Soviet delegates united in voicing concern at the lack of adequate information provided by the American side indicates a suspicion of its tactics. Not all was gloom, since the FEC began its history by endorsing much of what the United States was attempting to achieve in Japan and the ACJ propounded reform policies that played their part in changing the entire character of Japanese rural society.[20] Yet, during most of the occupation period, MacArthur's staff were jaundiced in their opinion of the FEC and ACJ. American personnel (taking their cue from the supreme commander) rarely disguised their views on these international organizations and regarded obstructionism as the best defence against even well-intentioned criticism.

General MacArthur could not and did not attempt any such open defiance with regard to instructions from his home government. By the autumn of 1945 MacArthur was sixty-five years old and at the height of his career. Military historians have been highly critical of his leadership in the Pacific[21] but his public reputation both during and after the war made it most improbable that any administration would readily wish to cross him. MacArthur had by 1945 become an American legend. He continued during the occupation to be widely popular with the public and regularly headed Gallup polls as the most admired figure in the world.[22] His reputation was a mixture of valour, military accomplishment and signal failure; his determination to succeed was driven by political ambition.[23] President Truman, doubtless fearing the domestic opposition if MacArthur were overlooked, accepted that MacArthur was to be the supreme commander for Japan. Certainly Truman had never liked him and would confide to his diary in June 1945 that the general was no more than 'Mr Prima Donna'.[24] Yet when others challenged Truman's judgement the president could be quick to defend his appointment[25] and the relationship probably survived until the Korean War by each man studiously avoiding the other. Geography and MacArthur's repeated claim that pressure of occupation business made it impossible for him to return to a hero's welcome in the United States undoubtedly assisted to this end.

MacArthur's orders were both detailed and discretionary. He was issued with a lengthy set of directives on how to conduct the occupation, yet the intent from Washington was more to clarify MacArthur's powers than to propound specific policies. The first sentence, for example, of the Basic Initial Post-Surrender Directive

12

spoke of intending to 'guide' MacArthur. A number of 'general principles' were spelt out, but the Joint Chiefs of Staff had no wish to shackle their representative with instructions that might appear irrelevant in the field. (There was also the difficulty of dealing with an officer who had himself been appointed Chief of Staff in November 1930.) MacArthur was told that, aside from 'the conventional powers of a military occupant' of enemy terrain, 'you have the power to take any steps deemed advisable ... to effectuate the surrender and the provisions of the Potsdam Declaration'.[26] Indeed, it would be slightly absurd to look for grounds of conflict between the JCS and SCAP, since both generally knew the opinions of the other and a great deal of communication passed between Washington and the Dai-Ichi building in Tokyo before MacArthur's orders were officially transmitted to him. This arrangement insured that MacArthur frequently got what he wanted. His directives reflected much that he wished to carry out.[27]

MacArthur's first orders were sent to him on 29 August during a period of immense confusion as the United States government scrabbled together a series of policies for the forthcoming occupation. Two vital questions immediately emerged that were to have an impact on all that was to follow. These interconnected issues concerned the future of the Emperor and the nature of the administration of occupied Japan. The twin topics had long exercised the minds of planners in Washington both because of their impact on American activities in Japan and for the domestic scrutiny they were expected to receive. President Truman had himself written privately at Potsdam in scathing terms of Japan and though he had agreed that the atom bomb should not be dropped on either Kyoto or Tokyo he had predicted that the Japanese cabinet would not take up the Potsdam offer to surrender.[28] Yet his administration, perhaps because of the pressures of the moment, had largely accepted the proposals of those authorities on Japan who were less inclined to be vindictive towards their recent enemy. These planners (led by former ambassador to Tokyo Joseph Grew) won the day not so much by routing the hardliners through superior policies but by the fact that Roosevelt's death had altered the bureaucratic power balance. This gave the edge to the Japan-hands in the State Department and left those groups associated with Secretary of the Treasury Morgenthau with less influence.[29] Not for the last time in this survey can Japan reckon itself fortunate. American public (and therefore Congressional) opinion was all for keeping the Japanese under. One third of those polled in June 1945 thought that the Emperor deserved to be executed, over half wanted to see strict

13

postwar controls on the Japanese people and few had any scruples over using the atomic bomb.[30]

The Emperor, along with Tojo and Tokyo Rose, was one of the very few Japanese known to the American public. His assumed divinity and supposed importance in deciding government policy made him a convenient symbol for the American war effort. For over forty years after Japan's surrender he remained a figure of obvious attention in Japan and the West. Interest has inevitably concentrated on his activities over Japan's decision to go to war in 1941 and in the days that led to surrender in August 1945. The contrast between the relative weakness of the Emperor in 1941 and his greater assertiveness in the summer of 1945 continues to be noted. What was, however, apparent to some American and Allied officials in these hectic weeks was the potential usefulness of the Emperor to the occupation. His determination to persuade a divided inner cabinet of the futility of further warfare and his recognition that defeat would leave his personal fate in the hands of the conquerors was not lost on the American planners. Only through Imperial rescripts did Japan surrender. The Emperor's language may have been elliptical but the fact of defeat was recognized through his statements. Instructions to the Imperial forces to lay down their arms and warnings to the citizenry that the hardships ahead would have to be accepted ensured that there was little resistance to either defeat or military occupation.[31] The Emperor's message ended the Pacific war and focussed Japan's attention on the new goal of reconstruction.

The Imperial rescripts provided valuable ammunition for those who maintained that the Emperor (and his government) should be employed as agents of the Allies to promote the objectives specified on the Potsdam Declaration. Yet this was no automatic decision. It took considerable courage for the administration to suggest that the Emperor could assist the United States when many Allied governments, such as the Soviet Union and Australia, expected him to be arraigned and Japan strictly controlled as punishment for its recent past. For an American president to order policies that appeared relaxed towards one of those held responsible for the day of infamy was no easy matter, given that the anniversary of the attack on Pearl Harbor remains perhaps the best recalled date in American history after 4 July.

The issue of the Emperor was too important a matter to be left to the discretion of the supreme commander; the opinions of the Allies had to be taken into account. Here the total diversity of views between those who wanted him at least arrested and those who suggested

clemency indicates the very real difficulties that an effective international division of power would have faced.[32] Events in Japan
worked swiftly to confirm the advantages of leaving the Emperor
alone. The call by him on MacArthur in late September created a
favourable impression on MacArthur and left Japanese readers only
too well aware of the contrast between the open-shirted head of the
occupation and the diminutive white-gloved Emperor. The palace's
activities were scaled down and attempts were made after the new
constitution had been promulgated to present the symbol of state as a
family man and conscientious limited monarch. His dignity was not
lost on MacArthur and some of his conquerors as he adjusted to his
new role and moved swiftly off to the wings.[33]

Firmly linked to the Emperor question was the related issue of how
to administer Japan. Once again there had been considerable work
prepared on the subject in Washington by pre-surrender planners, yet
obviously there were limits to the ability of any staff officer to correctly
anticipate conditions when Japan capitulated. Few specialists could
have imagined that the American commander would be sufficiently
confident of his abilities that he could announce as early as 17
September that 'a drastic cut' in troop levels would follow.[34] Truman,
facing difficulties from Congress over presidential proposals to maintain selective service, was angry at the implication that the United
States would in future be relying on the Japanese government for
American policies and that cut backs on troop levels 'would lead to the
general belief throughout the East that American power in the Far East
was being liquidated and that we intended to rely solely on Japanese
good faith'.[35] MacArthur, however, was correct. It might be unfortunate news for the Joint Chiefs of Staff attempting to prevent the
peace-time military from shrinking too fast, but the gamble of landing
relatively few soldiers in the initial days following surrender had
succeeded in that outward Japanese resistance was minimal. This in
turn, while not precluding direct, military government, made
American willingness to use the Japanese government and bureaucracy more probable.

Indirect rule was only one of a number of options. The degree of
international supervision, as we have seen, had yet to be regularized
and the original American plans suggest that military government was
the first American scheme. This appears probable from the remarks
made by General Sutherland (MacArthur's chief of staff) at the initial
meeting with Foreign Minister Shigemitsu following Japan's formal
surrender that the US army would rule directly and that US military
scrip had already been printed up for immediate circulation. To

15

reinforce American intentions it was clear that English would be the official language of the occupation and notices were due to appear over the establishment of military courts.[36] It is possible that MacArthur was already impressed by the initial Japanese reaction to the beginning of what might have proved a violent occupation and that Shigemitsu's pleas to let his government demonstrate its worth to American objectives left SCAP swayed by this case. It may, in contrast, have been bluff. It remains certain that this experimental system could be revoked if and when MacArthur judged fit and that 'the Emperor and government were in a sense hostage for their good behaviour'.[37]

The advantages to both sides of allowing Japan to retain both its Emperor and government were considerable. MacArthur's statement that the cost in manpower and financial terms to the United States would be enormously reduced by working through the Japanese state was accurate, though politically less than astute when made a mere fortnight after Japan's surrender. MacArthur and Eichelberger, who had already spoken of ending the occupation within twelve months, thought first of protecting their forces and ensuring that conditions within Japan returned to an approximate normality as fast as possible. Only the Japanese government and its bureaucracy could achieve this end, since the US Army had neither the experience nor the ability (with the exception of some linguists who MacArthur immediately shunted off to South Korea) to govern unassisted.

Yet Japan stood to gain the most from indirect rule. It would then be in a strong position both to influence American policies and their implementation. This would be Japan's second advantage following the determination of the United States to force its own control on Tokyo without attending overmuch to the views of its Allies. The evident restriction on other Allied troop arrivals certainly benefited the Japanese state, since it precluded the voicing of widely anticipated anti-Chinese sentiment of returning soldiers. The Suzuki cabinet had expected the Soviet Union to garrison Hokkaido (earlier American plans had considered this option) and the Chinese to have a role in Kyushu.[38] American unilateralism and Japanese placidity reinforced each other and got the occupation off to a good start.

The structure of SCAP's general headquarters was established in October 1945 on the premise that the supreme commander would transmit his orders to the Japanese government via its Central Liaison Office. Implementation was to be achieved through 'frequent informal conferences between Special Staff Sections of this Headquarters and the appropriate bureaus within the Japanese Ministries'.[39] Compliance at the prefectural and local levels was to be the responsibility of the misnamed Military Government teams. These groups were small inspection units that attempted to observe and report back to the SCAP GHQ on grassroots activities. Attention, however, was usually concentrated on the national developments and the contradictions and confusions in the towns and in the villages of Hokkaido and Shikoku rarely received all the consideration the regions warranted either by SCAP GHQ or from the American press corps safely ensconced in a more salubrious Tokyo.

MacArthur's command was organized, not surprisingly, along military lines. The details appear even more precise when expressed in published diagrams with neat lines of responsibility drawn from SCAP to his chief of staff and then running from the host of sections to the occupation forces themselves housed, at least in part, in former Imperial army barracks. Yet the clarity and style of such channels could prove misleading. Seniority and position were no guarantee of influence; rivalry and dissension can hardly show up on charts. All staff sections were not equal and the rapid turnover within these myriad units further complicated the story. For the history of US–Japan relations, three areas of contact were especially important. These were: first and foremost, the overriding ties between SCAP GHQ and successive Japanese governments; next, the constant influence of Government Section (after General Courtney Whitney was appointed to the head of the section in December 1945); and finally the military links that gradually emerged between some American officers and the supposedly demobilized Japanese military.

Recent studies have noted the paucity of Japanese planning for postwar Asia.[40] Given the increasingly desperate military plight of Japan from 1943 onwards, however, this should hardly be a cause for surprise. Similar disarray marked Japan's thoughts on the occupation where circumstances simply did not permit detailed reflection. The difficulties and dangers of obtaining peace against the objections of the Imperial forces left little time for considering how to cope with the forthcoming occupation. Incriminating documents were ordered to be destroyed, surplus military equipment was sold off or appropriated and the beginnings of the disarming of the soldiery undertaken, but this was merely to create the right impression on the Americans. Active cooperation was the official approach to demonstrate that the Japanese state could still function and was committed to fulfilling what cynics termed its 'surrender drill'.

Aside from this ingratiation that relied heavily on the skills of former diplomats who were now to work in the Central Liaison office was an

17

attempt to suggest that responsibility for Japan's present straits rested exclusively on its disgraced militarist leaders. Efforts were made to avoid any action that might possibly incriminate the Emperor for deeds done in his name. Representation was quickly made to SCAP's Diplomatic Section to clarify events which led to Japan's surrender and the Emperor's intervention of August 1945. Opportunists from all walks of life saw the way the wind was blowing. It was simplest to castigate the military for Japan's recent past. The press, the nation's teachers and its businessmen were now transformed into born-again democrats.

The Japanese civil service was criticized by American observers for employing the same tactics. The acting political adviser wrote to Truman that '[p]ractically all categories of Japanese show or pretend a desire to cooperate with our military, but the civil officials and bureaucracy are the least sincere and effective'.[41] Yet the United States faced major difficulties in ruling Japan without the continuation of the Emperor and most of its experienced bureaucrats. Japan might not evolve into a democratic society if the Imperial line and its officials were permitted to remain in office, but the political instability that was predicted to follow moves to oust the Emperor and the resignation of senior bureaucrats left the United States in a dilemma. Even those who might personally wish to see the creation of a republic admitted that 'so long as we are using the Japanese Government to accomplish what we wish – or are permitting it to make its own efforts toward that end – it would not seem the part of wisdom to interfere at this juncture'.[42] Indirect rule, employing a combination of 'dictation and persuasion' was to remain the basis for American endeavours in occupied Japan. The Japanese state was able to continue in a manner that was impossible in South Korea and Okinawa where the United States elected to run things its own way through military dictat.[43] The Japanese mainland was spared any such experience and one may speculate as to whether the postwar alliance between Washington and Tokyo could have evolved as it did under the heavy hand of military rule.

Reliance on Japan's bureaucracy might be distasteful but the alternatives were reckoned to be too fraught to gain approval. The result was inevitably an accretion of power in Japanese hands. This can be seen negatively by the considerable reluctance of SCAP to remove civilian bureaucrats under the purge programmes. It was relatively simple to dismiss practically all military officers, although a few were quietly retained to oversee the demobilization of the others and told to write up campaign records until the day arrived when the prohibition of a Japanese defence establishment might be reconsidered. It was also more acceptable to change financial, economic and political posts than the key area of public administration. One American authority, who himself served in Government Section and appreciated the problems at first hand, has concluded that '[the] purge left the bureaucracy almost unchanged in the composition of its personnel'.[44] The necessity of working through competent Japanese officials and their tenacity at protecting their own from investigation combined to leave the elite largely untouched. Such acts have had far-reaching consequences. Contemporary Japan is still administered by bureaucrats who were then starting out in Government.[45] The continuities in personnel and privilege are as if the occupation had never been. Reform was something that happened elsewhere as Japan's bureaucrats increased in power and number under American sponsorship.

After the Joint Chiefs of Staff had forwarded their orders and the experts had had their say, it was left to MacArthur to get on with the job. As we have seen and as might have been expected given the problems ahead, he elected to administer Japan through the Japanese state. The speed and guarded optimism with which the venture opened can be demonstrated by the fact the 1,000 directives were issued by SCAP to the Japanese government between September 1945 and June 1946.[46] The ambition and confidence behind this attempt to remake Japanese institutions and society was extraordinary. It reflected both American satisfaction in its own values and its victory in the Pacific and the at least outward acceptance by many Japanese that reform was necessary. Total defeat and subsequent demoralization gave the United States the opportunity to press for change. Dissent, however, came from two quarters. First, not surprisingly, many conservative Japanese figures voiced their objection to measures that they claimed were most un-Japanese. Modification of the role of the Emperor, the release of imprisoned Communists, changes in the family system and limits on industrial conglomerates were all highly unpopular, yet the protesters had to be careful not to overstep the mark, since worse might follow and uncooperative politicians and entrepreneurs could easily be removed. Conflict also arose within SCAP GHQ. Policy differences and personality clashes abounded to reduce the clarity and direction of the process. As William Sebald commented later on the basis of his experience as the senior State Department figure in Japan for most of this period, it was inevitable that friction would erupt, given 'an undertaking the size of the Occupation and especially the SCAP GHQ'.[47] Yet it might be more profitable to recall what did get done and its lasting influence on contemporary Japan than to overstress the shifts in policy and the bureaucratic infighting.

The occupation from the outset was stamped indelibly with the mark of MacArthur. The Japanese government and people knew this immediately and so did those Allied diplomats who were obliged to report back to their foreign ministries that control was firmly in his hands. Later American historians have challenged this observation by suggesting either that any American commander could have done the job or that MacArthur's influence on events has been grossly exaggerated, but the revisionists have yet to make much dent in the authorized version. Their criticisms of his posturing, the sycophancy of some of his staff and their defensiveness towards MacArthur's every action are hardly new and tend to ignore the extent of his achievements. There were inevitably limits to his reform programmes that left some dissatisfied and his powers may have waned after 1949 but the consistency and determination to remake Japan and end the occupation both speedily and with Tokyo likely to remain friendly towards the United States was the work of a singular man.

MacArthur was quick to impose his power and personality on Japan. He was faced with an awesome task amidst the rubble, the near-starvation and the general uncertainty. Nor was he assisted in his duties by the conflicts between his instructions from Washington, the counterpressures from the other Allied powers for a decent share in controlling the occupation, and daily consideration of the opinions of a series of shifting and unstable Japanese cabinets. MacArthur, however, had his own ideas on how the occupation ought to be run and, while he took note, of course, of orders from his superiors, he interpreted commands from the Joint Chiefs of Staff in a decidedly personal manner. The deputy chief of the influential Governmental Section could write forty years after the occupation commenced that:

> I agree with the British Mission that it was MacArthur's occupation and that the staff was there to carry out his ideas. That is not to say that MacArthur did not solicit advice from staff sections but, once a command decision had been made by MacArthur, the staff's function was to put it into effect. In reaching his decisions, MacArthur considered the directives from Washington as guidelines and not direct orders to be carried out and he never hesitated to argue with Washington about any particular provision in a directive which he thought called for an unsound policy and his views during the time I was at GHQ were always accepted.[48]

This approach may have contributed to MacArthur's later dismissal, but for our purposes in analyzing US–Japan relations his cavalier style greatly simplified operations. It let all know where ultimate authority lay. Students of civil-military relations might look askance, yet the arrangement worked. MacArthur's detractors have been quick to point out his errors and his authority was challenged as the occupation lengthened, but to argue that this post was a 'sinecure'[49] is to fly in the face of much of the American, Allied and Japanese evidence. Equally, it is difficult to imagine that President Truman retained MacArthur in Japan for over five years merely to restrain him from activities potentially damaging to the Democratic party. Certainly MacArthur had political ambitions (quite how he would have explained his radicalism in Japan and squared it with the anti-New Deal and Fair Deal rhetoric of the Republican faithful remains unclear) and his eagerness to cultivate all and sundry who visited Tokyo was notorious but this behaviour hardly damaged the occupation. The MacArthur years in Japan provided at the very least the necessary catalyst for latent change. The occupation was something more substantial than merely 'Japan's American interlude'.

Central to MacArthur's record is the postwar Japanese constitution. The timidity of Japanese attempts to revise the 1889 document and the need to preempt the FEC from offering its own scheme prompted SCAP GHQ to produce its liberal draft under the fiction that it was of indigenous manufacture. Since it has remained in force for the past forty years without amendment the 1947 constitution acts as both a constant reminder of American democratic intent and a source of irritation to those on the right who regard it as an alien imposition. An Anglo-American version of government replaced the Imperial constitution with what was intended to be a model scheme that aspired through a hundred and three articles to create a new framework for a participatory democracy.[50]

The constitution was an imposed, alien document. It could claim few friends among the ranks of the conservative political groupings, though the ease with which the new Constitution was approved in the Diet belies this suspicion. Executive and legislative authority was now to be clearly based on the existing parliamentary structure rather than being associated with the benevolence of the Emperor. The cabinet structure was retained and an American focus added by the adoption of an elaborate committee structure. Universal suffrage, extensive human rights provisions and an independent judiciary were also incorporated to produce what had the potential to be a novel form of government. Such blueprints, of course, were only the beginnings for what was immediately termed 'MacArthur's Constitution'.[51] Operational realities would quickly test the new arrangements.

21

MacArthur himself held a relatively low opinion of Japanese politicians during his proconsulate and was less optimistic over Tokyo's prospects than his frequent self-congratulatory public statements suggest.

Few Allied observers shared more than a portion of Government Section's enthusiasm. British diplomats spoke of the inappropriateness of the document and foreign journalists were always on the look out for a good story on the return of supposedly discredited wartime figures to political influence. One British MP described the Constitution as reading 'more like sentiments expressed at the Zenith Rotary Club and is not the language which one uses in the East. It will be interesting to see how long the Constitution endures.'[52] It remains the symbol of what the United States hoped to achieve in postwar Japan, though its popularity has been greatest amongst those on the left rather than with conservatives who have governed without pause since the occupation ended. Ironically, some of the politicians closest to the United States have been in the vanguard of moves to rewrite the postwar Constitution. Former premier Kishi, for example, long campaigned for a more 'Japanese system' of government that would clarify the role of the Emperor and the constitutionality of Japan's military establishment. Effective resistance to any such moves (and the difficulties of the amendment process) provide a useful reminder of the extent to which the new Constitution can be said to have taken root in Japan.

American concern over the extent to which postwar Japan could be accurately termed a transformed society persisted throughout the occupation years and beyond. (It was, of course, an ever more pressing issue within Japan. In the summer of 1986, the newly appointed minister of education was highly critical of the educational changes of the past four decades without conceding that an independent Japan had obviously opted not to make wholesale revisions in what had originally been a major American assault on prewar Japanese educational practices and institutions.) Opinions differed widely in SCAP as to whether American objectives in occupied Japan could be entrusted to a series of mainly conservative cabinets. Yoshida Shigeru, the leading Japanese political figure of the first postwar decade and perhaps the architect of much of contemporary Japanese diplomacy, could be bitingly critical of MacArthur's men and methods. Yoshida never accepted parts of the occupation's design and continued to voice his objections throughout this period. He would appeal against purge directives, police reforms, educational changes and labour laws directly to SCAP. His cunning can be seen in an approach to

MacArthur in April 1951 when he called for what amounted to substantial changes in occupation legislation in order 'to secure democracy more firmly by adapting the existing legislation to the actual conditions of the country'. His suggestion that the changes be made 'for the sake of Japanese–American friendship' before the peace treaty was signed was rebuffed.[53] Yoshida's popularity was based on his stance as a determined nationalist who by 1949 was described by his American critics as a premier who 'will respond to no advice, pressures, and threats from anyone except General MacArthur. Even the latter's advice will have to be presented in writing if it is to be effective.'[54] Yoshida's powers waxed after his electoral victory in January 1949, while MacArthur's began to wane as Washington took an increasingly detailed interest in Japan's future.

Promotion of a reformed political system takes pride of place in any assessment of the occupation. Yet occupations by definition are finite and some officials at least in SCAP GHQ and Washington were prepared to reckon with the day when the United States would have to quit Japan and trust that its efforts at institutional and societal change might persist. It was a subject that MacArthur had decidedly strong views on and he argued strenuously with his superiors over the timing and content of peace proposals. He had from the early months of the occupation wished to limit the process, since he maintained that 'the absorption of the ideals of democracy, however firmly the seeds are sown will proceed slowly' under 'the shadow of foreign bayonets'. Once the more constructive major reforms of Japan's political, educational and agrarian structures had been tackled it is difficult not to admit MacArthur had a strong case.[55] It was weakened, however, by the difficulties of the Japanese economy, which in turn were worsened in the opinion of some by uncertainties over reparation payments and proposed Zaibatsu deconcentration plans,[56] and the vagaries of international politics in east Asia. An unstable, inflation-ridden economy combined with an unarmed and vulnerable state was hardly the best recipe for success in the postwar world. Japan could under such a handicap jettison its recent ties with the United States or discover that threats to any newly-gained sovereignty might require some changes in both its domestic and foreign orientation. Washington was not prepared to accept the risk. Japan's independence would have to wait until the economy had been shored up and its position within the international environment clarified.

The process of repairing the economy and debating Japan's strategic posture took time. Such delays to ending the occupation also jeopardized the goodwill that the United States had endeavoured to build up

23

in Japan and might prove counter productive should peace be excessively delayed. If the occupation's reform were completed, in the main, by 1948, the period from then until 1950 can be best seen as a preparatory stage to the eventual peace settlements with SCAP GHQ increasingly taking a less active role in supervising the Japanese government. The two exceptions to this gradual relaxation were over economic stabilization schemes and the first hesitant moves to revive the Japanese military. In both cases, the United States faced considerable unpopularity over its actions. The need to contain inflation in order to move Japan a step nearer peace and generally dismantle what some economists saw as a 'greenhouse' economy left the Japanese government in a stronger position than might be imagined. The State Department and SCAP Government Section officials agreed in February 1949 that '[a]s long as the Japanese know that come "hell or high water" the U.S. will feed and clothe Japan in the interests of U.S. politico-strategic objectives, no amount of threats can evoke from the Japanese the responsibility, direction and drive necessary for carrying out a successful stabilization programme'.[57] Not for the last time would the Japanese cabinet shunt off the blame on the United States for insisting eventually on unpalatable medicine. The results, however, of what was popularly termed the Dodge line (after the Detroit banker who had offered similar prescriptions to the Germany economy) were generally favourable and the disinflationary, perhaps even deflationary, impact on sections on the Japanese economy considerable.[58]

Measures to alter the direction of the Japanese economy and shift it from what had been termed 'democratization' goals to greater stress on national recovery were unwelcome to many in SCAP. Trust-busting, anti-monopoly acts and Japanese labour legislation that was more advanced than in the United States sadly found fewer friends in Washington as criticism of 'SCAPitalism'[59] and the costs of the occupation to the American taxpayer mounted. Change did occur, however, and resulted in a degree of stabilization through controlled budgetary expenditure, a fixed (undervalued) exchange rate that was to endure until 1971 and tax reforms. Dodge rather than Yoshida received much of the blame from the Japanese public for the resulting austerity, though Japanese corporations welcomed the deregulatory aspects of the programme and the new opportunities to establish links with American corporations and the prospects for greater international trade. A balanced budget, reduced inflation and massive procurement offers from the United States following the outbreak of the Korean war saw the Japanese economy in a healthier position as the peace process reached its final stage.

24

The Japanese government and its bureaucracy[60] were obliged to work closely with American officials during the occupation in order to appear cooperative and hasten the day when the Americans might go home. (It was hardly coincidental that three of the four prime ministers during this era were former diplomats of the Anglo-American school within the prewar foreign ministry.) As the Cold War intensified there appeared to be advantages to both Japan and the United States in attempting to perpetuate these existing links into the post-treaty period. It would, presumably, ensure greater economic assistance and technological transfers for Japan, while retaining Japan's presence in an American-led grouping. Not for nothing did Yoshida stress to MacArthur in the summer of 1949 that 'Japan's Conservative bastion against Communism is secure'.[61] But any such pro-American stance for the future could also present considerable dangers to Tokyo. Making peace might realize Japan's sovereignty only at the cost of incorporating it into a subservient partnership with the United States; the necessarily unequal relationship of the occupation might be continued indefinitely. It was immediately apparent that Japan's freedom was likely to be far from absolute.

Yet the Japanese government's ability to manoeuvre had increased as the occupation lengthened and the eventual agreements should not be seen as an automatic decision. Much would depend on the terms, though the benevolence of the United States during most of what the Japanese diplomat attached to the headquarters of Eichelberger's forces in Yokohama later described as 'that trying period'[62] was in Washington's favour. Yoshida had rarely disguised his criticism of parts of the American design, but he was hopeful that the United States might conclude an agreement whereby Japan's security might be guaranteed and the necessary economic and financial crutch provided to ensure his nation's reconstruction. He spoke of the continuation of the postwar Pax Americana much as he had earlier in his diplomatic career praised the Anglo-Japanese alliance. Yoshida's respect for this central plank of late Meiji foreign policy has been attributed to parental influence (his adopted father was Jardine, Matheson's agent in Yokohama and Yoshida himself was later to be condemned as 'America's man in Japan') and to his opposition to Japanese continental aggression. Yoshida inherited the 'trader's mentality' that regarded cooperation with the West as central to Japan's reemergence as a power in a hostile, bipolar world. Yoshida, for better of worse, was the key Japanese figure with whom the United States was obliged to cooperate, since, with the exception of a disappointingly brief and inadequate period of Socialist and coalition rule in

1947–8, the conservative groups were to dominate Japanese political life.[63]

Yoshida might be unpopular with SCAP's Government Section for his beliefs (and indolence) but he held cabinet posts for practically all of the first postwar decade. His many detractors have to explain how a politician often out of favour with important elements in SCAP GHQ and supposedly out of tune with the more liberal atmosphere of all but the final period of the occupation gained and retained his powers. The answers, aside from a goodly portion of luck over the purging of the prewar political boss Hatoyama Ichiro, may suggest that the bulk of the Japanese electorate was (and has remained so until today) less aroused by the rallying call of reform than some Americans would have wished. Yoshida's determination to ally his nation to the United States, while simultaneously attempting to preserve options over east Asian policy that were strongly discouraged by Washington, must be examined next. The road to San Francisco was far from easy or assured. The ending of the occupation was to be a protracted business that eventually produced the framework for much that would follow in the Pacific alliance.

2 PEACE: THE SAN FRANCISCO SETTLEMENTS

> The central American objective ... is taken to be a stable Japan, integrated into the Pacific economy, friendly to the United States and, in case of need, a ready and dependable Ally of the United States.
>
> John Davies Jr to George Kennan, 11 August 1947

> Our material might was exemplified by the atomic bomb; our moral might is exemplified by General MacArthur. I am confident that when the hour of decision comes, the Japanese people in the light of these exhibits will elect to become dependable members of the world that is free.
>
> John Foster Dulles, Tokyo, 22 June 1950

Occupations have to end. The United States government fully appreciated the disadvantages that prolongation of its rule might cause for future US–Japan relations, yet it was far from easy to devise a peace treaty that would secure American objectives in Japan, retain Tokyo's goodwill and gain the necessary consent of Washington's allies. The divisions within the American bureaucracy and with its friends overseas made progress desperately slow; it also risked the danger of the Soviet Union embarrassing the US by courting Japan and calling for a treaty on its own terms. Yet, despite pressure from General MacArthur, the State Department and the British government there was no peace. Moves that had begun in MacArthur's case shortly after his occupation had secured its initial objectives came to nothing because of dissent in Washington and subsequent uncertainties in east Asia following the establishment of the PRC and the emergence of the cold war in the region.[1]

The failure of SCAP and the British Commonwealth to persuade the Truman administration of the advantages of an early termination to the occupation in 1947 reveals the limitations of both MacArthur and the United States' closest allies to get their way when key issues concerning Japan's future were involved. Much of the period from

1948 onwards may be seen as a holding operation (revisionists continue to assert that such a description more accurately applies to the entire occupation period) where Japan waited for its destiny to be decided. Certainly the delays contributed to increase Japanese leverage on the US authorities but influence was no substitute for independence. The extension of the occupation was devised as necessary for the United States to safeguard its political and military positions in the post-treaty years. It was motivated by a new appreciation of Japan's worth to American goals in Asia. The nature of Japan's future as an American ally was suddenly a central concern to American planners. This objective, however, was not to be secured by jettisoning the bulk of the reform baggage accumulated since 1945. The fate of this occupation legacy would be for the Japanese government and electorate to determine.[2]

Examination of the international context is necessary for explaining the nature of the San Francisco settlements. It is not possible to trace the evolution of the treaties merely in American–Japanese terms, since American peace diplomacy had wider concerns. It would, however, be poor history to imagine that there was a linear progression in American thinking over Japan and its destiny. Part of the problem was, as George Kennan, perhaps, enjoyed pointing out to his colleagues in 1947, that 'it would be highly dangerous, it seems to me, for us to enter in on discussions of peace terms until we know precisely what it is we are trying to achieve',[3] yet governments are invariably divided and equally unlikely to be granted the power to foretell the future in a changing international environment. Under the circumstances neither the delay in reaching agreement among rival American bureaucracies nor disputes with Washington's allies is particularly surprising. Dean Acheson was to write later that differences within the American government were more taxing for the Truman administration than troubles with the Japanese government or the many other nations, who minutely scrutinized American actions. The dispute between the State Department and the Pentagon over the best approach to the peace problem dominated American treaty formulation moves. Preparation of a Japanese settlement began and ended in the United States, but all parties based their cases on strategies that weighed up the appropriate response to complex international circumstances.

The rejection of MacArthur's peace suggestion in the spring of 1947 was merely the first of a number of initiatives that were spurned because of regional uncertainties. Such delays risked jeopardizing US–Japan ties but the fact that the American administration was prepared to postpone any detailed peace debate suggests either considerable confidence or a degree of foolhardiness on its behalf. The key to American thinking between 1947 and 1950 was the demise of Nationalist China and the increasingly bitter state of global relations with the Soviet Union. What Washington had to devise was a scheme whereby a weakened Japan might survive in a hostile environment as a friend of the United States. The repercussions of this strategy, it hardly needs emphasizing, are still with us today to colour the entire picture of international relations in east Asia and beyond.

Yet even despite these unfavourable trends there can not be said to have been any radical about turn in occupation policies. Important sections of SCAP economic aims were certainly changed but even the deconcentration programme that altered the anti-zaibatsu rulings was no more than modified. It was altered without much concern for either the Cold War or pressure from any amorphous 'Japan lobby'.[4] What determined the shift in policy was anxiety that Japanese industry might suffer to the extent that economic recovery would remain an impossibility, at a time when the Congress wished to limit the very substantial subsidies required to keep Japan afloat. There was no reverse course. Certainly the ideology of some senior officials in Washington played its part in reducing SCAP's economic controls but a crippled industrial structure was hardly the best recipe for building a new democratic state. The only threat that Japan posed in 1948 was to itself. It could hardly provide for the welfare of its own citizens, let alone present a danger to its neighbours. While always a potential power it lacked any great confidence in its future, in marked contrast to its recent position in Asia. Japan's political and social divisions were deep; its economy little better than in the early 1930s, and to support its larger population without its empire or assured markets was to test its industrialists and bureaucrats to the hilt. It was one thing for the United States to call Japan once again the workshop of Asia, but quite another to discover how this transformation was about to take place given the fragility of its economy and doubts on overseas outlets. If Japan was not quite the orphan it imagined, it certainly appeared ill-equipped to provide the locomotion for alleged American grand designs in Asia. A great crescent supposedly based on Tokyo and stretching from northern Japan to the Indian subcontinent could be little more than a rope of sand in the early 1950s.

Central to American thinking over any Japanese settlement was a wish to guide the probable economic and military policies Tokyo might embark upon. Japan's only friend was the United States. This had less to do with the Cold War, though this obviously influenced some nations greatly, than memories of earlier Japanese trading behaviour and the recent disgraceful conduct of its military. Japan was a pariah state. Only the United States displayed much real magnanimity, though some others found it expedient to dole out a degree of sympathy in order to be seen to be supporting Washington on occasion.[5] The limits to Asian and Pacific goodwill were clearly apparent in the final peace negotiations.[6] Washington's support for Japan as its Asian protégé was distasteful to others, who felt that their past loyalties justified more urgent claims to American favour.

The starting point for the eventual San Francisco conference was the policy paper approved by the National Security Council (NSC 13/2) in October 1948. It was here that portions of the final peace outline were drafted. Yet despite this attempt to clarify the differing political, economic and military options open to the United States it was to be a long haul. The explanation for delay is two-fold. First there were acute differences within the branches of American government both in and between Washington and Tokyo and secondly the uncertainties of international relations constantly made it tempting to put off a treaty until trends were clearer. Prevarication was the easier way out, though this assumed that America would be able to maintain its occupation without undue Japanese dissent.

We shall concentrate on the evolution of American policies, since the decisions of its officials in Washington were at the heart of the matter. The rest of the world knew this to be patently the case and acted accordingly to gain a hearing. General MacArthur, in time, came to accept this unpalatable truth. His famous attempt in the spring of 1947 to persuade the American government to launch a peace offensive was the first and possibly most serious setback MacArthur received from Washington. Thereafter, although he continued to urge speed, his voice was never decisive and he tended to shift his view on issues, such as Japanese rearmament, after being consulted by visitors from Washington. MacArthur, of course, remained a factor in American analyses but the initiatives after the rebuff he received in 1947 came from across the Pacific. Hopes that London and Canberra might be able to attach themselves to SCAP's coat tails and gain a hearing through his influence also faded as it became increasingly clear that Washington was not about to be hurried into any decisions over Japan's future.

The critical caesura was between the State Department and the Pentagon. Certainly to present these differences as between two equally united and farsighted camps is a distortion but there remained throughout the occupation two separate bureaucratic versions of how best to grant peace and win Japanese post-treaty friendship. Their rivalries and concerns show clear demarcation. For most of our period the US military had the upper hand. Their forces were garrisoning Japan and some officers were making preliminary contacts with the embryonic postwar Japanese security forces. Sections of Japan's mis-named Demobilization Ministry, for example, had begun before the Korean war to consider a new naval organization; obviously clandes-tine activities of this nature could hardly be formulated without encouragement from elements within the US Navy.[7] The US Army for its part had a number of senior spokesmen, notably General Eichelber-ger, equally prepared to argue that Japan required an army to safeguard the islands from Communism. Eichelberger spoke in March 1950 of 'Red Russia and Red China, cowering behind their hundreds of divisions and pointing to a completely disarmed Japan!'[8]

NSC 13/2 was an incomplete document, though certainly a neces-sary first step in drawing attention to some of the issues. There were to be numerous logjams *en route* to the peace ceremonies. Yet the international situation only compounded the American dilemma; it did not create the question of how and when peace might be granted. The Japan question was an argument for doing nothing only to those who were perhaps less familiar with Japanese developments. George Kennan's PPS report began by urging caution rather than speed. These findings were not the blueprint for rebuilding Japan as America's new partner in Asia that some would have us imagine. It was highly uncertain in tone (unlike the personality of its author) and its key recommendation on strengthening the Japanese economy was hardly sensational, depending for its implementation on a greater political will by the Japanese authorities and encouragement from SCAP GHQ. To gain economic change in Japan was the principal objective of the US government following NSC 13/2. The Kennan mission had hedged over its other two instructions concerning US security needs in the region and the issue of an 'early' peace.

The problems of how to formulate the American government's position persisted, though MacArthur rightly dismissed these con-cerns as exaggerated, since efforts to promote domestic change to improve Japan's ability, in Kennan's words, 'to resist communism after the occupation period' took time. In the ensuing discussion the American military had a clearer picture of its objectives and a stronger position to build on. It might not be certain of its support from General MacArthur, who initially was firmly convinced that Japan, given its postwar constitutional renunciation of war, could be left neutral and American forces shunted off to Okinawa, but the US military's political power in Washington was considerable. British diplomats in the USA saw that the Chiefs of Staff and the senior figures in the Department of Army still had the whip hand in the winter of 1950.[9] It is difficult not to agree with their conclusion that without substantial Japanese rearmament and US–Japan agreement on bases for the US military in the post-treaty period the work of the occupation would be put at risk. Given Japanese vulnerability and understandable wariness towards rebuilding its armed forces and over permitting the Americans to remain the JCS made haste slowly. It appeared to be better to hang on to what had been gained.

This approach brought out the latent jealousy within the State Department to the administration of Japan. Its own record during the first four years of the occupation had not been as distinguished or even as important as it would have liked. From this summer of 1945 SCAP GHQ had found it relatively simple to politely exclude all but a handful of State Department officials from any substantial role in occupation affairs. George Atcheson Jr. made some headway as MacArthur's political advisor but after his unfortunate death in a plane crash off Hawaii in 1947 his successor William Sebald had a harder time of it. Admissions of impotence by 1949 reached the stage of confirming 'how little our top State Department man in Japan is consulted or even in fact given copies of State Department telegrams directed to him'.[10] This humiliation cannot be said to have spurred the department into united action. America's diplomats made little impact on the occupation and were slow to work towards an agreed peace settlement. The department lacked anyone capable of galvanizing its differing divisions into forming a coherent set of policies. There was drift and defeatism in its corridors. It was easier to criticize from afar than to propound alternative policies. In the peace debate, for example, there were major divisions with the State Department that persisted until 1949/50. Some favoured unarmed neutrality for Japan,[11] others thought the entire problem ought to be shunted off to the United Nations, while a third group advocated that Japan's own behaviour and US interests warranted a peace without delay since, as Edwin Reischauer rightly pointed out, the response of the Japanese people to the occupation would be an important factor that ought to preclude excessive change in American policies for Japan. In part the bureaucratic confusion within the State Department only mirrored the differences to be found in the Navy and Army departments, JCS, the Treasury, Department of Occupied Areas and American members of the FEC. However, it was eventually to be the view of President Truman by May 1950 that Secretary Acheson and his officials should be responsible for the agenda.[12] It was only after John Foster Dulles had been appointed special ambassador for the peace issue that the State Department came into its own.

Dulles' role was to ascertain how peace could be best attained. His task complemented the domestic economic changes taking place within Japan and his efforts were only possible within the context of the improving economic position and recognition from the Truman administration that greater attention had to be paid to Japan. The unpopular but effective Dodge reforms provided the framework for the peace settlements, since Washington was not about to permit Japan to obtain its independence without a modicum of internal stability. Dulles seized his unexpected opportunity. It was perhaps to prove his finest hour. President Truman's appointment of an internationalist Republican, who had seen his prospects of being named secretary of state dashed by his party's defeat in the 1948 presidential election and his personal debacle in the 1949 New York senatorial race, was a godsend to Dulles' career. Solving the Japan question was to permit Dulles to work his way back to party and public favour. He began cautiously by checking with his Republican colleagues before accepting the post from a president under severe attack for his 'loss' of China. The shift in American policy was made public by President Truman's press conference of 18 May 1950 during which he hoped that peace with Japan would be possible before too long and announced the appointment of Dulles as advisor to the State Department. What should not be overlooked, however, was Truman's need to stress that Secretary Acheson had primary responsibility for the forthcoming negotiations. It would appear that this was required to dampen down persistent speculation over the position of Secretary of the Army Louis Johnson, and his proposed visit to Tokyo the following month where, accompanied by JCS chairman General Omar Bradley, he intended to consult with MacArthur. The Western press correctly noted that the delays and divisions within the American government had not yet to be papered over. There was nothing foreordained by Dulles' selection.

Yet, in retrospect, Dulles' appointment was the end of the beginning. The president had felt sufficiently emboldened (or desperate) to announce a new bipartisan initiative on Japan. He judged that the selection of a prominent Republican whom he regarded initially with some suspicion would placate the opposition, dampen down the increasingly shrill attacks from Senator McCarthy and provide the necessary evidence to America's allies that the peace question was under serious consideration.[13] More importantly, perhaps, it implied that the US military now would have to reconsider its objections to a peace treaty with Japan. For the first time the JCS and their advisors were under presidential pressure to justify their objections to granting peace with Japan. The contrast in press coverage between, for example, the *New York Times* headlines in mid-May provides a striking illustration of this shift. James Reston could write in the *New York Times* on 12 May an account of the State Department's difficulties subheaded 'Acheson Still Does not Have Backing for Firm Policy From Joint Chiefs or Truman', while less than a week later his paper began by crying 'Truman Optimistic on Japanese Pact'. Yet, however the press and foreign envoys might assess the importance of the presidential announcement, it would require feats of energy from Dulles to produce an acceptable agreement. He certainly was, as his most recent biographer has shown, 'a relative newcomer in intensely worked territory',[15] but this was to be to his advantage. A fresh approach and the knowledge that he had presidential support were to make remarkable changes on a subject that had long festered.

Dulles' initial thoughts on a peace settlement corresponded approximately to the current view of many in the State Department (and British Foreign Office) that a relatively generous treaty ought to be gained in the near future. Before Dulles could work out his ideas in depth he paid a visit to Japan and it was during his stay in Tokyo that he heard the news of the outbreak of fighting on the Korean peninsula. Peace for Japan immediately lost attention as the administration committed itself to massive intervention to assist South Korea. Dulles was quickly convinced that the fighting was part of a Communist attempt to overrun all of Korea in order to challenge the United States' hold on Japan. In one of his better metaphors Dulles spoke graphically of Japan at risk. If the Soviet Union and its allies were to capture all of Korea, then, recalling also the Soviet position on Sakhalin, 'Japan would be between the upper and lower jaws of the Russian Bear. That obviously would make it more difficult to provide the Japanese people with security as self-governing, unarmed members of the free world.'[16]

Negotiations recommenced in the autumn of 1950 on three fronts simultaneously. President Truman's statement in September 1950 that members of the Far Eastern Commission were to be informally sounded out by the US on the peace question suggested that sufficient progress already was being made in the American and Japanese negotiations. Such remarks reflected Dulles' efforts to gain an approximate consensus within the US and hinted at possible American attitudes towards Japan. Sympathetic treatment was implied in Truman's remark that '[I]t has long been the view of the United States

Government that the people of Japan were entitled to a peace treaty which would bring them back into the family of nations'.[17] It was certainly Dulles' opinion that Japan had earned the right to independence. He might become exasperated by talking to Japanese figures in Tokyo, but his judgement that Japan had to be treated as a potential ally, despite American and Allied remonstrations, rarely wavered. It was the only strategy that might pay dividends; anything smacking of a Carthaginian settlement would fail to last. What others held to be excessive generosity certainly was to disrupt Dulles' plans, but his determination and skill in speaking on occasion out of both sides of his mouth kept up the momentum. A small professional staff, succinct briefings and considerable travel also played their part in Dulles' offensive. Dulles practically invented shuttle-diplomacy. His frequent visits to Tokyo, London, Canberra and Manila eventually bore fruit.

Dulles' greatest difficulty was over the question of Japanese security. He can not be said to have been particularly satisfied with his negotiations with the Japanese government on this score. The seemingly endless prevarications by Prime Minister Yoshida and his inability to think through a consistent approach left Dulles despondent. The eventual compromise was to postpone many issues and to provide the grounds for decades of future dispute. Despite the United States' strengths over Japan, Dulles gained less than he intended from a stubborn Japanese government that pleaded pacifism and poverty in response to earnest suggestions that Tokyo faced a hostile environment with little but American aims and questionable international goodwill to preserve its territory. Dulles, for all his very considerable disappointments over the limited degree of Japanese rearmament he was able to persuade Japan to institute, quickly became a spokesman for a peace settlement that was in many ways in advance of opinion in sections of the American government and most of the Asian-Pacific region. Dulles in September 1951 had achieved much that twelve months earlier he had defined to the head of the British mission in Japan as the 'essential' gaining of 'the cooperation and good will of the Japanese people. Japan . . . should be encouraged to develop cultural, social and economic relations with the rest of the world as soon as possible. There were, of course, risks in restoring Japan's full freedom of action. Nevertheless the risks must be faced, and the alternative course of repressing Japan was bound to fail.'[18]

The risks for Dulles were also considerable. He wished to retain the confidence of Republican leaders, endeavoured to listen to MacArthur's views,[19] and wanted to at least appear fair-minded to his

35

overseas hosts on the diplomatic round. He had also to go through the motions of discussing some peace questions with the Soviet Union. This ultimately came to nought and the contents were leaked by Moscow to the press. Over the question of inviting the People's Republic of China to the conference table Dulles was even less flexible. The circumstances of the Korean war made this the necessary American approach, though it led to serious disputes with Britain and contributed to the absence of a number of Asian delegates from the final peace conference. The only temporary consolation for those who felt that Beijing ought to have been invited was that Britain effectively blocked Taiwan from also attending at San Francisco.[20] This proved small comfort to London, since shortly afterwards Japan made its own separate peace with Taipei and continued to obey the United States by cold-shouldering the PRC for a generation.

The views of Japan on the necessity and terms of a peace settlement were both simple and complex. On the general wish for a treaty there was unanimity. Successive Japanese cabinets and opinion across the entire political spectrum held firmly to the necessity for an early and equitable treaty. Diet resolutions merely voiced what the public demanded. Sebald reported to the State Department in November 1948, after receipt of one such resolution, that Japan saw a treaty as 'a kind of magical formula by which many of the economic maladjustments now plaguing the nation will be automatically solved'.[21] Rising Japanese expectations came up, however, against what was perceived to be American dilatoriness.

This preoccupation had to be accommodated. The United States, therefore, commenced hiving off portions of its responsibilities onto the Japanese government. This reduced the role of SCAP without satisfying more than some Japanese aspirations. The crumbs it gained were rarely sufficient. There were, as we have seen, greater economic freedoms and some previously tainted figures were now depurged and declared person grata. The United States Army, however, wished only to go to the brink and devised (on paper) schemes for granting Tokyo a semi-peace. This would have left most internal affairs in Japanese hands without disturbing the positions of American bases or Washington's control over Japan's external affairs. The seriousness with which such extraordinary plans were drafted says much for the unreality that existed by 1949 in some official American circles. A half free and a half dependent Japan would inevitably have invoked memories of the unequal treaties that had dominated Japanese foreign policy from the forcible opening of Japan in the mid nineteenth century until their final removal in 1899. The certain nationalist reaction can be imagined. 'Peace without a peace' could have wrecked long-term American aims in Japan.

Although by the autumn 1950 it was probable that peace was in the offing, the more difficult issue of its exact nature had still to be determined. Yet the United States had begun to make up for years of relative neglect and officials concerned with North-east Asia suddenly found themselves sought after figures with views worthy of attention. The ensuing months were to prove a rare period of drama in postwar US–Japan relations. Dulles' movements began to be covered in detail by the press. He was now in the limelight in much the same manner that MacArthur earlier had been the figure to quote and photograph. Dulles' speeches were subject now to careful scrutiny and his remarks poured over in the world's chancelleries. His energy and caution tended to offset each other, though on occasion he could be blunt when facing rebuffs.

The mounting American commitment and military difficulties in Korea were regarded by Dulles as no excuse for neglecting the Japanese peace question. He warned Secretary Acheson that any substantial delay might lead to a situation where 'we may lose in Japan more than we can gain in Korea'. Dulles suggested that '[i]t is probable that one of the purposes of the Korean attack was to break up United States planning of a peace treaty for Japan. This makes it particularly important that we should exhibit the confidence and resolution needed to proceed with our plan and not allow the Communist move to achieve its objective with reference to Japan'.[22] Dealing with the Japanese government had, however, to be given a lower priority to finally establishing what the United States wanted from the peace process.

To gain answers to this question Dulles placed the Japan issue in a broad international context. He stated in October, as the chairman of the Japan Study Group report of the Council on Foreign Relations, that the treaty could not be isolated from 'the prevention of the overpowering of the free world by the Soviet world'. He felt that '[t]he Communist offensive was probably aimed at getting control over Japan, for had Korea been conquered Japan would have fallen without an open struggle'[23], though this, of course, disregards the possibility that it was Communist fears of a rearmed, independent Japan that may have lain behind the North Korean offensive. For Dulles it followed that Japan must retain its pro-Western links through a policy of according Tokyo equality with the West, employing the precedent of the Anglo-Japanese alliance. Dulles sensed (or at least his staff did) that 'the Japanese have a certain contempt for the peoples of the Asian

37

mainland and a deep-rooted fear and distrust of Russia'[24] that would have advantages for the United States in steering Japan to stand with Washington against Communism but left the question of how best Japan might deal with the other Asian camp. It would, for example, have to trade with some one on the continent; a point that the British government had long appreciated, without knowing whether this could be achieved other than at its expense, particularly if the PRC were to be ignored.

Dulles committed himself almost immediately to a generous approach to win Japanese friendship, though he was not certain it would succeed in the long-term. This hesitancy may present problems for those who claim solid and lasting Pacific bonds stretching back to the liberal Anglo-Americanism of the 1920s and on automatically into the distant future. It was, however, the only strategy that might convince the Japanese government to stay firm. There were to be territorial restrictions, but no reparations, economic barriers or opposition to 'the recreation of a navy or air force'. Dulles was to insist on these objectives in the midst of assaults from American and Allied critics. He reckoned that no peace would 'of itself assure that Japan will remain within the orbit of the free world' but it could demonstrate that the Japanese 'are equals of the peoples of the West'. It was to be, with the exception of military business, a nondiscriminatory peace.

'The United States and Japan are the only significant sources of power in the Pacific, we actual, they potential': Dulles' explanation to MacArthur in March 1951 on the necessity for a positive approach was the theme behind American actions. The United States had to accept Japanese sovereignty in all areas except defence. Here Tokyo was not to be free to do as it pleased. Dulles, displaying the temper that was usually kept in check, was not about to accept Japanese excuses as adequate, given the changed international environment following the clashes in Korea. He found Yoshida's behaviour over Japanese security little short of absurd when the United States was eager to end the occupation and reach a peace settlement favourable to Tokyo. Opinion within Japan was sharply divided about the wisdom of accepting Dulles' advice, since the Pacific war and the recent denunciations of militarism could not be ignored by the Japanese bureaucracy. Those sections of the Foreign Ministry that attempted to prepare peace drafts that encouraged Japanese rearmament received an angry reception from Yoshida, in much the same way that his prevarications gained a cool response from Dulles.

Yet public opinion could not be entirely discounted. The Japanese response to the peace settlements was far from enthusiastic. At best it might be described as a sense of relief, at worst very considerable disappointment turning to active opposition in some cases. Those, however, protesting against the treaties were divided among themselves with the Socialists badly split over the issue of Japanese rearmament. Not everyone was prepared to uphold the party's earlier commitment to a total peace with all its occupiers, to remain neutral and prohibit foreign bases on Japanese soil, when the proximity of peace inevitably led to questions of Japanese alignment in a divided world and the need for self-defence. The left-wing Socialists argued that any remilitarization would leave Japan a hostage to foreign powers and predicted a repetition of the horrors of the Pacific war if Japan were to build a new military establishment. Merely to start to protect Japan might also lead to another 'dark valley' with repression at home and the loss of the newly-won democratic institutions. The gains of the occupation years might then be swallowed up in a general mobilization. Such assertions suggest both a lack of confidence on the left in the roots of the newly-proclaimed democratization of Japan and recognition that power was not going to be easily attainable by the Socialists. Distrust of the conservatives lay at the heart of the matter. The attempt to gain neutrality had widespread public support,[25] despite dissent within the Socialist party on the direction of Japanese foreign policy that would lead to unbridgeable rifts later on the left.[26]

Mass demonstrations throughout the 1950s against American military bases persisted and led eventually to the greatest public protests of the postwar decades in the spring and summer of 1960. Those who saw the need for some form of Japanese rearmament and security arrangements with the United States could rely on a majority in the Diet to endorse their views but precious little active support was forthcoming in the first decade following independence. Critics gained all the publicity; supporters of the security pact tended to keep quiet. To be seen to befriend the United States was a liability when Japan was popularly regarded as subservient to American Cold War strategies and beholden to Washington for economic favours.

The administrative agreement was perhaps the most politically damaging part of the peace settlements from the Japanese government's point of view. It was hardly an area where Tokyo could claim to have substantially altered the American's determination to retain broad legal rights. As with the issue of US bases in Japan there were senior officials who opposed the American demands but once again the United States won the day.[27] Foreign Minister Okazaki Katsuo failed to gain a diminution of American rights to use its bases pending a final agreement between the two nations; Japan, had, in effect, to promise to accept that its soon to be assumed sovereignty would not alter the bases' status quo. Much the same inequality continued over the controversial issue of criminal jurisdiction for US servicemen and their families. Japanese officials gained little in these encounters.

No Asian state welcomed Japan back into the region. Asian attitudes could hardly be described as cordial towards the newly-independent Japan. This uncomfortable reality was to persist for a considerable period. It was an inevitable consequence of the war years and recently presumed American favouritism towards Tokyo. Japan's greatest concern was over the attitude of the Russians. The Soviet Union refused to sign an American-dominated peace treaty and has yet to conclude a formal agreement with Japan. Its delegates attended the San Francisco conference only to use the venue as a convenience for launching barbs at Japan. This was all highly predictable and much less disturbing to Washington and London than to the Japanese foreign ministry, since Soviet invective served to underline the State Department's point over the ideological division of the globe and the Soviet military threat to the Japanese islands. The fact that the Soviet occupied northern territories could be seen with the naked eye from Hokkaido bore more heavily on the Japanese public than the US Congress.

Moscow's vision of Japan as an American satellite, capable at a later date of a repetition of its recent militarism in partnership with the United States, persisted. The impression that the Soviet Union continually presented to the rest of the world was that Japan could not be trusted. It was in many respects similar to the view of others in the region who (unlike the Soviet Union) had experienced at first hand the realities of Japanese imperialism and occupation. Comments from Moscow on Japan's ability to get round the imposed Allied reforms and return once more to the Asian mainland and Pacific waters were also the small change of endless conversations in Manila and Melbourne. Chinese and Australian criticisms of Japan during the public debates of the Allied Council for Japan paralleled on more occasions than the United States would have wished the sentiments of the Soviet delegate. It was not only the Cold War but also the Pacific war that divided the Asian-Pacific region. It was the need to reassure the United States' allies over Japan as much as fear of the PRC that led to the ANZUS and Manila pacts. The past would not go away.

The Soviet Union's objectives in occupied Japan are not entirely clear. It is, however, generally reckoned that Moscow wanted to gain support from groups within Japan sympathetic to Communism and to do what it could to paint the US–Japan relationship in as unpleasant a light as possible. It had little chance, presumably, of seeing its friends gain power but may have had higher expectations of causing a degree of nuisance. The Japanese Communist Party would not repeat its electoral successes of 1949 when it won 35 seats to the alleged consternation of Yoshida and his men. As with earlier rice demonstrations, the conservatives were not above depicting the prospects of Communism as a danger that might threaten the stability of occupied Japan to gain favours from the United States. Some on the right did have such nightmares[28], but MacArthur took a more relaxed view of this spectre.

It would be false to imagine simply because the United States had prepared carefully for the occupation of Japan that things automatically fell into place once the American forces landed. The 1947 Constitution, the retention of the Emperor, the nature of land reform and the details of educational change were crucial pieces of the American design that had had to be worked out under pressure after the occupation had begun. To assume that other Allies and the Japanese government played no role in either prompting or delaying American schemes is simplistic, though it was not in doubt that the United States was entitled to the final word, since it had won the war and rightly led the occupation. Likewise, drafting the peace treaties could not be done single-handed if the USA wished to win a degree of Japanese support and Allied assent. The length of time involved and the effort expended by the United States to devise a satisfactory series of peace settlements suggests that Washington was fully conscious of the obstacles that had to be overcome in a manner that might win friendship from a wary Japan and hesitant Allies.

Even at the end the United States was unable to gain quite the approval it had hoped for from the rest of the world. While it is certainly true that American diplomats were able to whip in a large number of nations to vote for its text, the fact remains that twenty of these signatories came from Latin America. Chile and Colombia had done little to defeat Japan. India and China who had contributed a great deal more were absent from San Francisco.[29] The State Department's view, made in the euphoria of gaining its goal, that the acclaim from supporting delegates 'bore effective witness to the genuinely collaborative nature of the treaty negotiations and of the final text' is somewhat misleading.[30] Only eight of the thirteen members of the Far Eastern Commission and two out of four ACJ members actually signed the peace treaty. There were several disappointments as well as numerous successes in the peace process. Even conquerors and occupiers have to discover the limits of their power, though Truman

41

was correct to ask in an unsent letter to the columnist Arthur Krock in September 1952:'[w]ere the Japanese Treaty and the Pacific Agreements blunders?'[31] The answer, despite the unsatisfactory absence of major Asian states and the half-hidden difficulties over the security pact, has to be in the negative.

In any analysis of the peace treaty, the US–Japan Security pact and the administrative agreement it is difficult not to regard Washington as the power that had gained most from the negotiations. Given the United States' position in Japan since 1945 and its strengths in the region the outcome was broadly in line with existing power realities. The peace terms spelt out at San Francisco reflected the United States victory in the Pacific war, its domination of the occupation and its determination to maintain its influence over Japan. There were few surprises. It was hard to deflect Dulles, Rusk and Allison from their objectives. Isolated concessions were granted to Tokyo but these only reinforced the clear impression of both sides that the United States held firm to its basic goals. The Japanese, of course, had spent a great deal of time from the winter of 1945 onwards considering peace problems (what else was there for officials of its rump foreign ministry to do than ponder Japan's future and the related fate of their careers?) but the paperwork signified industry rather than influence. Task forces abounded; alterations to American drafts were rarer birds. It has even been questioned whether the bulk of this material got any further than SCAP's Diplomatic Section which was not exactly the boiler room of GHQ.[32] Even if portions were accepted and digests later transmitted back to Washington their impact on Dulles is likely to have been marginal at best. After 1950 what mattered was the more personal diplomacy conducted by the Japanese prime minister, who could be notoriously secretive in his handling of peace issues. Yoshida may have known what he wanted but his officials and colleagues were often kept deliberately in the dark. This was not simply a result of Yoshida's sense of vanity that he was the best man for the job, since the Gaimusho was itself divided over, for example, the highly sensitive issue of US bases in Japan following any peace treaty. Some of its proposals on Japanese security provoked nothing but Yoshida's easily ignited anger.[33]

The most critical part of Japanese peace diplomacy concerned the serious question of economic reconstruction. Here, too, planning had commenced with the surrender, but the concentration of talents brought about by the immediacy of Japan's destitution was greater and the consequences for Japan's future very considerable indeed. The need to resolve some of Japan's enormous economic difficulties was obvious when Tokyo looked like an extended charnelhouse in September 1945. Blitzed neighbourhoods, bullocks on the Ginza and general privation told their obvious story. Food, clothing, some sort of employment and rough accommodation were the national priorities throughout the occupation years. Japan was indeed to get its second innings later but this was very far from predictable in the aftermath of total war and unconditional surrender. National recovery required a herculean popular response, astute planning, American economic assistance and a goodly portion of luck. It was, however, still a weak and uncertain Japan that regained its independence in 1952. American officials thought there would be little that its country could purchase from Japan given the parlous state of Japan's export trades, yet access to the American market was vital for Japan. American aid, technology and free trading arrangements with the United States formed the basis for Japan's post-San Francisco links with Washington, in Japanese eyes. Japanese poverty and the lack of alternative markets for gaining the foreign currency with which to purchase essential imports underpinned the relationship with the United States. This led the State Department to confidently predict in September 1951 that 'Japan's dependence on the US for economic assistance will to a large extent automatically assure her alignment with the free world'.

The claim of some students of the occupation that Yoshida was responsible for Japan winning the peace after losing the war is suspect.[34] The details of the peace treaties rarely support the frequently made suggestion that Japan was able to gain more at the negotiating table than objective circumstances warranted. Certainly Yoshida rejected advice from many quarters on the inadvisability of linking his nation too closely to the United States but the terms under which Japan regained its statehood were onerous. Yoshida, the Anglophile, had to make the best deal he could with a nation with which he had few personal sympathies. His bitter disappointments over the course of the occupation and the nature of the peace were however partly submerged because he could foresee no alternative. Since the United States had so clearly replaced Britain as the leader of the West in Asia it would be necessary for Japan to align itself with Washington. It was not pleasant for Yoshida but he saw no other way that his nation could rebuild its economy and gain the necessary protection amidst the tensions of the region. Yet his hopes of retaining some links with the PRC were rejected by Dulles on senatorial advice, he was obliged to consent to the principle of rearmament in depth and assurances over economic assistance from the United States were less generous than he had hoped. This was hardly the handiwork of a national saviour.

43

Yoshida's successes are hard to find. His personal courage is not in doubt – he alone signed the unpopular US–Japan Security pact to stress his own responsibility – but events were in the saddle once he had decided that Japan's redemption could only come about under American aegises. There were strict limits to what any Japanese politician could achieve.

Immediate American assessments of their work in occupied Japan were more modest than some later accounts would have us believe. General MacArthur entertained few illusions about future difficulties for the new Japan. He was uncertain as to whether there would be any lasting positive legacy and told Sir George Sansom in January 1951 that he did not think Japan had become a democracy. He merely said, after making due allowance for alternations after the peace treaty, that 'the Japanese would not revert to unqualified militarism'.[35] MacArthur's caution was balanced by two factors that would persist in later years. He thought that a reversion to authoritarianism was improbable because '[t]hey could not, even if they wished, so long as the Allied Powers could use economic pressure' and 'in any case he believed that there was, since 1945, a growth in the feeling for freedom among the Japanese people and this was bound to play a part in domestic politics in the future'.[36] Equally low-keyed was Dean Acheson's remark to the Senate Foreign Relations Committee the previous year when he went no further than saying '[w]e have, I think, not done badly at all in Japan'.[37] Doubts abounded as to the strength of Japan's commitment to the West. It was perhaps in part a reflection of recent American disappointments in China and a recognition that much would have to be taken on trust against an uncertain international backcloth and limited prospects for Japanese overseas trade.

Japan's attention was inevitably narrower than the United States. Its primary objective for over the past six years had been to gain an end to the occupation. It saw less reason to place itself immediately within what Dulles termed 'the framework of a larger problem, namely, the prevention of the overpowering of the free world by the Soviet world'.[38] Yoshida was too astute a diplomat not to miss the opportunity to bargain presented by Dulles' need to secure Japanese membership of what he spoke of glowingly as the Western club.[39] Any reevaluation of Tokyo's worth to the United States would clearly mark up Japan's stock, but formal discussions had hardly begun before 1950. The Japanese government could observe at first hand the development of the Cold War through American criticisms of the Soviet member of the Allied Council for Japan, yet neither side can be said to have been particularly forthcoming. The whimsical and secretive behaviour of Yoshida made the situation no easier. He could only too easily annoy senior American diplomats by producing a succession of contradictory, impulsive remarks on the peace question. No wonder that Dulles found Yoshida infuriating when he might outline mischievous schemes for permitting the Allies to decide Japan's policy towards China (knowing, of course, that Washington and London were hopelessly split on the issue), or speak of neutrality one moment and a fully-fledged alliance with the United States the next. Yoshida and Dulles had their largest disagreement over the so-called 'Yoshida Letter'. Here, Dulles had to operate under the rubric of senators anxious to prevent any backsliding from Japan over the non-recognition of the People's Republic of China and, therefore, requiring cast-iron guarantees that the future Japanese state would deal only with Taiwan. Yoshida attempted to evade such a commitment, only to be hoist with his own petard by despatching personal delegates to Taipei without adequate instructions. What Yoshida had hoped would be no more than a promise to Dulles for a treaty with the Nationalists became a stronger document thanks to Taipei's insistence on a peace treaty with territory that might yet become Chiang Kai-shek's if he were to make his triumphant return to the mainland.[40]

The issue of China was only one of a considerable number of difficulties that had to be faced over gaining agreement at San Francisco. Since it was apparent that the Soviet Union would be highly unlikely to sign a treaty so obviously intended to bolster American interests in east Asia, Dulles wished to emphasize that his draft had a wide-range of support from lesser powers in the region. This he was largely unable to achieve. It was asking much of newly independent states to turn the other cheek and make peace with a Japan guilty of so much recent barbarism and now transformed into the favourite son of the United States. Neither then (nor later) did recognition of the horrors of Japan's own wartime occupation of Asia sink very deeply into the Japanese mind. It has been easier and more comforting for the Japanese to equate Pearl Harbor and Hiroshima rather than to reconsider Nanking and the reigns of terror in South-east Asia.

There were two factors that further reduced the impact of the American occupation on the Japanese public. The first was the omission of any reference within the treaty to the moral aspirations that had been behind some of the initial American programmes for Japan. Edwin Reischauer, when examining the 'psychological questions involved in the draft Japanese peace treaty' in the autumn of 1949, had rightly noted that it would be possible to 'capitalize on this Japanese idealism and not suddenly shift to a coldly practical tone in

45

the peace treaty'. This unfortunately was ignored in 1951 and it has become a force of lesser importance in Japanese society as the occupation era has faded from public consciousness. In a period following the disgrace of defeat it might have been sensible to have incorporated reference to the principles of what Reischauer termed 'high idealism and universal and timeless concepts'.[41]

The second issue was more damaging for American interests. The occupation had been a military exercise and some of the activities of its soldiery had hardly endeared the United States to the Japanese public. General MacArthur might speak favourably of his GIs as ambassadors to Japan but such statements were made for export only. The reality in Tokyo, Osaka and Kobe could be very different from the picture presented in the *Stars and Stripes* and home-town newspapers. There were, of course, serious students of Japanese affairs (some of whom would retain their interest and swim to the surface later as authorities on Japanese literature and politics) but equally there were serious problems. It was said of one black unit in Kobe that its officers only saw their men at pay parade and court martials.[42] The remarks made by General Ridgway to US forces at the moment the occupation ended suggest that the military authorities were fully aware of past antisocial behaviour and the hazards ahead.[43] Comfortable housing, abundant food, PXs and ready cash highlighted the divide between American soldier and Japanese civilian. The conquerors seemed to hold most of the cards. All too often the expansion of US military installations and the arrival of dependents created a bloated establishment where 'to a casual observer it appears that the occupation is principally engaged in taking care of itself.'[44] No wonder the State Department was eager to end the whole business and the military equally determined to hold onto a good thing. The issue of the United States' security relationship with Japan was fated to hold centre stage throughout the 1950s.

3 INEQUALITY: THE 1950s

The Japanese themselves are to some extent still living in a dream world.

John Allison, November 1952

What I am worried about is that when Japan is attacked from the outside the Japanese people will be playing 'pachinko' because the United States armed forces will be taking care of defense. Is that the plan of the Government?

Ashida Hitoshi, July 1953

The most important thing to avoid in conversation is the temptation to give advice.

State Department advice to Secretary of Defense Charles Wilson prior to his visit to Japan, May 1954

The United States concluded its occupation successfully. Minimum American goals had been met, since prospects for continued friendship with Japan were satisfactory, the 1947 constitution was in place, Japan's economy had been greatly boosted by the Korean War procurements boom, and guarded expectations were held of contributions by Tokyo towards its own defence. The contrast in the state of relations between the United States and Japan at the end of the Pacific bloodbath in the summer of 1945 and the civility of 1952 was both stark and reassuring.[1] Responsibility for this extraordinary shift in attitudes is clearly shared between the two nations, but it would be churlish not to assign the lion's part to American officials stationed in Japan. Even the most critical of Yoshida's many opponents might have been prepared to admit in private that events had not turned out as badly as most had feared when the first American troops had landed. Japan was once again in a sovereign state, its economy was recovering and a host of enforced changes had begun to transform Japanese society.

The left, of course, was not about to remain silent over what it saw as a partial peace and subservience to American imperialism in Asia, yet such opportunities for open criticism and protest were in them-

47

selves an important reflection of a new Japan. The occupation had liberated Japan through a bloodless (if necessarily incomplete) revolution. Whatever the complaints of the right and the doubts of the left there was not unlikely to be any large-scale retreat to the prewar order. Certainly the same figure was still on the throne and some ministers and bureaucrats had hopes of altering parts of the occupation's handiwork but any major move was improbable in the light of new public expectations and constitutional requirements. Many of the occupation's reforms took root. It could all have been a great deal worse.

What would happen next would inevitably depend on a host of diverse factors. Some would be beyond Japan's control but part of the answer was assumed to lie within the orbit of the Japanese government. It was generally reckoned that, in the verdict of the British Foreign Office at the coming of the peace, 'never again will America occupy such a dominating position in Japan as at present'. This prediction was soon proved correct, without, however, any realization by other powers that they too might begin to influence Japanese developments. The ending of the occupation saw instead the eventual reemergence of Japan as a force to be reckoned with in the Asian-Pacific region in league with the United States. Yet it was a gradual process that frequently exasperated Washington and left many Japanese decidedly uneasy at the attempts made by the United States to persuade Tokyo that it ought to assert itself for the common good. Memories of the Pacific war and fears that Japanese rearmament might lead to a return to militarism in the land worked as powerful constraints on American pleas.

The 1950s provide a transition period for Japan between earlier subjection and later self-confidence. In terms of foreign policy the governments of this decade were ever-conscious of American pressures and protection. This led to both dependence on American military strength and a determination of some of Yoshida's successors to discover alternative paths for Japan which might well provoke American displeasure. The 1950s were to demonstrate both the scope of its ambitions and the limits of American power over Japan.

Tokyo's main anchor was obviously the United States. American impressions of Japan were slow to change from the images formed during the occupation era. MacArthur's damning conclusion in August 1949 that Japan was 'not even a third-rate power' would long persist.[2] Those in Washington who were following events in Japan tended to assume that Japan's 'basic national objectives will be to rebuild its national strength and to enhance its position in the Far East' through 'close cooperation with the US, at least during the next two or three years'.[3] Intelligence estimates in 1952 reckoned that 'the most probable long-term prospect' would see Japan remaining within 'the framework of a generally pro-Western orientation', though 'seeking to eliminate the basing of US troops in Japan and seeking to attain increased influence and leadership in Asian affairs of joint US–Japanese concern'.[4] Those in the West who adopted the opposite approach and were eager to see Japan reappear as a regional power would have their hopes dashed time and again, since it was domestic reconstruction that remained the key to Japan's future. The uncertainties of economic recovery and the political scene in the early 1950s left little ground for the realization that '[t]here can be no stability in the Far East unless Japan stands on its own feet and plays the part of a great power'.[5] John Allison summarized the realities best when he cautioned 'it is difficult to make any quick, easy statement . . . about whether the situation in Japan is good or bad. All sorts of things could go wrong politically, economically and other ways'.[6]

Linked to American doubts over Japan's future were Japanese reservations over the extent of Washington's interest in supporting and protecting Tokyo. General Ridgway wrote to the Department of the Army that '[t]he most vital factor in the achievement of US objectives in the Orient is the continued maintenance of Japanese faith in our commitment to guarantee the essential security of Japan, until it is capable of assuming that responsibility of a sovereign state'.[7] Ridgway wished that the American commitment be clearly spelt out to the Japanese government, since the Japanese people, like others outside the Communist orbit in Asia, are 'ever alert to any indication of a weakening in our political or military policies towards them. Japanese response to US leadership will be predicated upon a constant realistic appraisal of US intentions and commitments on a positive and long range basis. What they think our intentions are, may be even more important than what these intentions actually are.'[8] Speaking in April 1952 'of the imminent and unlamented demise of SCAP', he concluded that 'we must by word and deed do everything within our power to overcome any feeling in the oriental mind that our interest in Asia is casual, temporary or overshadowed by our interests in other regions'. The language and sentiments of MacArthur clearly lived on.

A relationship of sorts was in the making. Both sides had now to work out the details behind their professions of military and economic cooperation. The greatest difficulty facing the Eisenhower administration and successive conservative cabinets in Japan during the 1950s was undoubtedly the issue of the security treaty and its possible

49

modification. All other problems in US–Japan relations between the San Francisco peace settlements and the eventual revision of the security pact in 1960 pale into insignificance against this running sore. Negotiations over an appropriate level of Japanese rearmament and a more equitable basing arrangement for United States personnel stationed within Japan provide a continuous thread woven tightly into the decade. Security diplomacy was to have an importance in US–Japan relations during the 1950s that would later be replaced by an equally strong mutual obsession with trading ties. The difference, of course, between the two national responses to security revision in the 1950s and trade disputes since the 1970s has been the reversal in roles; it was the Japanese public that took to the streets to campaign against the American (and Japanese) governments in 1960, while today it is US Congressmen and their constituents who are up in arms at Japanese trading behaviour.

Disagreement over security affairs had been clear during the occupation era. The San Francisco peace settlements made it all too apparent that Japanese society was badly split over the issue to the extent that senior State Department officials were obliged to report to Washington that 'Yoshida is wobbly about rearmament. He gives lip service to the necessity for some form of Japanese defence force but does not recognize the realities or know how to start.'[9] The response from most Japanese politicians during the 1950s was not dissimilar. It led to an almost continuous series of exchanges between the United States and Japan without either side gaining much satisfaction.

The gravest Japanese suspicions over rearmament would persist far beyond the 1950s, but the subject was inevitably of the greatest public concern in the years immediately after surrender. Yoshida himself apparently avoided all public mention of the word defence (*boei*) until January 1951 and the Japanese penchant for coy euphemism was to be given endless scope in the realm of security statements.[10] There remains to this day no official recognition that the Japanese army, navy and air forces are anything beyond Self-Defence Forces, whose role, at least to the public at large, is consigned to emergency relief operations in the case of summer typhoons, earthquakes and coastal accidents. In the years following San Francisco, the title, function and strengths of the rearmed military units changed as the result of American persuasion and gradual acceptance by (at the least) the Japanese government that the subject would not go away. Yet Yoshida employed a host of arguments to deter the United States and was able to delay rearmament in depth during his tenure as prime minister. His successors were rarely any keener to follow the Pentagon's logic.

Much of the subsequent embarrassment felt by many Japanese over the creation of a postwar military establishment stems from the opposition expressed in the early 1950s to the tripod of agreements reached with the United States on Japan's security. The mutual security pact, bases agreement and military assistance programmes emphasized the obvious point that Japanese rearmament would take place only with the active encouragement of the United States. The nature of the protracted negotiations that had to be accomplished before agreement could be reached on all these issues suggests once more that the Japanese government had serious reservations to the steps it would reluctantly have to undertake.

The majority view in Japan during the 1950s was undoubtedly to keep as much distance as possible from linking a degree of rearmament with larger American plans for Japan's security and wider regional schemes. Those who maintain influential Japanese politicians and military personnel had plans from 1947 onwards for a coherent defence build-up risk ignoring the ever-present popular suspicion that Japan might be on the march again.[11] Even Ashida Hitoshi, the figure who perhaps pressed the hardest for Japan to possess its own military once more, admitted in January 1951 that public opinion might well reject a constitutional amendment over alteration to article 9's renunciation of war.[12] The debate over the San Francisco settlements saw both future premier Miki Takeo (then of the National Democratic Party) and Yoshida's own attorney general argue that Japan ought not to rearm. There was no national consensus over the wisdom of reestablishing a new Japanese military (however termed) and widespread dissatisfaction at Yoshida's consent to the stationing of US personnel on Japanese soil.

Security diplomacy continued throughout the 1950s as Japan and the United States attempted to gain very different objectives. Only after violent protest in 1960 was the United States prepared to substantially amend its earlier security pact and take more careful note of the objections of considerable sections of Japanese politics. For much of the decade, however, the United States government, acting on the advice of its military leaders, was reluctant to alter course. It seemed at times as if Washington was more interested in holding onto what it had gained through the peace settlements than recognizing that ultimately no agreement would be worth the paper it was written on if domestic support were to collapse. European observers wrote scathingly at times of the ham-fisted style of American negotiations with Japan and felt that the Pentagon had too large an influence on entire American policy towards their Japanese 'oyster'.[13]

51

The temptation to insist on retaining the advantages gained from the Japanese government after arduous bargaining was understandable. The US military had no desire to surrender the privileges of the occupation era; it may have tended to remain mentally within the confines of the past. General Ridgway certainly spoke emphatically against such attitudes in September 1951 when he cautioned that the 'new era' would bring 'a marked change in the personal relationship between each of us and the Japanese people. The Occupation ends. We become guests in their land which joins the ranks of the free nations of the world.'[14] But Yoshida had no great wish to regard membership of the Western democratic group as requiring an onerous military contribution from his nation. The agreement to some degree of rearmament and the bases arrangements appeared to him to more than suffice. He faced continuous sniping over security matters throughout the last two years of his rule in damaging confrontations with both the Eisenhower administration urging him forward and his opponents telling him to retreat. Where Yoshida stood personally has been the subject of debate. Western diplomats generally portrayed him as not wanting to do more than the minimum since he felt his country could not afford the expenditure and equally unwilling to offer any leadership or explanation to the public of the realities facing Japan.[15] Yoshida's reluctance to come clean on defence was part of his wider difficulty in adopting to parliamentary politics. He fell, in what was in effect the British ambassador's obituary on Yoshida's lengthy term as premier, because he 'failed to make even the remotest effort to keep the Diet, his Cabinet colleagues, the press or the public on his side'.[16]

Yoshida's reputation would grow later to the extent that even in the late 1980s all rival candidates for the post of Liberal-Democratic president (and thereby automatically prime minister) would shelter under claims to be the rightful heir to Yoshida's 'mainstream' conservatism[17] but he left office under a cloud. He probably delayed his departure too long and was badly hurt by a succession of political scandals endemic to postwar Japanese politics. Yet valuable parts of Japan's external relations were laid in place by Yoshida and his stock rose later when the American alliance was judged in a more positive light and the domestic economy came good.

Undoubtedly the basic planks for the US–Japan relationship were the responsibility of Yoshida's cabinets. Some assessment of his years in office is now required. Yoshida's own view of his record centred on his work to gain a peace treaty for his nation. His numerous critics complained that the costs of regaining Japan's sovereignty were excessively high, but this is to ignore the very considerable limitations on Yoshida's freedom to manoeuvre. He saw that the choices facing Japan over peace negotiations were constrained by American strength and a hostile regional environment that had existed since 1945 and was to be further exacerbated by the outbreak of the Korean War. Yoshida's cooperation with the United States, which has earned him the 'good loser' tag, was created largely by circumstances beyond his control. It was, however, to his credit that he made the best of a bad job and gained politically and economically what he lost militarily. The trade-off between advantages for Japan's recovery through American assistance necessarily involved concessions over American strategic considerations. Yoshida's later defenders have reason to argue that Japan's reconstruction can hardly be ascribed merely to national determination to conquer austerity and that to denigrate Japan's principal politician for the first postwar decade is to be overswayed by criticism from his opponents.[18] It will not do to regard Yoshida merely as an old man enamoured with the Anglo–Japanese alliance who muddled Japan through from the occupation to independence. His undoubted nostalgia for an earlier era did not prevent him from binding his nation to a newer international scheme.[19] Yoshida was a realist who appreciated that Japan's weaknesses would take time to correct and that a degree of dependence on the United States was the only valid strategy worth pursuing for the present.

Yoshida's policies were acceptable, however grudgingly, to the bulk of the Japanese people. Opposition was certainly vocal but a premier who was able to boast of the formation of five cabinets should be given his due. When the peace treaty was sent to the lower house of the Diet for approval it was passed by the overwhelming votes of 307 to 47 and even the security pact sailed through by 289 votes to 71. It was not only the conservatives who gave their consent. It is not, therefore, entirely accurate to suggest that all on the left attacked the San Francisco settlements or were totally opposed to Yoshida's links with the United States and alignment with the West in the Cold War. More Socialists voted for the peace treaty than against it, though both groups united to reject the security pact.[20] The National Democrats, after a great deal of intraparty discussion, agreed to vote for the twin treaties and, despite their suspicions of a secretive and stubborn Yoshida, did display a degree of bipartisanship that appeared improbable in 1950. Public opinion may have been more apathetic than angry at Yoshida's actions. Surveys in the press suggest that the stress of the left on either a pro-Communist line or a neutralist foreign policy had far less support than those who either welcomed the peace or had no views on international relations.[21] There was perhaps widespread if unenthusiastic agreement in Japan that the peace settlements were the best that could be obtained. Yoshida may have been speaking for many in Japan when he told one senior British government representative at San Francisco that 'it is more generous than I expected'.[22]

The security pact was clearly less well received than the peace treaty. Yet there was an expectation on both the Japanese and American sides that it might prove to be a merely temporary arrangement. It was, of course, likely that American figures would stress the future possibility of termination of the security treaty as a ploy to sweeten the pill, but such statements did raise at least the prospect of change. This opportunity, however, was dependent on Japan assuming action over its own defence. It placed the onus on Tokyo to provide more substantially for its national security. To complain of the unequal peace and yet to continue to oppose rearmament was precisely the irresponsibility that angered the Eisenhower administration. Even a rearmed Japan at the levels proposed by the United States would have presented a flimsy basis for Soviet and Chinese complaints in the mid-1950s. As it was, the degree of Japanese remilitarization was far less than Washington had hoped for and a threat to no one in the region. Red Star and the People's Daily might thunder on but the rampant nationalism and expansionism that Moscow and Beijing claimed to detect was largely a mirage. It is difficult to see in either the San Francisco peace treaty or the ensuing military arrangements much evidence to bolster Gromyko's assertion in September 1951 that '[t]he American–British draft is not a Treaty of Peace but a treaty for the preparation of a new war in the Far East'.[23] Such fears were indeed widespread within and without Japan, yet objective evidence is hard to come by that Japan was anything but reluctant to shoulder even a portion of the defence burden. The United States throughout the 1950s was more in the position of constantly chastising Japan for its ineffectiveness than building up a new force in east Asia that might threaten its neighbours. Yoshida led a Japan that was hesitant indeed to dance to the American drum. It might be more profitable to note Yoshida's attempts to delay effective response to demands from the Pentagon than to decry his agreement to permit US forces to remain on the Japanese archipelago. He was not able to brush off more than some American recommendations but it is apparent that Yoshida's diplomacy was not mere shadow boxing.

Agreement on the security pact was only reached after considerable debate. Dulles' difficulties over Japan in the peace negotiations were a taste of what he would have to confront on several occasions with

Japan during his lengthy term as secretary of state. Much of the pressure for an accelerated rearmament came from the American side and most Japanese politicians were exceedingly wary of obliging the United States. Yoshida's procrastination was based on his contempt for Japan's prewar officer class (with good reason given the way he was treated in 1945) and his concern that remilitarization could bring a return to the recent past. He backed these views up by claiming that Japan could not afford rearmament, in the same manner that he had most undiplomatically informed the San Francisco conference that Japan faced 'huge difficulties' in complying with its reparations obligations.[24] Poverty was a convenient excuse for avoiding what other nations pressed on Japan. Yet, it was not the state of the economy but the attitude of the public that made for such slow progress over defence. The economic arguments, probably genuinely held by Yoshida whose knowledge of the discipline was slight, were far from convincing given the rapid improvement in Japan's industrial output in the 1950s. The nation that led the world in shipbuilding capacity and design technology would have had little difficulty in converting its yards to naval work. Diversion of resources to military programmes would hardly have imperilled an economy that by 1955 had already exceeded its prewar peak. What was lacking was not the necessary finance but the required leadership and national will.[25]

Yoshida attempted to straddle the gulf between American entreaties and Japanese hesitancy. The evidence from the later occupation years onwards suggests that he would have made even less effort without American pressure. It was General MacArthur who, after Yoshida had voiced his personal doubts, ordered the establishment of the National Police Reserve (Kokka Keisatsu Yobitai) in early July 1950 in the weeks following the outbreak of increasingly unfavourable fighting in Korea.[25] This paramilitary force (and strengthening of the already existing Maritime Safety Agency) found little favour with Yoshida's cabinet who were under a premier that only days previously had informed Dulles in Tokyo that rearmament was quite out of the question. If Yoshida did indeed regard the Korean War as 'a gift of the gods'[26] he would later have to discover that the undoubted economic advantages that were to flow to Japan weakened his case that Japan was illequipped psychologically and materially to assist in its own defence. Dulles maintained sufficient pressure on the Japanese government to carry out at least part of the commitment made in February 1951 to create a Japanese defence force (separate from the National Police Reserve) and a Defense Planning Staff (akin to the Joints Chiefs of Staff).[27] But the determination of Yoshida to dig in his heels was a constant source of disappointment to the secretary of state.

The differences between Japan and the United States were vividly seen in the Ikeda–Robertson talks of October 1953 that eventually formed the basis for the Japan–United States Mutual Defense Agreement of March 1954. It was a compromise that resulted in Washington accepting a figure for Japanese troops levels far below what had been desired, but it did gain the acceptance of limited rearmament, the establishment of an American Military Assistance Advisory Group in Japan and changes in the legal position of Japanese forces. The length of the talks and the differing glosses placed on the outcome showed the continuing problems facing the two nations. Yet it was, in the opinion of Ambassador John Allison, an accomplishment that Yoshida's cabinet 'had crossed a major stream in the presentation of current defense plans to the Japanese Diet and in recommending a change in the assigned mission of the Japanese forces'.[28] American diplomacy was getting results. Undoubtedly, the bait of offering US economic assistance made the military aspects more palatable to the Japanese government. In addition to this ploy there were American hints that if no satisfactory agreement could be reached then it might prove necessary to withdraw American forces from Japan. Certainly, the possibility of this eventuality was discussed by President Eisenhower in the National Security Council in February 1954, though the president appeared to regard that prospect as being of little immediate likelihood.[29] It was one thing for Yoshida to adopt a relaxed view of Japan's predicament in the politics of the Cold War in east Asia,[30] but quite a different matter if American troops were actually to depart. It was not difficult to lecture the United States on the amphibian and aerial limitations of the Soviet Union and the People's Republic of China (facts which, presumably, the JCS were fully aware of), but to lose American protection might present domestic and overseas challenges of a greater magnitude. Ashida had a point when he argued that 'camouflaged' rearmament misled the public into assuming that little needed to be done by Japan itself.[31] Pacifism and poverty tended to be employed as a crutch to resist American proposals and led Dulles to complain in August 1953 that 'the Japanese were neither willing to make an effort to defend themselves or to put their economic house in order'.[32]

The Mutual Security Assistance agreement went some way to placating the Eisenhower administration, though onlookers still noted that Japan remained a weak military power dependent on the United States for much of its security needs. The relationship was indeed unequal, but Yoshida and his successors felt that it was politically impractical to accede in any rapid manner to American proposals. This voluntary acceptance of inferiority was unsatisfactory to both nations without either being able to solve the issue unilaterally. Under the MSA Japan committed itself to no more than 165,000 troops (a figure far less the American hope of 325,000–350,000 men) but promised that it would be a balanced organization with an air force to be added to the ground and naval units. By the spring of 1954 with the passage of MSA and two important legislative bills (the Defence Agency Law and Self-Defence Forces Law) the Japanese government had moved far from the supposed restrictions of article 9 and was now in a considerably tighter relationship with the United States.

There was a gradual improvement in US–Japan security relations by the late 1950s, despite the frequently voiced private dissatisfactions of Dulles and the JCS that Tokyo was reneging on its commitments. The process by which Japanese officials began to build up their military establishment is both controversial and complex. State Department papers tend to criticize the slowness of Japanese moves, while later studies by American officers have demonstrated both Japanese initiatives and a degree of alacrity to assume a more substantial defence role. It is perhaps significant that James Auer, later to be military attaché at the US embassy in Tokyo during the Mansfield years, divines four 'points of departure' during the 1950s whereby Japanese naval forces gained wider responsibilities in the brief period from 1953 to 1957[33]. His study claims that the progress made by the Maritime Self-Defence force in devising long-range defence programmes was not inconsiderable. No wonder, therefore, that demonstrators in 1960 would denounce the US–Japan security treaty and public opinion surveys in the late 1950s show a clear preference for 'rice before guns'.[34] Those who would later note that many in the West have downplayed (or even virtually neglected) the growth of the postwar Japanese military can point to the 1950s as the crucial decade in this reemergence.

To reassure the United States' allies in Western Europe and Australia, to say nothing of the understandably widespread apprehensions of east and south-east Asia, the general American stance over Japanese rearmament was to stress its defensive nature. This satisfied some nations. Churchill, for example, instructed his chiefs of staff in April 1953 that he was, 'in principle in favour of the re-armament of Japan within carefully considered limits and under United States guidance. This might well be the only effective manner of balancing the growing power of Communist China in the next decade'.[35] Others, such as

Australia, were sufficiently eager to improve commercial ties that their governments downplayed talk of Japanese revanchism.[36]

For the United States in the 1950s, Japan was rarely a nation of any particular import. It was only the subject of rather fleeting notice in the higher reaches of the Eisenhower administration. The president, it is true, could make an occasional reference to Japan that might suggest he had more than a passing awareness, but this was not sufficient to provide anything as coherent and coordinated as a sustained set of policies for Japan. Japan tended to become a topic of debate only when the United States was about to be faced with unpleasant decisions over the islands. Eisenhower in June 1954 was reported by his personal secretary to have warned aloud that 'we could *lose* [underlined in original] Japan', but the spasmodic nature of attention given to Tokyo suggests otherwise.[37] There was rather a general tone of complacency throughout most of the decade. This may explain in part the American unpreparedness for the 1960 crisis. American officials in general tended to hold rather uncomplimentary views of post-treaty Japan and initiatives to strengthen ties with Tokyo were rarely productive. There was, however, general agreement on Japan's value to the West and some recognition that international trading agreements ought to be designed to incorporate Tokyo, despite the lingering doubts of many in Europe and Australasia over Japan's economic behaviour. Yet Washington's efforts to support Japan were limited, since foreign aid was reduced, trade with the PRC remained banned and south-east Asia was hardly about to be in a position as an alternative market to soak up large quantities of Japanese exports. There was yet no substitute for lost empire.

The most dramatic political crisis before the turn of the decade concerned a small Japanese vessel called the *Lucky Dragon*. (It was more serious than the usual reference term of 'incident' would lead one to believe.) Recent researchers have suggested that both Washington and Tokyo were at fault, but the initial errors were undoubtedly caused and then compounded by the United States.[38] Contaminated with the radioactive fallout from the first American test of its new hydrogen bomb in the Pacific on 1 March 1954, the *Lucky Dragon* quickly became the centre of a damaging dispute with the United States. The issue was mishandled by American officials on both sides of the Pacific. Ambassador Allison was not particularly attentive of understandable Japanese sensitivities over nuclear matters and his position was hardly helped by differences within the Washington bureaucracy and the seemingly casual manner in which the president followed events. Eisenhower and Dulles did not have a firm grip on events in Japan, though in partial mitigation it has to be said that other issues were necessarily foremost in their minds. The *Lucky Dragon* controversy occurred when the secretary of state was deeply involved with the collapse of the French position in Indo-China and the associated difficulties of trying to gain European cooperation. The future of south-east Asia occupied Dulles' waking hours in March and April 1954. Crises rarely turn up in neat, self-contained succession. Others, unfortunately, proved inept at handling the Japanese dispute with the result that the *Lucky Dragon* business smouldered on until January 1955. Only after the final, long predicted demise of the Yoshida era was a solution achieved that answered some of Tokyo's complaints. The Eisenhower administration maintained that the Japanese government failed to give the American embassy in Tokyo sufficient cooperation to contain the issue, but the Japanese authorities were themselves under pressure.

Allison's strident opinion was that 'emotionalism' inhibited any fair debate and he insisted that the 'weakness of the [Yoshida] government, [the] entrenched position of government scientists and bureaucrats, and jingoistic sensationalism of the press'[39] made his task difficult in the extreme. No doubt a number of Japanese played up the crisis in order to embarrass both Eisenhower and Yoshida, but the case against the United States was a strong one. Changes in wind patterns had exposed the crew of the *Lucky Dragon* to fallout and at least one member's death was attributed by some to irradiation. Differences over the details of financial compensation dragged on for far too long, the United States did not alter its nuclear test schedule as a result of the crisis, and the entire Japanese fishing industry faced collapse when the Tsukiji fish market had to close temporarily as consumers panicked. A Japan without safe supplies of fish thanks to the behaviour of its chief ally and protector was indeed a state in turmoil. Allison would reflect later that the crisis was 'one of the worst periods we had to endure during our four years in Japan'.[40]

The eventual agreement demonstrated the ability of the Japanese bureaucracy and two successive cabinets (Hatoyama had finally replaced Yoshida in November 1954) to employ pressure to strike a bargain with the United States. Compensation was granted, though the delays suggest that Tokyo's hand was not particularly strong and that anti-nuclear demonstrations were not as yet seen to possess significant political influence. This, however, would change and the *Lucky Dragon* crisis 'began in earnest' a twin campaign against nuclear weapons (usually American ones) and the existing US–Japan security treaty.[41] Later protests against American intervention in Vietnam cleverly exploited the *Lucky Dragon* affair by installing the restored vessel in a commemorative museum on reclaimed garbage land in Tokyo Bay.

Japanese criticism would have been even stronger if it had learnt of Ambassador Allison's opinions of the attacks made on the United States. He informed the State Department in late May that, 'although [f]ull implications may not be known for years . . . certain conclusions of critical import to US policies are now possible'.[42] He felt competition among Japanese bureaucrats, indecision by the Yoshida cabinet and regional developments in Korea and Indo-China all combined to bring out the worst in the nation to which he was accredited. He blamed the Japanese government for failing to take sufficiently strenuous measures to control first the medical profession and the media (the original scope by the Yomiuri was followed by less restrained reportage by its rivals) and then the left that quickly 'moved into [a] situation that was made to order for them'.[43] Allison's charges involved virtually the entire Japanese administration and the lack of governmental discipline over the presentation of the American side of the case. (The crewmen, with the exception of the radioman, escaped any permanent disabilities and nearly all were alive thirty years later.) It was, indeed, a period of national hysteria. The public thought that the 'ashes of death' from the Bikini nuclear tests presaged a second disaster for Japan and the ambassador sensed that any opponent possessing the bomb might succeed, if it could mount an effective 'psychological-military operation' to gain its objectives, through threat alone that would leave American bases isolated and the nation leaning towards neutralism.

The American embassy in Tokyo was surely correct to note that even a stronger Japanese government would have distanced itself from the United States over the *Lucky Dragon* crisis. The State Department was informed rightly by Allison that the problem was essentially a political rather than a legal one. Ultimately what mattered was not an agreed compensation figure, though this was in itself an important issue, but closer relations and some degree of mutual cooperation by both parties. The difficulties of 1954 may have had a salutary effect on both the State Department and the Ministry of Foreign Affairs. It seems that Washington officials, temporarily at least, did take Japan more seriously as the crisis deepened. Yet the storm blew itself out, assisted by a change of government in Tokyo and an American willingness to grant Japan a far larger sum in compensation than it had originally rather grudgingly proposed.

An end to the *Lucky Dragon* crisis was protracted because of the

United States' close involvement in Japanese politics. It was felt to be in the national interest for American diplomats to wait till Yoshida had finally (and ungracefully) resigned. It was also in the interest of the new premier Hatoyama Ichiro to both boast of his success in gaining a settlement and, in the light of very apparent anti-Americanism, to display a degree of public truculence before the forthcoming general election scheduled for March 1955. Hatoyama, a major prewar politician who had waited impatiently in the wings to gain office before shortly succumbing to ill health, agreed to US$2,000,000 as damages for the Bikini radioactivity fall-out. The premier, ably assisted by Shigemitsu Mamoru, the former war criminal and signer for Japan of the surrender documents on board the Missouri in Tokyo bay, was indeed to benefit from the improved offer.

The end of the Yoshida era was an opportunity for both the United States and Japan to repair their differences and reassess their positions. The omens appeared propitious. Yoshida had hung on to power too long for his own good and for that of the feuding conservative groups he had nominally led. A new cabinet might be better united and clearer in its foreign policy objectives. For the United States it was hoped that the past hesitancies over Japan's role in regional affairs might be replaced with some degree of concerted action. Dulles told Yoshida, during the premier's final inglorious visit to Washington in November 1954, that Japan ought 'to develop the spirit and strength to resume a place as one of the great nations of the world' rather than 'to coast along' as a dependent state.[44]

Expectations, however, that Hatoyama's men had aspirations for a more assertive stance in international relations could backfire. It was all very well for the American embassy to pass on assurances from highly placed Japanese politicians that the new cabinet 'will, for [domestic] political purposes, talk a great deal about regularizing relations with USSR and Communist China and increasing trade with [the] Communist bloc but that in fact little will be done'. It was also encouraging to learn that there would be few changes in economic policy, though Allen Dulles could not resist teasing Secretary of the Treasury George Humphrey in front of the National Security Council that Hatoyama had a reputation as 'an inflationist'. But activism towards normalization of relations with the Soviet Union and a new dialogue with the People's Republic of China would almost certainly conflict with American policies in east Asia and only demonstrate the weaknesses of a supposed united front among the Pacific allies. The Hatoyama period illustrates the American dilemma only too well. A subservient Japan was felt to be overreliant on American political, military and economic support, while a brasher government in Tokyo might opt to take its nation into newer terrain.

The wish of Hatoyama to distance himself from the Yoshida regime led to strains in the US–Japan alliance. Hatoyama's disassociation from existing conservative policies inevitably came to be seen as implied criticism of existing ties with the United States. Even those members of the Yoshida entourage who were seen as more or less well disposed towards the United States had been obliged to attack Washington's Cold War fixation and its wish to view the region as a ring of military alliances to contain the double-headed forces of continental Communism. The Minister of International Trade and Industry Aichi Kiichi wrote privately that Communism was better resisted 'as much, if not more, in the political and economic fields as in the military'.[45] Miyazawa Kiichi later described Japanese public opinion at the end of the Yoshida era as sensing that the United States was equated with 'war-loving America'.[46] Exaggerated or not, the new government was cautious about being thought to be too close to Yoshida's stance on the alliance. Left-wing figures in Europe were equally suspicious of Japanese rearmament and subordination to the US. Aneurin Bevan, when interviewed by the Asahi Shimbun's representative in London early in 1954, cautioned Japan against becoming regarded by others as a partner in 'White Imperialism in the Far East'.[47] It was next to impossible in Bevan's view for Japan to escape being tainted by the rest of Asia as a satellite of Washington. Bevan's point was reinforced shortly afterwards with the reemergence of the PRC as a major power through its role in the Geneva conference that settled (temporarily at least) the division of the former French territories of Indo-China and its behaviour under the spotlights at the Bandung non-aligned meeting. Rival powers in the region now made their move to attract Tokyo away from its American moorings.

Hatoyama's cabinet sought to display its diplomatic skills in this contest for the allegiance of Japan. It realized immediately that Japan was playing for high stakes. By absolute standards Hatoyama's diplomacy with regard to the Soviet Union failed. It was not, however, for want of trying to distance his nation from the politics and advice of the United States. Some of the hurdles obviously were not all cleared – in 1991 Japan has still to establish a peace treaty with the USSR – yet a degree of progress was accomplished and it would be wrong to regard the Hatoyama period as barren. There was a substantial improvement in Soviet–Japanese relations and those who saw at the time that Japan had played a weak hand with a degree of skill are surely correct.[48] Much did change, and for the better. Some issues, however, could not be resolved then and the outlook over thirty years later remains uncertain. The 'northern territories' question has yet to be clarified.

Public attention on the issue of normalization was heightened by feuding between the feuding conservatives and Hatoyama's dislike of Yoshida and all his works. The new premier, therefore, announced in December 1954 that 'Japan desired, without prejudice to her cooperation with the "Free World", to normalize relations with the Soviet Union and China on terms mutually acceptable'. Hatoyama may have impulsively dreamt up the wish to get closer to Moscow as an effective electioneering ploy that successfully confirmed his hold on power, but he had next to see the issue through. This proved hard to accomplish. He was challenged from within his own party and without by those critical of his diplomacy. Hatoyama's actions continue to excite the historian and opinions differ sharply over his handiwork.[49] In some ways the optimism of sections of the Japanese public and the press was disappointed. The protracted negotiations that began in London in June 1955 and ended eventually at Moscow in October 1956 both failed and succeeded. Lengthy talks failed to persuade the Soviet Union to alter its control over the small but strategically important islands to the north east of Hokkaido, yet Hatoyama did return personally from Moscow with important concessions. The ailing prime minister, who resigned shortly after his announcements over normalization, brought back a joint declaration that ended the state of war between the two nations, and led to the establishment of diplomatic relations, initialled an important fishing agreement (in itself 'bait' successfully prepared by the Soviet Union and put down at a crucial moment in the negotiations), gained the release of Japanese POWs still in Siberia and ensured Japan's entry into the United Nations.

Certainly these prizes failed to satisfy some in the conservative ranks and the in-fighting led to the demise of the Hatoyama government but this is to belittle the premier's efforts. He won a great deal, despite divisions at home and his inability to gain the northern islands. Controversy since has centred on whether a compromise arrangement, whereby Japan might have received the Habomais and Shikotan, ought to have been grasped by the Japanese negotiators. The question is further complicated by the intervention of Secretary Dulles in a State Department note to Tokyo in early September reminding the Japanese government that the terms of the San Francisco peace treaty prohibited Japan from transferring 'the sovereignty of the territories without the consent of the signatories of the San Francisco treaty'.[50] Hatoyama's diplomacy had been crafted to deal with the 'easier' issues first and by deliberately leaving the territorial question until progress had been made elsewhere he was probably resigning himself to gaining only half a loaf.[51]

Certainly intra-party splits damaged the Japanese hand, but Hatoyama's strategy and the known views of the American government ensured that it would never have been likely that maximum Japanese goals could have been met. To have acquired the southern-most islands alone would have been indeed an achievement given the American view, the dissatisfaction of parts of the Japanese public and press at anything less than all the islands and the Soviet determination to concede only at a substantial price. It is true that Moscow failed to gain a peace treaty with Japan, but this appears to be less of a defect against the security advantages of retaining the northern territories, successive fishing arrangements that benefit Moscow, and the exercise of full diplomatic privileges in Japan.[52]

Japan may have contributed to this highly complicated outcome by shooting itself in the foot. The factional disputes and business community disagreements over the correct posture to adopt led to important changes in Japanese approaches to Moscow that left Tokyo's ambition of presenting a united front in tatters.[53] The hoped for major shift in Japanese external relations collapsed. It was clearly a retreat once Hatoyama had said in an interview in June 1956 that it

> does not appear possible for us to regain immediately the [Northern] Territories; of course, I will try hard. As long as the Soviets do not agree with us on that, I think we have to consider the second best formula. Namely, I will try to [first] solve other issues than the territorial one, those issues which have been already agreed upon in London, such as the release of the Japanese interned in the USSR. It means that I have to leave only the territorial question as a pending issue for the future.[54]

It is still pending. The death of Stalin had made little difference to Soviet approaches to the question in the early 1950s and it is not yet certain that President Gorbachev will be any more relaxed than his predecessors over making concessions. Improvisation is doubtless the driving force of any nation's diplomacy much of the time, but no Soviet regime will voluntarily surrender territory without exacting its just rewards. Moscow may have toned down its criticisms of Japan and what it saw as its subservient and dangerous relationship with the United States to coincide with the normalization process, yet it was rarely prepared to shift far on the northern islands question. Its legal rights to the area in dispute are stronger than Japanese public opinion realizes and its political control unchallenged.

The extent to which the United States urged Japan to stand out for all the islands is not easily discovered. Published evidence on Secretary Dulles suggests he was extremely cautious on the matter of the northern territories. He reported to the president in December 1954 the uncomfortable reality that 'I do not know anything we can do to get the Russians out short of war'.[55] Only when he was advised that a thaw in Japan–USSR relations might occur did he attempt to influence Tokyo's behaviour. Allied observers in Tokyo felt at the time that Dulles' move may have been counter-productive, although it was claimed that he spoke out only in response to requests from Shigemitsu for ammunition to deploy against Moscow. His lieutenants informed the British embassy in Washington shortly after normalization that though the earlier State Department aide-memoire remained policy, there was a great deal of legal juggling at work and relief that 'the thorny problem of the Kuriles' was unlikely to be brought up in the near future.[56] An additional reason for Japan to leave well alone was a warning to Hatoyama's negotiators in Moscow that any discussion of the northern islands question would be linked by the Soviet Union with the issue of American-occupied Okinawa and the Bonins. The fate of Okinawa had not been considered at Yalta and linkage of the two problems would clearly embarrass the United States. Equally on the basis of article 26 of the Japanese peace treaty, which stated that no alterations to the settlement were to be made without the consent of the signatories, the US threatened to remind Japan of the Okinawa issue. It was surely sophistry for the United States to claim that Etorofu and Kunashiri were not part of the Kuriles and should 'in justice' be handed over to Japan. The Soviet Union could hardly fail to complain, given that Japan had renounced its rights to the Kuriles at San Francisco, though it was correct to note that final determination of Japan's borders was to be left to the future.[57]

The final outcome was to leave Hatoyama well pleased with his settlement but bereft of his job. He resigned, as previously promised to heads of the newly formed Liberal Democratic Party, since the discord within the party was all too plain. Factional bosses said one thing, while the government did another. The squabbles, however, should not be overemphasized. They may have discredited Japan's position abroad and made it impractical to realize additional goals but Hatoyama returned from Moscow with much more than a scrap of paper. His successors have made little subsequent progress.

During the negotiations between the Soviet Union and Japan it was not only the United States that watched developments with considerable attention. The People's Republic of China was also interested in improving its relations with Tokyo and, therefore, greeted news of the normalization by editorials that spoke cordially of Soviet behaviour, warmed to Japan's 'independent development' and looked forward to Sino-Japanese rapprochement. American obstruction, however, was seen by the 'People's Daily' as certain to increase. Its review of the postwar decade insisted that Washington wished 'to perpetuate its occupation of Japan, turn Japan into its colony and war base for aggression and try by this means to keep up tension in the Far East'.[58] Whatever the emerging differences between Moscow and Beijing there was sufficient outward unity for both to commit themselves to attempting to divide Japan from the United States. Paradoxically Japan made little political headway with the People's Republic of China, despite the enthusiasm of important elements in Japanese society, and was to achieve far less in the 1950s with the PRC than it did towards a Soviet Union that was held in low esteem. Equally the PRC attempted far more than the USSR ever did to gain the goodwill of the Japanese people. It failed in its efforts to gain diplomatic relations with Japan and had instead to be content with modest trading links and some two decades of so-called 'People's diplomacy'.[59] This Trojan horse rarely threatened to subvert the Japanese commitment to the American alliance. Japanese guilt over wartime behaviour, prospects of gaining a larger share of the chimerical China market, and ideological support by some on the left for the experimentation of the PRC were no match for the rival claims of Taiwan and the United States. It was to remain an uneven contest till President Nixon and Henry Kissinger went to Beijing.

Hatoyama certainly wished to advance towards the PRC but he was constrained by electing to tackle the Soviet question first, the frigid response of the Eisenhower administration to the Japanese government's attempted rapprochement and major policy differences within the LDP over the China question, particularly from the Yoshida faction. All that was achieved, despite the ambitions and hopes of the cabinet, was the beginning of economic and cultural links. The Cold War largely determined the predictable American response to Hatoyama's tentative moves and it says much for Japan's enfeebled position in regional affairs that little active resistance to Washington's sharp reminders of its influence on Japan was encountered. It was simply a non-issue for many Japanese who continued to vote according to local and regional prescription. As late as June 1967 only half of those polled knew that Japan had yet to establish diplomatic relations with the PRC.[60] Foreign policy could be safely left to others to concern themselves over. Against this seemingly constant background of general apathy by the public at large and caution by the bureaucracy and LDP it is hardly surprising that Sino–Japanese estrangement continued till 1970s.

It may be that the PRC bent its principles rather more than the LDP in the 1950s as Beijing searched for means whereby it could accommodate Japan. China's rhetoric had been toned down even before Hatoyama gained power and much of Japan's 'security diplomacy' of this decade was received with remarkably mild comment by Chinese diplomats and official publications. Beijing might still denounce Tokyo as the lackey of the United States, but Japan's entitlement to possessing its own military forces was rarely questioned. The 'two Chinas' position of Japan was rejected, yet by instituting semi-official trade arrangements (the so-called Liao–Takasaki agreement of November 1962 followed in the wake of a succession of private trade accords that had at least indirectly involved the Japanese government) the PRC was perpetuating the policy. Japan continued to have full diplomatic relations with Taipei and limited economic ties to Beijing.

The United States gained its way over Japan–China policy in the 1950s. It is apparent from the series of measures that Washington was able to insist upon that Tokyo remained generally subservient to American wishes. The amplification of the US–Japan security treaty and the signing by Japan of its peace treaty with Taiwan in 1954 indicated clearly where Japan stood. The same year Dulles also prepared a US–Taiwan mutual defence treaty and hoped that his regional anti-Communist front, the South-East Asia Treaty Organization (SEATO), would further drive home to Beijing its isolated position in Asia. A concerted attempt to ban most Western trade with the PRC was an additional ploy that Dulles used to contain what he saw as an aggressive regime.[61] Western allies of the United States were more vocal in their complaints against the economic blockade imposed on the PRC by the United States. The suggestion of recent commentators that Japan was capable of great diplomatic finesse in perpetuating its two Chinas policy may also need some re-examination, since it was a decidedly unbalanced set of arrangements that benefited Taipei and Washington more than Beijing. Whether 'Japan's postwar China policy has been subtle, sophisticated, and largely successful'[62] is questionable. It has frequently been reactive and cautious, following in the wake of the United States, rather than 'a creative adoption to the Cold War'.[63] The evidence to refute the enthusiasts is not the personal views of the Japanese leadership that (with some notable exceptions such as premiers Kishi and Sato) frequently attempted to wrestle with American hegemony over the PRC, but the cold realities of international politics in the 1950s where Japan simply made little headway.

The much touted policy of *seikei bunri* (the separation of politics and economics) produced few dividends. Commercials links with the PRC in the 1950s were weak, even though President Eisenhower himself conceded that Tokyo ought to have at least some economic contacts with the PRC.[64] The limited state of China's modernization programmes largely foreclosed the China market. It was not political differences (though they hardly helped) but economic levels that shut Japan out.[65] Tokyo's industrial rivals were equally disappointed that the PRC failed to live up to the more extreme predictions of British, German, and Canadian businessmen. China was no El Dorado. Its own economic handicaps were larger impediments to international trade than American restrictions.

Hatoyama's difficulties over the China question, the Soviet normalization issue and his illness combined to end what was at least an attempt to get out from under the skirts of the United States. His successors were to prove more cautious in external affairs and decidedly more wary of confronting the United States. The fall of Hatoyama, which was clearly something of a relief to the State Department both because of the premier's objectives and his medical history, saw a switch in focus from regional issues to bilateral ones. The security treaty next emerged as the bone of contention between the United States and Japan. It was a subject that inevitably aroused immense controversy in Japan and would lead to the most severe crisis in postwar US–Japanese relations.

4 CRISIS: REVISION OF THE SECURITY TREATY

Japan has been a modern state for less than 100 years. It has been traditional in Japanese life for the people to look for guidance, assistance, and support to some wealthy, influential patron. The United States could exploit this attitude to our mutual advantage.
Finance Minister Ikeda Hayato, 16 June 1954

Mr Kishi is, perhaps, the first post-war Prime Minister who is getting to act, or is beginning to act as though he wanted Japan to become again a great power and to become such a power in friendly relations with the free nations of the world.
Dulles press conference, 28 April 1957

The [p]eriod of [the] next few months is probably the most critical juncture in US–Japan relations since the war . . . This period will be of decisive importance for formulation of [the] main lines of our subsequent policies towards Japan.
Ambassador MacArthur to Secretary of State Herter, 9 October 1959

For most of the 1950s the United States took Japan for granted. The eventual confrontation in 1960 marked the end of an era where Washington could any longer presume to gain its way in Japan without overdue respect for Japanese sensitivities. In retrospect, it is not difficult to suggest that pressures to create a more equal relationship were virtually inevitable given some American attitudes and the fact that the decade coincided with a period of very considerable international tension. Opposition within Japan to the links to the United States combined doubts over American intentions to encourage a militarily strong Pacific ally and the dangers of being drawn into international crises over which the Japanese government would have little or no influence. The personality of Prime Minister Kishi and his ministerial role in the conduct of Japanese imperialism in the early 1940s added yet more fuel to this fire.

Dissatisfaction with the US–Japan relationship and the conduct of American foreign policy during a period of cold war rivalries between the US and Communism was widespread in Japan. President Eisenhower was informed in 1956 that Japan's international predicament was likely 'to be shaped more by the policies of the Great Powers than by any positive moves by Japanese leaders'.[1] Unlike, it was maintained, the Western European states, who had necessarily to look on the Soviet Union as their principal protagonist, Japan had to encounter three powers in devising foreign policy. In addition to the United States and the Soviet Union, Tokyo was obliged to reckon with 'mainland China, which the Japanese tend predominantly to view as an *Asian* power, rather than necessarily a *Communist* power in the Cold War context'.[2] This triangular vision, in the view of State Department material commended by Dulles to the president, left Japanese public opinion far from convinced that the United States knew best or that following Washington was necessarily in Japan's self-interest. A litany of complaints over American behaviour with regard to nuclear weapon testing, the retention of Okinawa, US military bases in the Ryukyus and in Japan proper, coupled with slim prospects for disarmament, left the United States decidedly unpopular. Neutralism had legions of supporters, while the Japanese Government found it impolitic to sing the praises of its Pacific ties.

Fears that the United States would be able to build Japan as its principal military ally in the region against Communism had led to what one top secret State Department report in April 1952 warned might be 'explosive' repercussions on Japanese domestic politics.[3] In reality, the degree of impact that Japan would have, either alone or in tandem with the United States, 'in redressing the Far Eastern balance of power' was considerably less than critics maintained and some senior American diplomats at least thought little of Japan's 'counterweight' capabilities.[4] Opponents of the US–Japan security arrangements in Tokyo, Moscow and Beijing exaggerated the Japanese role in the alliance and paid little or no attention to the forces in north-east Asia that were hostile to a newly-sovereign Japan. For fiscal 1954, Japan had only the most rudimentary of US assistance in the form of minute mutual security funds for promotion of the beginnings of a Japanese air force, while the American sources reckoned the PRC possessed in December 1952 '2,500 aircraft, including about 1,300 jets'.[5] A handful of Japanese training planes was not much to pit against MIG fighters piloted by Korean war veterans. Only in the late 1950s did Japan begin to develop some naval and air strength at the moment when the United States in 1958 decided to pull out its remaining ground forces.[6] This was not, of course, the view of Japan's left or many within the LDP, whose anxieties were directed against

Washington, since its military was stationed in Japan where many citizens were convinced the United States was storing nuclear weapons. The propaganda battle was lost before it could begin. The Soviet press was quick to warn of the 'extremely dangerous strategic vulnerability of the Japanese islands and the extreme danger to its population not only from atomic bombs but simple incendiary bombs [which can] start devastating conflagrations in Japanese cities and [cause] mass destruction of the population'.[7] The Soviet Union next protested to the Japanese Foreign Office over reports that its American ally had introduced atomic missiles and carriers into Japan and warned that any such weapons would 'menace the peace and security of the Far East'.[8] Khrushchev also informed Haragui Yukitaka, the chairman of the General Council of Japanese Trade Unions, that Japan would be safe from nuclear attack provided its territory were not used as the base for foreign aggression against the Soviet Union.[9] It was rare for Japanese commentators to point out how regional instability might also be the product of Soviet militarization and that constant diplomatic and press involvement by Moscow to coincide with the forthcoming Japanese general election was not exactly a demonstration of goodwill towards Tokyo.

The PRC sought, too, to bolster the left in Japan by adding the verdict of Foreign Minister Chen Yi who, in November in a widely reported speech, denounced the security pact as a 'unilateral, unequal treaty with which American imperialism enslaves the Japanese nation and brings it nearer to the brink of war created by the United States'.[10] North Korea and Mongolia also joined in the press barrage, while repetitive Chinese accounts carried by Hsinhua News Agency spoke of the Kishi clique as a paper tiger that, somewhat contradictorily, could still cooperate with American ruling circles and might employ a new security pact to revive militarism, suppress the Japanese people and assist US monopoly capitalists. Evidence to fuel such criticisms was seen in remarks made by Kishi to a reporter from NBC in October when he spoke in favour of abolishing article 9 and argued that 'Japan must be prepared to play her part in preserving the Free World'.[11] Opponents in the Diet immediately denounced the premier for this statement, which was regarded by Socialist member Narita Tomomi as exposing 'the militaristic spirit with which he is imbued to the core'.[12]

The speed and scale of Japanese rearmament in the 1950s was deemed disappointing by the American government, yet, given the domestic opposition within Japan, a start was made. Tokyo, however, could hardly defend itself – some would argue that it saw no great threat to its territory and therefore made only half-hearted efforts

71

merely to placate the United States – in the first post-treaty decade. It was never easy to explain Japan's security predicament to the public and numerous politicians went out of their way to avoid antagonizing a nation that felt in its bones that Japan's behaviour in the Pacific war must never risk being repeated by establishing a new officer corps and military. Even when Prime Minister Kishi spoke in less elliptical terms than usual to a foreign news agency on the advantages of a fresh security treaty and the abrogation of article 9, which prohibits the despatch of troops abroad, he was predictably quick to claim immediately afterwards to the Diet that he had been 'misrepresented'. For most Japanese the problems of Asia were regarded as someone else's difficulties. The Japanese nation wished merely to get on with the job of economic reconstruction and recommence effective trading links with the Asian–Pacific region. The provision of an international framework within which such prosperity might be cultivated was regarded as the responsibility of other powers. Japan was more than delighted to opt out of the great game.

State Department-sponsored studies in Japan in 1952 had correctly pointed out that the best that could be said of the US–Japan security schemes of this era (and beyond) from the Japanese point of view was that they were 'a necessity for an otherwise almost defenceless Japan. At the same time, these arrangements are subject to varying degrees of criticism based partly on their domestic impact on sovereignty, but also to some extent on their implicit negation of any possibility of a neutral position in the event of war.'[13] The Psychological Strategy Board, itself a title surely possible only at the height of the Cold War, maintained that '[f]or many Japanese, the prospect of immediate involvement in another war is viewed with decided revulsion, a circumstance which injects an emotional and irrational element into popular opinion regarding rearmament'.[14] Irrational or not, the State Department was obliged to note that neutralism had its advocates, who would argue that this might best protect Japan's sovereign independence and reflected 'a marked sensitivity' feeding on nineteenth-century opposition to extraterritoriality and the trappings of Western imperialism.

Yet the same study found that 'the attitude of most Japanese toward the United States is friendly'[15] and cited appreciation of US aid, leniency during the occupation and the non-punitive peace treaty as evidence to support its case. This may have been something of an exaggeration, given that the commentary spoke also of acute Japanese irritation over jurisdiction in cases involving US military personnel off base and the economic differences that had arisen on American determined security export controls towards the PRC. The familiar Japanese complaint (still alive and well nearly forty years later) of the average American as supposedly 'shallow, materialistic, and lacking in cultural values'[16] also contradicted the State Department's optimism over US–Japan ties. It was probably nearer the mark when suggesting that the Japanese approach to occupation reforms was to cooperate in 'the realization that they had no other alternative'. While clearly less true after independence had been regained it still served as an appropriate strategy to guide Tokyo in the 1950s. The United States was obliged to carry Japan during the 1950s in the hope that at some future indeterminate date Tokyo would be prepared to enlist on the American side 'in the fight against Communism'. This hope, in retrospect, was rarely seriously entertained by any Japanese cabinet until the 1970s. The American embassy in Tokyo cautioned the chief of staff of Far East Command in September 1954 that 'the United States cannot, no matter what it does, make Japan either rich or militarily strong' and suggested as an alternative, 'that we will attain, as a minimum, without the indefinite large scale expenditure of American funds, a Japan which while not necessarily an active ally is nevertheless strong enough and independent enough to remain out of Communist clutches other than as a result of full scale war'.[17] Such sentiment by Ambassador Allison clearly disappointed the Pentagon but was, it will be seen, to prove an accurate assessment of Japan's future ties with the United States in the area of security at least, while American assumptions on Japan's economic prospects appear to have been universally gloomy in contrast to the defeatism of sections of European industry to anticipated Japanese competition.[18]

In place of pressing Japan to rearm in depth the State Department argued that it made better sense to shore up both the economic and internal security positions first, since '[i]f Japan cannot be made politically and economically stable, no investment in its defence sector is desirable or justifiable'.[19] The crux of the matter for the embassy in Tokyo was seen to be the working towards gaining 'the basic requirement of the long-term US–Japan relationship: a strong, stable conservative government in Japan'.[20] This wish to assist what it termed 'the moderate conservative movement' was to be assigned 'absolute and urgent priority', although the Japanese government was hardly regarded with any great confidence by American diplomats.[21] Alterations in US behaviour might, however, yet end 'the stagnation which has taken place in Japan since 1952'. Such frankness suggests that the first years after San Francisco had yielded remarkably few

73

dividends for the United States in its initial relations with Japan. There never was a honeymoon.

Doubts over Japan's reliability as an ally and its future political economy abound in American official reportage from Tokyo in the 1950s. Hostile press comment over the signing of the administrative agreement set the tone for an era that was to end in the 1960 security crisis. The hesitancy of the Japanese media left the US embassy recognizing that it would have to face 'the task of selling the Agreement to the Japanese press and public opinion'.[22] This was never to prove a realistic goal, since complaints and suspicions were far too deeply embedded in the popular mind for anything but major reform to stand any chance of altering the national psychology. The American prediction that 'the under-current of dissatisfaction on these issues will remain' was soon confirmed.[23] It was virtually impossible for the United States to hope (in telegraphese) to 'teach Japs "facts of life" re true nature of Commie threat to Japan and futility of trying to carry on "business as usual", both politically and economically, with Sov-dominated Commie govts' or to 'convince Japs that basic US foreign policy particularly in FE is wise, firm and consistent both as to its aims and to means of their achievement, and that it will continue to take Jap interests fully into account'.[24]

Much that was predicted by American officials in 1952 on the factors likely to produce 'an adverse effect on post-Occupation Japanese attitudes toward the United States' was certainly realized in part by 1960. There was also, as Ambassador Robert Murphy pointed out, an American preoccupation 'with what the United States did for the Japanese' after the war and a neglect of 'what the United States also did to Japan'.[25] Yet, for all the American pessimism and the Japanese indignation, the partnership survived. Attention was rightly focussed on security issues, but even here the fears of the United States government were exaggerated. The US–Japan military links would later grow closer. General Bradley's remark at the moment when Japan regained its sovereignty that '[o]ur position in Japan is temporary' or General Collins' view that the Japanese 'are not going to want US troops in Japan indefinitely'[26] were, however, the received wisdom in the early 1950's. Japan might not stay loyal; it was, therefore, all the more essential to retain Okinawa. Hedging one's bets said little for Japan but bespoke of military and diplomatic caution in an era where 'Japan may not always be in our corner'.[27]

By 1956 the American embassy in Tokyo was sufficiently concerned over relations with Japan to argue at length on the need for a 'fresh start'. Some may have thought the suggestion melodramatic, but

Allison insisted that 'Japan is on the verge of slowly slipping away from us'.[28] Thus attention to 'signs of Japan's discontent' was seen as necessary, since 'when they become striking it will be too late to retrieve the situation'.[29] Japan was regarded by American diplomats (or at least those in Tokyo) as the only major nation in Asia 'with which we have any prospect of building lasting close ties. Either we do without a senior partner in this half of the world, or it must be Japan.'[30] Interestingly, perhaps, in the aftermath of the Bandung nonaligned movement conference, Allison regarded Japan as of higher potential value to the United States in 'non-military aspects of the world struggle' than for its strategic worth. The ambassador claimed that Japan 'can contribute as no White partner could toward working constructively with the fermenting new nationalisms' of the Asian–African world and supposedly 'energizing their resistance to subversion and helping them attain the stable progress which such resistance presupposes'.[31] In somewhat schoolmasterly fashion, Allison then graded Japan as having 'the makings of a good ally, ambitious, industrious and, when committed, dependable'.[32] Tokyo appeared to have earned itself a respectable Beta plus.

Yet the American analysis suggested much was amiss with America's friend. Allison attempted to balance his criticism by explaining to the State Department that in the economic field there had been progress and that 'Japan should be judged by Asian, not European standards', particularly while undergoing convalescence 'from the immense and still only partially digested shock of defeat and occupation'.[33] The new assumption was that, 'it will take longer than we hoped and, above all, it will require a fresh start with methods better designed to rate the necessary sense of mutuality'[34] to retain Japan's friendship. Allison argued, as ambassadors invariably will, that Japan deserved a higher priority and a 'concrete gentleman's agreement' with Japan's leaders at a 'meeting of minds about ways and means of developing Japan as our senior partner in Asia' was called for. The embassy paper also attempted to look at relations through Japanese eyes and view the disappointments the Japanese felt at rough treatment which went so far on occasion to seem as though she were still an 'enemy'.

'Mutuality' was the term employed to define the hoped for alterations in the handling of Japan so that, for example, consultations might be forthcoming over 'Pacific nuclear tests or troop redeployments to or from this country' issues at present on which 'we seldom provide more than the casual courtesy of a few hours advance notice, and sometimes not that'.[35] Initiatives by Japan in improving relations with its neighbours in north-east Asia from the mid-1950s can be seen as a reaction in part to such unpleasantries from the United States. When the Hatoyama cabinet attempted to gain a peace settlement with the Soviet Union there was public evidence that Washington would do what it could to remonstrate with Japan, as when Dulles was reported in the press to have threatened to keep Okinawa permanently under American control if the Kuriles were conceded to Moscow.[36] The State Department tried to dissuade Hatoyama from proposing to visit Washington on his return from Moscow, though earlier in the year Japanese officials had been outwardly welcomed when they attempted to argue that the restoration of diplomatic relations with the Soviet Union would not impair Japan–US solidarity.[37]

By 1956 members of the State Department were well aware of the need for change. Prompted, no doubt, by Hatoyama's normalization schemes with the Soviet Union, the Division of Research for the Far East compiled a lengthy series of intelligence reports on perspective foreign relations of Japan for the next five years.[38] Portions read today as an accurate and well reasoned series of predictions that the British Foreign Office conceded were 'a lot of good sense'. Institutional, political and national forces were identified that suggested it would repay the United States to tread warily in the future. Japan, the reports cautioned, was shedding its old skin and deserved to be handled in a gentler manner. It would be necessary to recognize that there were deep changes at work within both the confined and divided Japanese political system and the public at large. The identification of these factors and acceptance that American attitudes associated with the occupation era had to end left the State Department's anonymous authors perturbed. There would need to be 'evidence that the US is prepared to place its relations with Japan on a new basis of mutuality' in order to convince Japan that its pro-Western alignment ought to continue. The intelligence officers put forward in the clearest of terms the problems likely to disrupt the Pacific alliance. It was apparent that divisions within the LDP, increasingly vocal complaints from opposition parties and external changes would combine to lead to a situation whereby 'the Japanese public will reexamine its attitudes toward the US and the Communist bloc, largely in reaction to policies adopted by the great powers toward Japan'. The assumption throughout the reports was that 'Japan can be expected to drift toward a more peripheral association with the West, world tensions permitting, unless it can obtain a more equal stature in such terms as restoration of Japanese administration over the Ryukyus and Bonins

[and] modification of the US–Japanese alliance'.[39] Storm cones were being hoisted.

Prophecy and policymaking are differing skills, but the State Department's warnings in 1956 testify to a degree of professionalism and concern. An independent Japan, it stressed, would have to be treated as an equal. The assumptions were that the American government had an uneasy conscience over its earlier handling of Japan and that change ought to be possible. Both premises were to be soundly tested in the next half decade. The journey to revision of the US–Japan security pact was to be rougher than most imagined. To plot this chart we need to begin with an analysis of Japan's internal dynamics, since the 1960 crisis was spawned in Tokyo; the American contribution will then be added and a critique attempted that draws on the domestic and external forces at work. Whatever one's conclusions, it may be a little hard to accept the title of one of the more distinguished accounts of the crisis – that the events of 1960 were, merely, 'Protest in Tokyo'.[40] It was, rather, a national reassessment of Japan's entire post-surrender history.

Japanese politics in the 1950s was concerned with two issues. The first was economic reconstruction and the second was the alliance with the United States. It was the success of Japan's bureaucrats and industrialists in improving dramatically the standard of living in the 1950s that cleared the decks for greater concern with issues of foreign policy. The achievement of hyper-expansion by what one prominent figure would later term the 'virtuous circle of accelerated growth'[41] was the undoubted goal of the Japanese state in the years from San Francisco to the 1960s and, indeed, beyond. It was no easy task, but it was aided by an extraordinary national determination to recover from defeat, occupation and poverty. External factors also contributed to Japan's recovery, though instances of American generosity and self-interest tended to be downplayed by a Japanese public increasingly conscious of its burgeoning affluence. The expansion of international trade, an undervalued currency and American procurement programmes also contributed to Japan's advance, even if many still claim the reemergent phoenix to be exclusively home-reared.[42]

The evidence, as the decade lengthened, that Japan was successfully pulling itself up by its own bootstraps left the opposition parties and their unionist backers in a quandary. It would have been political suicide to attack the LDP's economic policies head-on. New (if fragile) prosperity was also widely seen by the Japanese public as intimately connected with the American alliance. Trade to and from the United States was perceived by both American and Japanese leaders as a vital rationale for continuing friendship between their two nations.[43] Many who had serious reservations about the US–Japan defence arrangements found it impractical to ignore the economic benefits that had accrued to Japan throughout the 1950s and saw the American market as vital to continuing Japanese economic growth. Favourable international economic circumstances, governmental policies and the activities of both management and labour combined to produce an enviable improvement in Japanese living standards.[44] To object to Japan's policies towards the United States was to risk jeopardizing all.

Subordinate independence, under American leadership was, however, an emotive rallying point. Dulles' remark to British ministers and diplomats in the summer of 1951 that the coordination of impending US–Japanese defence plans 'amounted to a voluntary continuation of the Occupation'[45] was precisely the objection of the Japanese left in the late 1950s. Little had changed by then to alter the San Francisco arrangements. The consequences for Washington of a slow response to Japanese domestic opinion were decidedly unfortunate. The diplomacy of the revision of the security treaty is our main concern, but it needs to be placed within the political context of the Kishi years. The gulf between the two newly-formed major political parties, the LDP and JSP, was hard to bridge. The opposition's continuing electoral difficulties (at best the JSP could barely scrape together one third of the Diet's seats) and fears that this would lead the LDP to curtail some of the reforms of the occupation period showed the vulnerability of a badly-divided party and the hopes of some at least in the LDP. The result, as has been frequently noted, was that the United States was reliant on a political party that had severe doubts about the postwar changes imposed on Japan and which faced opposition groups that would appear to be closer in sentiment to the United States in at least domestic policies, though widely divorced from Washington over foreign and defence issues.

The domestic political situation grew worse after the 1958 general election. The prospects for dialogue between parties that might listen to each other had never been likely, but tempers and rhetoric took on a harsher tone as politicians and portions of the public concentrated their minds on the security treaty. The election of 22 May 1958 had given some important pointers to both the state of public concern and the parties' attitudes towards the USA. The gains made by the JSP were smaller than had been anticipated and the Kishi cabinet felt sufficiently confident to proceed with legislation over education and police issues that were offensive to many on the left. It seemed to some that Kishi, designated a class A war criminal, though never tried, and a senior minister during the Pacific war, was intent on returning Japan to the repression of the recent past. His close involvement in the war and recent rapid ascent within the LDP suggested to many that he was unprincipled and prepared to serve any master in the pursuit of power.[46]

Once Hatoyama had resigned his office, the fundamental question of how to correct the Japanese disquiet over security arrangements was unavoidable. Kono Ichiro had already hinted to Ambassador Allison in the autumn that adjustment would be helpful and from 1957 onwards the subject moved to the head of the agenda. It was no longer possible to duck the issue. Working parties now met and policy papers were composed in the light of this and other 'troublesome' issues and indications of 'decreased Japanese dependence on the United States amidst the advent of more independent Japanese policies'.[47] It was accepted that, in the carefully qualified language of Ambassador Allison, relations 'would bear re-examination', though he hastened to add that 'he thought it was premature to consider any drastic changes in present treaty arrangements'. Yet American shifts were, in fact, overdue. Panel discussions, and press interviews in the Japanese media amongst those supposedly friendly to the United States made this apparent. There could be no turning back after the Kishi cabinet had been formed. The private sentiment of conservative leaders was also conveyed to Washington. Quiet pressure was applied on American officials to stress the seriousness of Japanese demands in the light of electoral losses by the LDP caused by defections among younger voters and the need to present a fresher image in future political contests. The American embassy warned that 'the majority of conservative politicians share with the people at large' the conviction that 'the present relationship to the US is "unequal"'. What was yet unclear was the probable pace of Japanese diplomacy and the precise nature of any negotiations. A great deal of exploratory work now followed with both sides probing and weighing each other's remarks and proposals. It was, however, improbable that anything short of treaty revision could be the long-term goal of the Japanese state. The crucial legacy of the occupation era was about to begin to be reworked.

Recognition of the need to accommodate Japanese opinion was, of course, a very different item from immediately granting Tokyo all or even a goodly portion of its wishes. Omens for a new start to US–Japan relations were improved by the appointment of Douglas MacArthur II as American ambassador and the resignation of Prime Minister Ishibashi Tanzan through serious illness shortly after he had gained the post (Ishibashi was probably the least pro-American of the main

LDP leaders). MacArthur and Kishi took office together and were fated to share an uncomfortable period that would end for them both in high controversy. They rose and fell together.

Kishi was the Japanese politician on whom American officials placed most of their hopes in the late 1950s as both sides worked at sounding out the other party. Kishi began by attempting to overwhelm the new ambassador with a picture of what he termed Japanese sentiment towards the United States. MacArthur replied by holding him off and requesting immediate comment from the State Department. It was an opening gambit by Kishi designed clearly to keep the new ambassador under pressure. Washington's response was cool to this attempt to test the United States. MacArthur was instructed to stall.

Kishi and his advisors wanted to both press the views of public opinion and yet distance themselves from the clear anti-Americanism that 'no small number of Japanese people (including unbiased scholars and press circles and even the vast segment of conservatives, but excluding of course opinionated or opportunistic elements) is to varying degrees critical of or in certain circumstances opposed to the policies, foreign policies in particular, of American government'.[48] It was not a particularly subtle method of attempting to change the administration's approach to Japan, but it does appear to have made an impression on MacArthur, who cabled to Washington that

> in subsequent meetings, I will present my line of thinking and certain suggestions to which, it is sincerely hoped, US Government will give most sympathetic consideration. Once mutual agreement is reached thereon, [the] way will be paved for eliminating obstacles, and I believe that I shall be able [to] undertake full responsibility to further strengthen and promote cooperative relations between [our] two countries.[49]

The prose and confidence of its author has a slight family echo.

By any account Kishi spoke up bluntly. He provided evidence to show the constraints his government would face to prevent the existing pattern of US–Japan ties from continuing. The discussion papers left with MacArthur by the Japanese delegation noted that the 'basic relationship between Japan and the United States' was hindered by Japanese suspicion that American foreign policy in the far east was badly flawed. Kishi's notes listed four features of this 'antagonism'. These were

> (A) Japanese aversion to war as against global policy of US, particularly its military policy towards Japan. (B) Resentment against Japan's subordinate position to US under Japan–US security treaty

arrangements. (C) Antipathy arising from territorial problems. (D) Disappointment over restrictive measures against Japanese goods in US and dissatisfaction over embargo against Communist China.[50]

What MacArthur termed this 'candid statement' then went on to draw the conclusions that

> many Japanese have come to believe that [the] foreign policy of [the] US is ultimately a policy of war aiming at overthrow by force of Communist bloc, and that Japanese–American cooperation under existing formula amounts to subjugation [of] their country to US policies that may lead Japan to war. This sentiment of [the] Japanese people has been fully exploited in peace offensive of [the] Soviet Union and Communist China and also by left-wingers in Japan in their anti-American propaganda.[51]

Greater detail on the 'Japanese aversion to war' was next provided, that suggested the 'intensification of [the] Cold War' had produced an even stronger determination within Japan to avoid conflict and a belief that 'war is evil irrespective of cause. It may be stated without exaggeration that they detest war more than Communism.' (Kishi added parenthetically '[that] this contrasts with [the] situation in West Europe where Communism is believed [to be the] greater danger'.)[52]

In what must rank as one of the more extensive and valuable Japanese communications during the 1950s with the representatives of the American government, the premier continued by expressing the 'Japanese view of US military policy'. This was politely introduced by the remark that '[i]t cannot be said that all Japanese people appreciated US military policy for maintenance of world peace', since the US seemed to count on maintaining 'at all times America's military superiority' over Communist states and wished 'positively to display that superiority'.[53] Postwar Japan regarded the supposedly policy of deterrence as likely to lead to the 'ultimate overthrow of Communist powers by means [of] war.' The Japanese side noted that prewar Japanese governments had built up their military might 'under [the] pretext of "self-defense", only to bring upon herself military domination, culminating in disastrous defeat. In [the] minds of Japanese people, haunted by this evil memory, [the] term "armament" itself immediately arouses hatred of militarism and war, and any emphasis put on importance of military policy serves only to fan that hatred.' Kishi's paper warned that the 'presence of US forces and various problems arising therefrom, such as expansion of bases, impress Japanese people as symbolizing such military policy. It is generally felt that US has no interests in Japan other than military.'

In connection with Japanese objections to the security pact the

81

message was once again clear. Kishi's paper stressed that 'even among those of [the] Japanese people who recognize [the] necessity of security arrangements of some sort between Japan and [the] US, [the] overwhelming majority holds [the] opinion that [the] security treaty arrangements should be reviewed now that Japan has built up considerable self-defense capabilities and has been admitted to [the] UN.' Beyond the obvious issue of dissatisfaction over the existence of US military bases and the legal arrangements surrounding them and their users was a wider difficulty. The Japanese text warned that the 'severest criticism is that [the] security treaty grants [the] US [the] right to use forces regardless of intention of Japan and in certain cases for purposes irrelevant to [the] direct defence of Japan, thereby involving Japan in such hostilities as might occur somewhere else in [the] far east'. Tokyo might yet be embroiled in quarrels not of its own making. Kishi's lengthy presentation, reflected a more defiant approach by the Japanese government towards its relations with the United States. It reads at times as more of a declaration of independence (and obviously dispenses with the diplomatic circumlocutions) than an aide memoire to one's closest ally. The need for change was going to be hard for the United States to refute, particularly when Kishi adopted such a firm stance.

MacArthur's reply to the Japanese premier centred on correcting what he defined as the 'false impressions' of the Japanese public. He began by explaining the reactive nature of American postwar foreign policy in the face of Soviet 'force, violence, threats and subversion', citing American attitudes during the Suez crisis as a recent example of how Washington rejected the use of military might to settle international disputes and contrasted this with the continuity of Soviet behaviour 'since the death of Stalin, as events in Hungary and recent campaign of intimidation against Scandinavian nations clearly indicated'. MacArthur rejected any need to apologize for his nation's foreign policies and stated firmly that he found it 'difficult [to] appreciate how there could be such misunderstandings among [the] Japan[ese] people as to [the] aims and purposes of US policy and realities of [the] world situation'. The ambassador then wondered aloud whether the fault might not lie either with the 'previous Japanese governments' for not having 'tried sufficiently to explain [the] world situation and facts of life to [the] Japan[ese] people in terms of Japan's own long-range interests' or the hostility of a 'one-sided, anti-US and anti-Western press'.[54] For an ambassador still in the process of familiarizing himself with Japan this was strong stuff and it can not be said that his masters in Washington entirely shared their representative's approach. Dulles instructed MacArthur to play down any expectations that Kishi may have held over the nature of his proposed visit to Washington and the 'unwarranted' view that his forthcoming 'conversations' would lead to American 'acceptance [of] Japanese views'. Dulles stressed that Kishi's arrival in the United States, for which it was obvious that the Japanese government was far more advanced in its preparations than its American counterpart, was not to be taken as the signal for negotiations to commence but merely to serve as an exchange of views. To underline this point MacArthur was advised to meet less frequently with Kishi and refrain from detailed debate on Kishi's memoranda.[55] MacArthur, of course, next agreed with the State Department, though he had noted in fairness to Kishi that the premier was preparing for his Washington visit 'with [the] utmost seriousness based on long-term thinking, a radical departure from [the] practice in past Japanese visits'.[56]

More detailed 'general guidance' from the State Department soon followed that refuted large portions of the Kishi papers by noting that there was considerable feeling in US that '[the] Japanese [are] too sanguine about [the] threat represented by international communism both in Asia and world as [a] whole'.[57] It was '[d]ifficult for Americans to understand why Japan, with unparalleled economic prosperity and higher standard of living than other Asian countries, is either incapable or unwilling [to] exert greater effort in mutual defense of [the] free world whose trade and whose aid has made Japan's economic recovery possible'.[58] The American counter-attack continued by pointedly contrasting the Japanese 'complaints against US administration of Okinawa and Bonins which is provided for in the Peace Treaty and which US has repeatedly expressed is only [a] temporary measure' with American surprise that 'Japanese ignore unilateral confiscation of their former northern territories by [the] Soviet Union'.[59] Differences between Tokyo and Washington over trade were also described to MacArthur. It was pointed out that 'Japan imports few products from US which are competitive with Japanese industry', while 'Japan exports few products to US which are not competitive with US industries which make restrictions more spectacular in the public mind but no more real in final effect'.[60] American dissatisfaction over Japanese textiles was seen by the State Department as an issue where both sides were at fault, but it still expressed the hope that future Japanese 'exports [should] not be concentrated on [a] single product within [a] short period'. Regardless of the claim of Dulles' advisors that MacArthur could '[c]oncur with Kishi that fundamental interests of the two nations are closely akin, we would hope identical', it was apparent that differences over international affairs and 'growing competition in manufacturing and trade' had produced 'considerable area[s] of friction . . . despite identity of basic long term interest'.[61] It was clearly a far from happy assessment and one that would do little to encourage Kishi over his schemes to alter the entire relationship. Rival American and Japanese diplomatic forays suggested that, if, as Fukuda Takeo claimed to MacArthur, '[t]he Japanese people are pinning their hopes on Prime Minister Kishi' there might well be disappointments in store.[62]

Orders to stonewall by the State Department also produced changes in MacArthur's assessments of Kishi. The more their talks were drawn out the less optimistic the ambassador became. By mid May he would cable that in conversations with Kishi the question arose of whether Japan would 'accept responsibilities which go with mutuality? As I looned [sic] at revisions Kishi had proposed I could not see any clear indication that Japan was prepared [to] assume the necessary additional responsibilities to make [the security] treaty mutual'.[63] MacArthur added that 'Kishi's proposals involved a few changes in [the] security treaty but essentially his proposal seemed to call for [the] termination of [the] treaty in five years with nothing to replace it. I saw no indication that his proposals were aimed at obtaining a mutual security treaty.'[64]

It was against this somewhat strained background that Kishi went to Washington to meet with President Eisenhower. The talks can not be said to have won for Kishi any great attention from the administration if judged by the follow-up activities, since the extent of the changes that the American government would permit in the summer of 1957 was slight when compared with Kishi's initial proposals of April and his eagerness to change the Pacific relationship. The establishment of inter-government committees to study US force deployment in Japan and consideration of Kishi's request that the Japanese flag be flown in the Ryukyus hardly suggests any great urgency had been engendered.[65] Neither limiting the requisition of land in Okinawa nor paroling B and C class war criminals was the purpose behind Kishi's visit, but debates on such issues provided a lesson in what the United States was and was not prepared to do in the face of Japanese requests. There were few signs of the promised new era.

In briefing papers prepared for Secretary of State Dulles before the arrival of Foreign Minister Fujiyama the list of priorities again suggested that security issues would remain buried beneath questions of US–Japan trade, the possible return of former Bonin Islanders and south-east Asian economic development. Few topics involving defence were seen as likely to be raised, with the exception of the implications of reduction in size of US ground forces that had already been announced in the communiqué at the end of Kishi's recent talks in Washington. Instead the focus was on the dilemmas facing Japan over its economic prospects and US fears that protectionist sentiment within the US at both the federal and state level would weaken Tokyo's links with Washington. Ambassador MacArthur reminded the State Department of the fact that Japan's *'basic foreign policy and alignments will ultimately and inevitably be dictated by her over-all economic needs, particularly access to foreign markets'.*[66] It was the issue of US–Japan trade relations that MacArthur insisted was 'the most important single item in our present and future relationships', since 'the nature of the Japanese economy' left Japan with no option but to 'trade to live'.[67] He suggested that '[t]rade with the United States is certainly uppermost in the minds of Japan's leaders' and that Washington ought to recall that 'Japan last year was our second best all-round customer and our largest market for agricultural goods. Her payments to the United States for goods and services were $1.1 billion.' While the ambassador's list of discussion topics was certainly appropriate (he also included China trade, and south-east Asian economic development schemes as probable items that would be raised by Fujiyama), the minimizing of security questions may be indicative of American reluctance to confront what was the major concern of the Japanese government.

Secretary Dulles was not in favour of responding with any enthusiasm to Kishi's proposals. Dulles advised Eisenhower, on the eve of the prime minister's visit to Washington, that 'this is not the time to renegotiate any of the specific provisions of the present Treaty. This process requires most careful study and preparation if it is not to precipitate strong Japanese public and Socialist Party demands for such sweeping revisions in the Treaty that our entire security relationship could be placed in jeopardy.'[68] Clearly American officials in Tokyo had made little impression on the administration and were at variance with their own master. Dulles would agree that 'we work toward a mutual security arrangement which could, we would hope, replace the present Security Treaty',[69] but his caution and unwillingness to be rushed were disappointing. Perhaps a little more urgency from the administration might have aided both Kishi's work and avoided some of the later problems. If Dulles did, in fact, believe that Kishi was Japan's ablest leader and the best friend that the United States possessed, this appears to be a strange way of demonstrating his faith. The belief that Japan was still an American vassal that could be granted the occasional concession if and when the United States government judged the moment opportune, had yet to be corrected. Opposition groups to American security goals in Japan would, ironically, soon achieve what Kishi and the LDP apparently could not do by themselves and demonstrate the errors of taking Japan entirely for granted. Dissenters rather than allies eventually got the security process moving; not before time it has to be stressed.

The United States government still maintained in the summer of 1958 that change in the security relationship ought to be contingent on 'Japanese willingness to accept a burden and responsibility of free world defense in the area of Japan'.[70] The complaint that Japan was not contributing to the common good was once again rehearsed and the example of American aircraft being left in storage in Japan due to lack of Japanese pilots and maintenance deficiencies noted.[71] On the controversial subject of deployment of nuclear weapons, the National Security Council was informed that 'Japanese feelings on this issue are still so intense that public introduction of nuclear weapons at this stage would be impossible.'[72]

Talks continued for the next two years. The American administration's timetable was based on waiting until its officials in Tokyo had reached some form of tentative agreement with the Kishi cabinet and then organizing a 'top level review' of US–Japan relations. American impatience with the frequently rehearsed views of Japanese politicians on the clear limits of Japan's ability to consider defence issues grew as Tokyo attempted to argue that new thinking was required from the Eisenhower administration. Secretary of State Dulles was hardly sympathetic when Finance Minister Ichimada pointed out that the reduction in US military personnel numbers in Japan had made it more difficult for Japan to accumulate dollars and balance its budget, saying merely that 'we are doing what the Japanese Government wished'.[73] Nor was the United States particularly interested in accommodating the labour problems associated with the employment of large numbers of Japanese civilians on American bases. MacArthur went so far as to claim that this was 'potentially the most explosive political issue involved in our military presence here'[74] and warned that Japanese figures felt that the US–West German changes to their administrative agreement did not necessarily appear to apply in the case of Tokyo parallel negotiations.

The results of the 1958 general election spurred Kishi forward. Having been cautioned by MacArthur to avoid discussing security issues during the campaign, the premier now felt sufficiently confident to confront the United States once more. Yet again MacArthur cabled to Dulles that Japan needed to be treated as a 'full and equal partner' and that the alternative to granting a new treaty would be an unwise resistance campaign that would 'make piecemeal adjustments in our security arrangements (i.e. on nuclears, deployment and use of US forces in Japan, etc.), giving in reluctantly inch by inch as the pressure and public opinion mount against us.'[75] This 'disastrous course' had to be replaced by a new deal, since '[w]hether we like it or not we are going to have to deal constructively with the problems of nuclears and deployment of Forces, etc.'.[76] The implication that the United States was at this time either stationing or considering the deployment of certain types of nuclear weaponry in Japan is apparent from such ambassadorial reportage. The need to recognize that in the future there would have to be change in at least the 'political' aspects of security questions was urged upon the administration by MacArthur, not least because if too little were done then 'we will be undermining the very leadership in Japan which holds the best promise for bringing Japan in the coming period into a long-term, durable alignment with the US and the free world'.[77]

Talks in Tokyo followed. The administration had belatedly agreed with the Japanese request since this would both 'strengthen Japan's alignment with the West' and avoid having to negotiate 'under pressure'. On 4 October 1958, the United States presented its proposals for a new security arrangement 'patterned after the other mutual security treaties in the Pacific. They included a commitment by the United States to aid in the defence of Japan, [phrase classified] and on the operational use of US bases, in return for Japanese agreement to allow the United States the use of its bases in Japan for the defence of the Free World position in the Pacific'.[78] Delays on both sides then followed, Kishi moved slowly because of the Police Bill crisis and LDP in-fighting. When Kishi returned to Washington in January 1960 to meet with President Eisenhower it was possible for them both to claim that progress had been made, but Eisenhower's remark that since the United States intends 'to consult with Japan under the new treaty fully, completely, and as equals . . . there was no need to add secrecy to our relations'[79] suggests that even then there were reservations on the American side.

In October 1959 MacArthur had reported, that the

> next few months will represent [a] particularly critical juncture in US–Japan relations, as [an] independent and fully sovereign Japan faces [the] choice [of] whether, in [the] face of major Sino–Soviet pressures and blandishments massively supported by Japanese socialists and neutralists, to move freely into voluntary and

> confirmed security association with the US, or to begin to extricate itself from this relationship and move toward neutralism and accommodation.[80]

The period about to follow was judged, correctly, by the ambassador to be 'the most critical juncture in US–Japan relations since the war'. He suggested that in the four areas of international relations, domestic politics, defence and economics a series of challenges would have to be faced and met. For the Tokyo embassy, what mattered most was the cohesion and determination of the ruling party to stand firm when tested by the Eastern bloc and to remain sufficiently united to avoid worse factionalism that might eventually end in a possible split within the LDP. To buttress the conservatives, MacArthur encouraged his government to treat Japan in a manner similar to that which guided Anglo–American and American–German relations.[81]

Surprisingly, at this juncture MacArthur insisted that in any review of US–Japan relations the greatest emphasis should remain, as he had long maintained, on trade. He asserted that

> [i]f Japan is to remain firmly aligned with the US in security and other fields, it is imperative that American economic policy continue to give Japan access to a fair and responsible share of the American market. It is also important that the US encourage other free world countries to do likewise. For Japan must, in the final analysis, end up where and with whom it can earn a living and if the US and other free world countries make this impossible by restrictionist trade policies, Japan will inevitably turn away from us and toward the communist bloc. A liberal trade policy is important in the relations of the US with many countries but in the case of Japan it is the foundation on which any really meaningful relationship must rest.[82]

This view was, perhaps, at variance with Japanese concerns over security and global economic realities. It was surely far from certain that the Soviet Union was likely to take on board yet another waif if trading ties with the United States were sundered by Japan. More important, for at least the immediate future, was Washington's need to gain Japanese cooperation over the proposed security treaty revisions. The 'great debate', as MacArthur rightly termed it, was critical to American military strategy in the region. He had earlier made the point to Washington that ultimately 'we have no alternative but to accept what the Japanese consider reasonable if we wish to retain our bases and facilities here'.[83]

Kishi's role in security treaty revision had begun before he attained the premiership. He had visited Washington in August 1955 as part of the entourage of Foreign Minister Shigemitsu. The communiqué issued at the conclusion of these talks had spoken clearly of Japan in assuming greater responsibility for its defence and 'that when such conditions were brought about it would be appropriate to replace the present security treaty with one of greater mutuality'. The implication was that revision would depend on the speed and nature of Japanese rearmament. Expectations within Japan now put the onus on the government and Kishi was able to point to the communiqué issued following his meetings with President Eisenhower in June 1957. He could inform the public that a new US–Japan committee would consider the future position of US forces within Japan, though the impact of this news was quickly dampened by Dulles' comment that treaty revision was not on the cards. Still a commitment to withdraw US ground forces had been obtained from Washington and a *quid pro quo* of sorts was being realized in that the Japanese SDF were increasing in size and capabilities.

On 9 July 1958, against a backcloth of extraordinarily complicated and persistent quarrels and manoeuvres within the LDP, the Japanese foreign minister Fujiyama Aiichiro proposed to the American ambassador that talks on the revision of the security treaty might commence. In response to American feelers on alternative schemes, Kishi replied the following month that a new treaty, rather than an amended one, would be necessary. The premier's decision signalled the beginning of the security negotiations and nearly two years of political controversy. Major differences were quickly uncovered and then multiplied both between and within Japan's political parties. Attention must first be focussed on the LDP, since its divisions, rather than the clamourings of the left, were decisive in determining the fate of Kishi's proposals. It was to be his own party that would eventually unseat him and to overstress the role of Opposition groups in the ensuing events may be to neglect the importance of the internal manoeuverings of rival conservative bosses and their factions.

The LDP was split over treaty revision. Kishi's rivals adopted stances that were critical of the prime minister, though generally tempered with sufficiently tepid notice of public eagerness to pursue the quest. The opponents to Kishi varied from those, such as Yoshida, who felt that 'his' treaty of 1952 was adequate to those, such as Kono Ichiro and Fujiyama Aiichiro, who were itching to topple the premier. Kishi made endless attempts to paper over the cracks within the LDP, yet the treaty and administrative agreement were used quite blatantly by Kishi's opponents as a football to be kicked at will. There was little substantial concern for consistency or thought of national interest. Party members reversed themselves as they saw fit to further their own political careers. Ikeda Hayato, for instance, switched sides and became a Kishi supporter once promised office in the reformed cabinet of June 1959. Criticism from within the LDP that the treaty had flaws and the administrative agreement even more disadvantages, played directly into the hands of the opposition groups[84] who maintained that if the government was still divided then it had no right to recommend treaty revision to the nation. The protracted nature of the serious LDP wrangling further benfited the left in that it gave certain parties more time to organize and cooperate. Kishi's immense difficulties elicited little sympathy from Japan's journalists and the public at large.[85]

Attention on the LDP's internal affairs tended frequently to obscure the fundamental issue of how to gain a more satisfactory series of security arrangements from the United States. Indeed, one unnamed (perhaps cynical) source within the Japanese Foreign Office went so far as to suggest that by December 1958, 95 per cent of the LDP's sound and fury concerned the scoring of political rather than diplomatic points.[86] Probably the ratio of rhetoric to substance was less than this, but the reactions of Japanese and American diplomats to the public statements from all sides can be imagined.

The all-too-public dissent within the LDP and the relative slowness and elitist nature of the conservatives' efforts to mount an effective campaign to defend the proposed treaty revision, in the face of well-coordinated criticism from left-wing parties, academics and student groups, severely tested Kishi's nerve and skill. Yet with his party holding a comfortable majority in parliament and the fact that the United States and Japan appeared to be ready to agree on a more equitable treaty the premier and his supporters might have seemed to possess cause for celebration. It was not to be. Kishi did, it is true, gain the passage of the new security treaty through the Diet, but this was only effected at a high price that left many observers concerned about the political maturity of the nation and the future of its relationship with Washington. The opposition surprised many by its effective organization and had a cause well worth fighting for, but the key to Kishi's demise lies within the LDP. Its naked power struggles did Kishi in. Public opinion during and after the 1960 crisis registered little change over its pro-conservative orientation.[87] Ties with the United States, while most certainly strained by events that culminated in the cancellation of President Eisenhower's intended visit to Tokyo, were not permanently damaged. Yet there were moments during the crisis when the final outcome was in serious jeopardy. We must return to the story.

Battle lines were drawn up by 1959. Much that occurred later was, to a degree, presaged by earlier confrontations between the government and a rapidly strengthening anti-Kishi coalition. The left, encouraged by its tactics in gaining the withdrawal of the Police Bill, put together an umbrella-like federation in March 1959 officially termed the People's Council for Preventing Revision of the Security Treaty. It was inevitably a loose grouping of organizations (led by trade unionists from the Sohyo federation) eager to attack Kishi but not necessarily agreed on how this might be best achieved. It spoke of rejecting the LDP's plans to revise the security treaty (arguing that this would merely perpetuate the US–Japan alliance), and wished to work for neutralism (an official aim of the Japan Socialist Party).[88] A united front of sorts was coming into place. Kishi was now faced with opponents who had gained confidence from street demonstrations over the Police Bill and who widely regarded the prime minister as the embodiment of reaction in both domestic and foreign affairs. Kishi's personality and the whole array of his policies formed the ideal bogy. Portents for confrontation were growing.[89]

Those eager to dethrone Kishi were next assisted by a piece of good fortune from an unlikely source. Two days after the formation of the People's Council, Tokyo District Court Judge Date Akio ruled that the US–Japan security pact was unconstitutional. The Japanese legal system had thrown an additional spanner into the works. Not surprisingly the government immediately appealed to the Supreme Court and hoped for a rejection of Date's view that those arrested for forcing their way onto the US air force base runway at Tachikawa on the edge of Tokyo could not be charged under laws designed to protect the security treaty when by its very nature this violated the pacifism of the postwar Japanese Constitution. The 'Sunakawa' case caused uproar and was highly embarrassing to the Kishi cabinet. Even the fact that the Supreme Court made quite unprecedented speed to hear the appeal and quickly (and predictably given the court's general timidity since 1947) overturned the District Court's verdict did little to end the debate. The publicity alone was a boon to the anti-Kishi groups who exulted in his misfortune and, while the final decision went against the left, it was widely noted that the bench had not ruled on the constitutionality as such of the Japanese Self-Defence Forces.[90]

Encouraged by the furore the opposition mounted fresh challenges to the LDP. Street demonstrations, strikes (usually brief in the Japanese fashion to avoid inconveniencing the public), constant speeches and the distribution of handbills coincided with the signing of the new 'Treaty of Mutual Cooperation and Security Between the United States of America and Japan' on 19 January 1960 in Washington.[91] The treaty was short, containing only a preamble and ten articles. It deserves to be analyzed carefully. The text began by stating that the US and Japan wished 'to strengthen the bonds of peace and friendship traditionally existing between them' and reaffirmed their mutual commitment to 'the principles of democracy, individual liberty and the rule of law', before noting shared economic ties, support for the United Nations and the 'inherent right of individual or collective self-defense' of its charter and their 'common concern in the maintenance of international peace and security in the Far East'. Article 1 stresses the commitment to the United Nations of both parties, Article 7 likewise states that the treaty does not affect the responsibility of the UN for international security. Articles 2 and 3 speak of economic and military cooperation. Article 4 simply says that the two nations will meet 'whenever the security of Japan or international peace and security in the Far East is threatened'. The heart of the pact is contained in articles 5 and 6. The area to which the two parties would 'act to meet the common danger in accordance with its constitutional provisions and processes' is firstly defined as 'the territories under the administration of Japan'. Article 6 then grants to the United States military facilities in Japan in order to contribute 'to the security of Japan and the maintenance of international peace and security in the Far East'. The text gave Japan a guarantee that if Japan were attacked or US forces were attacked on Japanese soil then the United States would defend Japan, although no provision was made for joint military responses or a unified high command.[92]

What happened after the signing of the revised security treaty could hardly have been foreseen by either the Kishi cabinet or the Eisenhower administration. Ratification was to prove a far more difficult and fraught process than it appeared in January 1960 when it was possible for the LDP to claim that the new treaty had removed most of the anomalies of the past and would 'foster an atmosphere of mutual confidence'.[93] The fact that the power of the United States to intervene with force in Japanese affairs had been scrapped, that the Japanese government could grant military rights to third parties at will and there was now a ten-year term for the treaty made no impression on the left. What were seen as substantial improvements by the government were dismissed as sops by its critics. Kishi was still denounced; the revised treaty had been signed by the man who had also put his name to the Imperial rescript's declaration of war in December 1941. Japan would be at risk as long as Kishi remained its head of government. Under such political tension neither the Kishi cabinet nor the opposition parties led by the Socialists were ever likely to compromise over the issue of ratification of the US–Japan security pact. The use of violence to prevent the passage of the pact was openly considered, following the precedent of the forced entry into the Diet compound on 27 November by groups of students, and unionists with the cooperation of Socialist Dietmen including Asanuma Inejiro. The JSP hoped to redeem itself in the public mind by appearing both determined and constructive in its parliamentary behaviour in the new Diet session. Kishi, for his part, wished to gain approval for the treaty and then receive President Eisenhower in Tokyo in June. Success would then leave him with the option of calling a general election, though he could never be certain of more than lukewarm support from some of the LDP factional bosses who had their own political ambitions to consider and were not averse to watching the prime minister stumble.

Debate in the Diet commenced at the beginning of February through committees in both houses with the Socialists doing what they could to delay proceedings until the close of the session on 26 May. The public was now subjected to an extraordinary amount of information on the course of Japan's postwar international relations. Speeches in the Diet, special meetings in provincial cities, and endless outpourings in the press all contributed to the charged atmosphere. The left tried to gain both clarifications from the government spokesmen (on, for example, the precise meaning of the 'prior consultation' clause contained in the Kishi–Herter exchange of notes following the signing of the security treaty) and to embarrass it whenever possible.[94] Kishi may have given as good as he got but was not regarded as having won over those not already firmly committed to the LDP. The prime minister had to admit that in some instances Japan would be obliged to rely on the good faith of the United States. He was surely correct since international agreements can never function in any other manner; however watertight the text may attempt to be, there are likely to be unseen eventualities, but this hardly appeased his critics.

Public interest in what constituted self-defence and whether, if the Japanese SDF fought together with American forces, this would violate the constitution was very considerable. The Socialists challenged the government on the minutiae of the text, while much of the press led by the Asahi Shimbun remained opposed to treaty revision.[95] The first six months of 1960 saw an attention on foreign policy that was to have no parallel in the postwar years. The subject was unavoidable for Japanese readers and viewers in 1960. Ominously for the Japanese government, international events in May were closely related to the security revision debate. News on 7 May of the shooting down of an American U2 spy plane over the Soviet Union was a godsend to the opposition and a further setback to Kishi. It was already public knowledge that U2s operated from Atsugi air base and the possibility of Soviet action against Japan for harbouring such planes was a cause of much discomfort. The Soviet prime minister then announced a week later that his nation had become the first to launch an artificial satellite in space and next compounded American misfortune by abruptly ending the Paris summit conference and any hopes that President Eisenhower might still be harbouring of a visit to Moscow before his term of office expired. Instead of going to the Soviet Union, Eisenhower would merely continue with his pre-arranged tour of east Asia.

Japan did not appear to be linking itself to the most competent of allies. Parliamentary events now came to a head. On 19 May the LDP extended the current Diet session for fifty days, despite sit-down tactics of the opposition parties and objections from a small minority within the conservative ranks who felt such a blatant show of force, whatever the undoubted provocations, would reduce still further any remaining hopes of a national consensus on the question of treaty revision. The use of policemen to eject Socialist members and the immediate extension of the Diet left Kishi's position in jeopardy. The roar of disapproval reached a crescendo when it became apparent that automatic ratification by the Diet would result in the treaty becoming law at the very moment when Eisenhower was scheduled to arrive at Haneda. The timing was all wrong.

The climax to the security treaty issue was seen in June. Protests and strikes continued against Kishi's anti-parliamentary behaviour, abusive treatment was meted out to Eisenhower's press secretary James Hagerty and the appointments secretary Thomas Stephens as they arrived at Tokyo airport on 10 June, and there were violent scenes outside the Diet Building on 15 June (leading to the death of a Tokyo university student). These all contributed to the eventual decision of 20 June, when Kishi was obliged to ask President Eisenhower to postpone his visit. It is probable that Kishi was encouraged to make this decision by voices within the American government. Despite the relaxation in tension epitomized by the joint declaration of seven newspapers on 17 June[96] and a general sense that unless restraint was now exercised the consequences would be incalculable, the presence of President Eisenhower in Japan would have put the alliance at risk. It was best that the visit be called off, although publicly this was explained as a decision made by the Japanese government. The chief executive of Japan's closest ally in the Pacific was neither welcome nor safe in Tokyo.

The contrast between what Eisenhower immediately after his reception in Taipei and Seoul described as 'tremendous (and exhausting) and the schedules crowded' and the action of 'a small destructive minority'[97] in Japan would have been a massive loss in prestige to both the American and Japanese governments. Cancellation was clearly likely after the demonstrations that occurred when the president's press secretary James Hagerty and his appointments secretary Thomas Stephens arrived at Haneda on 10 June. MacArthur, who was at the airport to greet his guests, reported to Eisenhower that the party had decided unanimously to 'proceed as planned in my car rather than sneak out of [the] airport by helicopter'.[98] MacArthur reasoned that 'if the leftists were going to resort to force and violence it was better for Japanese and us to know now rather than when [the] president arrives. Furthermore I felt that if force and violence were used against us, there would be a deep feeling of revulsion on [the] part of the great majority of Japanese which would seriously blunt the pro-Communist offensive here.'[99] The fact was that

> a mob spearheaded by Zengukuren students closed in on us stoning the car, shattering two windows, cutting the tires and trying to turn us over. Our situation was fairly uncomfortable for about fifteen minutes until [the] police reached us. Since it was quite impossible to proceed further by car the police eventually cleared a path for [the] helicopter to pick us up and we arrived at the embassy without further adventure and with none of the party suffering any real damage although unfortunately the helicopter was damaged. Hagerty and Stephens were superb throughout this trying experience.[100]

The ambassador hoped that this incident would have a 'most salutary and helpful result', since he felt that the

> Japanese press, intellectuals, business leaders and the conservative party have long needed some real shock to shake them out of their passive acceptance of use of force, violence and illegal action by a militant pro-Communist minority which is trying to paralyze parliamentary government and democracy in Japan. I am hoping that [the] Japanese reaction to this incident will be similar to [the] Japanese reaction to the violence on May Day 1952 and that net result will be a major setback for [the] Communist cause in Japan.[101]

MacArthur's reasoning appears suspect given the impossibility of guessing what the mob might do then or later and the risk that any sustained violence might result in the cancellation of the presidential visit. The left immediately termed the Hagerty arrival a test case for

95

whether Eisenhower's safety could be guaranteed and called the Haneda business provocative. The difficulties for Washington and Tokyo were already considerable, of course, prior to the Hagerty affair. Discussions had certainly begun between MacArthur and the Japanese ministry of foreign affairs by late May over the advantages of cancellation. Eisenhower told MacArthur on 26 May that he would still be prepared to come only, 'if it remains [the] considered judgment of Kishi that Presidential visit in June as scheduled is vital' but when the ambassador attempted to deliver this message he was thwarted by pickets. MacArthur told the Japanese foreign ministry that he thought 'various consideration[s] indicating postponement made sense' and correctly pointed out that the selection of 19 June as the date for Eisenhower's arrival was more than a little unfortunate since it coincided with the ratification of the treaty signed six months earlier in Washington.

The campaign against the revision of US–Japan security treaty provided both governments with a considerable number of lessons. The crisis in Tokyo forms a convenient moment to assess the first years of the post-San Francisco relationship. It goes without saying that the lack of domestic agreement on Japan's ties with the United States in 1960 revealed massive faults in the supposedly shared terrain. The degree of active opposition to the proposed revisions to the security pact must, however, have severely shaken both governments. It is certainly the case that both Tokyo and Washington had appreciated by 1956 that the late 1950s would be a time of tension as voices against the treaty were likely to make themselves heard, yet the size, fervour and organization of the anti-pact groups was remarkable. Thousands of previously uninvolved people took to the streets to denounce Kishi and his American allies. Portions of an entire generation of students and youth were mobilized for action. Not all, of course, participated but many became aware of the need to reconsider Japan's predicament. The occupation and post-San Francisco years were subject to reassessment and frequently found wanting. The Japan of 1960 surprised itself and outside observers by challenging much of its recent past. Parliamentary democracy was discarded in favour of direct protest; criticism of government behaviour frequently ignored parallel errors of an opposition that insisted that its acts were sanctioned by the intelligentsia and media.

For our purposes one salient fact deserves to be stressed. It was difficult in the turmoil of the crisis to hear clear, articulate voices in support of the US–Japan security pact. Supporters of the treaty were on the defensive in the face of a strong nationalistic mood, but the response from those in favour of the treaty was disappointing. Few appeared willing to court unpopularity, many equivocated. Hesitancy appears to have been the best response that many academics were able to manage. In reply, for example, to questions such as: 'Should Japan be Pro-American, Pro-Russian, or Neutralist?' it was felt that Japan could straddle all three positions.[102] Such contortionism was obviously of little use to a Japanese government desperate for support and beset on all sides by mass protests and the fear of a return to an earlier era when the assassin's knife foreclosed debate. Extremism of left and right should not be easily discounted, when Hagerty was mobbed, Kishi attacked, and in October the head of the JSP killed by a young follower of Akao Bin.[103]

Later authors have made the point that the alterations to the original security treaty by Kishi can be seen as the culmination of over a decade of quiet diplomacy by successive Japanese governments and might be interpreted as the successful completion of a formidable task.[104] International lawyers would correctly argue that the 1960 text was a different document from the one signed by Yoshida at San Francisco in 1951. Japan had, technically, gained a victory. The new treaty was much more than a modification of an earlier version, since, while it now guaranteed the United States' firm commitment to defend Japan, it was not a mutual pact in the sense that Japan had an obligation to assist the United States.[105] Its supporters would later claim that it represented precisely what Yoshida had attempted to gain in 1951.[106] Yet the left-wing in Japan continued to respond by repeating that any treaty would unwillingly place Japan at risk and increase the likelihood of their nation's involvement in regional confrontations between the superpowers. Neutrality was seen as safer than behaving as the American lapdog; only with the freedom to conduct an independent foreign policy could Tokyo move closer to its neighbours and reassure them of Japan's goodwill. (Ironically, one of the barbs launched against Japan by American scholars and European diplomats has been the tendency of Japan's foreign policy to remain concealed behind the United States since regaining independence. The alterations to the security treaty in 1960 did little to change what has been rightly termed 'policy immobilism'.)

Still, the fact remains that the treaty was ratified. Japan gained new security ties with the United States, though the role that was now expected of Tokyo was hardly very different than before the crisis. Not much would change in the ensuing decade because successive Japanese premiers were to constantly recall the recent eruption of anger at the Pacific relationship. The domestic foundations for a greatly increased Japanese stance over defence issues were judged not to exit by the LDP. Caution and cowardice were to ensure that there would not be any repetition of the June days. We will examine next how the US government sought to repair the damage caused by what it had confidently but erroneously expected, when it commenced negotiations in the late 1950s, would herald a movement towards greater equality and friendship. The new objective was to put the past behind both partners and begin a period of consolidation after the storm.

5 READJUSTMENT: THE 1960s

To many Japanese, an American general or admiral seemed much more of a genuine American than a Harvard professor.

Ambassador Edwin Reischauer

Japan is opposing the United States, and it's not only the Japanese Communist Party and the Japanese people that are opposing the United States – the big capitalists are doing so too.

Mao Tse-tung, 13 February 1964

It is difficult to draft boys from Kansas farms and Pittsburgh factories to send as riflemen to Japan which has a population of 95 million people.

Secretary of State Dean Rusk to President Johnson, January 1964

The shared objective of successive Japanese governments and American administrations in the 1960s was to avoid another major political crisis. Both sides, therefore, were more ready to identify common problems and to consult on means to solve issues before flash-point was reached. Memories of 1960 acted as a powerful constraint on pressing matters too hard and too far. New politicians and new diplomats took over from Eisenhower, Kishi and Ambassador MacArthur, as if to symbolize the new thinking that was presumed to be in the air. The degree of change that took place in the Pacific relationship must now be examined.

In many ways the replacements were fortunate. The immediate crisis had passed and the new security pact had been ratified. Washington could breathe again. Indeed, once Ambassador Edwin Reischauer had been selected and commenced his efforts to improve American–Japanese relations, the subject of Japan rapidly lost any priority with the new Kennedy administration. Japan would hardly feature in later memoirs of the early 1960s[1], since there was no repetition of the 1960 crisis and other incidents involving Japan tended to be dealt with competently by area specialists without the need for any but the bureaucratic handling of US–Japanese ties that had characterized most of the Truman and Eisenhower eras.

Ambassador Reischauer had written an article in *Foreign Affairs* shortly before his appointment which argued that 'despite the violently anti-American stand of the Communists and despite the tremendous opposition to the treaty with the United States and the visit of Eisenhower, there was no general anti-American feeling.'[2] Perhaps not, but Reischauer then went out of his way to cultivate elements within Japanese society that had been most vigorous in their criticism of American policies, if not American citizens. It may be clutching at straws to stress the distinction, since the widespread unease at the continuation of the US–Japan security pact did not go away and the idea that 'the US was not an inherently aggressive, militaristic country' remained dubious to numbers of Japanese. The new ambassador would write later that his personal mission was to correct misperceptions of American omnipotence and Japanese weakness. He claimed that both sides should 'look on each other as equal partners'[3] and he evoked the binocular image that would later be recalled by Japan as it in turn began to look down on other Pacific nations.[4]

Obviously there was a limit to what the United States could do to explain and promote its Reischauerian vision of a more cooperative relationship; much would depend on the actions of the new Ikeda cabinet that had replaced Kishi's government in July 1960. Ikeda's strategy was to downplay questions of national security and to concentrate on the further promotion of economic growth, something that the Japanese nation was already rather good at. In the circumstances it made sense, though it depended for success on both the continued competency of Japan's business–bureaucratic links[5] and an acceptance by trade unions and others that economic priorities were not to be derided as merely ploys to buy off the opposition parties and their supporters. Ikeda had to trust that prosperity would provide the necessary distraction and that time could be bought in which the US–Japan relationship might heal itself. In the event the conservatives were soon to reap the benefits of this strategy. The 1960s would prove to be the quietest decade of the postwar relationship.

The appointment of Professor Reischauer as President Kennedy's representative to Japan was intended to suggest that US–Japan relations were about to change. Possessed of Japanese reputation, language and wife, he benefited immediately from a good press. He worked hard to repair ties, but an important factor that assisted his embassy was the generational shift within the ruling LDP. Reischauer would later admit that his rapport with the old guard was slight and that he found relations with Yoshida and Kishi difficult. Their successors were apparently somewhat more open, though Reischauer in retirement said that his contacts with them were not helped by the bureaucratic background of Fukuda Takeo and the fact that Tanaka Kakuei was 'a wealthy, self-made man of modest education, entirely unlike any of the others' left in both cases 'too great a gap in our backgrounds to establish any real sense of intimacy'.[6] Ikeda and Ohira were apparently the two politicians in the conservatives' ranks that Reischauer felt closest to. Other American academics would endorse this assessment, but, of course, their government had to deal with a range of Japanese politicians whose thinking was less immediately attractive to Western intellectuals.[7]

Reischauer's version of a new relationship was impressive, but, unfortunately, ahead of the perceived realities of both the Japanese and American governments in the early 1960s. Neither side was willing to go as far as the ambassador would have liked to adjust to what may well have been his farsighted objectives. The difficulties were ones that persisted throughout the decade and on into the 1970s. On the American side the alliance was frequently seen as a military convenience with the United States entitled through its substantial presence in Japan to get its way on the Japanese cabinet. Tokyo, moreover, was unwilling to assert itself. The legacy of the 1960 crisis was to leave the conservatives with both justifiable fears (or at least good excuses) for remaining a trading nation relatively isolated from international politics. The opposition parties continued to object to the US–Japan security pact and would point to the American occupation of Okinawa and the increasing American involvement in south-east Asia, particularly in South Vietnam, as proof that Washington had not changed its spots.

The Socialist party did temporarily modify some of its objections to the direction of Japan's foreign policy, but this proved a momentary shift that resulted in only a short period of a more studied 'neutral' neutrality and the return to its traditional ideological stance was complete by 1965.[8] Even in its platform of November 1962, during the supposedly more liberal phase, the JSP had insisted that the Ikeda cabinet was 'subservient' to the United States and, therefore, remilitarizing Japan and 'leading the country to the path to nuclear armament'.[9] The belief that distinctions could be maintained between peace-loving Socialist states and the war-mongering West was too deep-rooted to be erased by attempting to condemn both power blocs for their military expenditures and nuclear testings. It was easier to attract voters and preserve party unity if the crude distinctions of

101

earlier years were maintained. The fight was still to gain 'the complete removal of US military bases and the withdrawal of US forces from Okinawa and Japan, toward the ultimate goal of abandoning the Japan–US Security Treaty'.[10] The election of Sasaki Kozo to the chairmanship of the party following factional struggles in 1965 saw the Socialists once more attacking the United States for its behaviour in Vietnam and for perpetuating a series of military alliances with reactionary governments in South Korea, South Vietnam and Taiwan. Neutralism may briefly have been assessed as an even-handed distrust of all great and regional powers in 1960 but the mood soon changed. It was supposedly better politics to criticize the United States than to note that it was not only the United States that was intent on proceeding with the arms race. The nuclear explosions by the People's Republic of China were, therefore, justified as defensive rearmament in the face of American intimidation, rather than the accession of the first Asian nation into the nuclear club, thus increasing the prospects of nuclear competition in the region, despite the beginnings of detente between the United States and the Soviet Union as expressed in their signing of the test ban treaty.[11] The nation that had strongly criticized Khrushchev for putting his signature to the July 1963 treaty as guilty of 'capitulation to US imperialism'[12] was able to explode its first nuclear weapon the day after Khrushchev was himself removed from power in October 1964. The deepening of the Sino–Soviet rift and the attainment of a more relaxed relationship between Washington and Moscow did little to alter the JSP's verdict on the faults of the United States, while leaving the party by the late 1960s unattached to either the USSR or PRC. Whatever the factional divides within the JSP it was safe to assume that most members were united in undisguised anti-Americanism.[13] This severely limited the wider electoral prospects of the party but provided a useful rallying cry when outward cooperation between rival factions was required.

The Liberal Democratic Party hardly required reminders from any quarter of the deep divide that persisted between itself and the opposition parties. Both the Kennedy administration and the Ikeda cabinet would have endorsed Reischauer's later recollection that '[m]ilitary matters ... were the area of chief delicacy in Japanese-American relations and therefore had to be subordinated as much as possible to political control'.[14] It was one thing for the LDP to criticize the Socialists for neutralism but quite another to claim that such a policy would in practice 'induce foreign intervention in our national affairs' when this was seen to be the practical consequence of Japan's ties with the United States. The existence of American military installations throughout the nation and lack of Japanese control of the Bonin islands and Okinawa also suggested to many Japanese that cooperation with the Americans did not produce all the advantages claimed by the LDP in the early 1960s.

Alterations to the US–Japan relationship took place in a decidedly gradual manner. Prime Minister Ikeda might visit Washington as part of the convention that newly appointed premiers ought to make a pilgrimage to the United States but beyond agreeing to hold annual US–Japan cabinet meetings and settling the question of Japanese payments towards postwar American expenditures involved in the occupation little of immediate importance was accomplished. Many Americans in occupied Japan would indeed have agreed with the widespread Japanese view that it would not be necessary for aid repayment of what (mistakenly) was seen originally as an American gift; but eventually, after protracted negotiations and the fact that West Germany was reported as having completed its own postwar debt repayments to Washington, a settlement was reached that required of Japan the payment of US$490,000,000 principal with a low interest rate attached to the unpaid balance. One source of aggravation at least had been removed.[15]

More important issues of Japanese security relations with the United States and the degree of economic support between the two nations were handled less successfully. Ikeda prevented any fresh deterioration in security ties but he can hardly have been said to have displayed any willingness to extend military links. Little was done to comply with American requests over substantial improvement to the size and capabilities of Japan's SDF. The impressions that Japan could safely leave most of its security affairs in the hands of the United States was itself endorsed by the LDP in its September 1960 platform for the lower house elections which spoke of the maintenance of 'the Japan–US Security System as a means for the security of our nation until the United Nations can replace it; and to possess the self-defence forces to the degree of minimum necessity'.[16] For some American officials the lack of Japanese commitment to improved defence capabilities was less important than 'shared economic interest and political ideals'.[17] Yet this Reischauerian view had many critics in the light of American expenditure on Pacific defence and the self-evident successes of the Japanese economy by the 1960s. The relaxed stance adopted by many of Japan's responsibilities over security and endorsed by some American officials may have been a mistake. If more had been asked (and more frequently) of Japan in the 1960s it would have been easier to break the old habits before it became apparent in the 1980s (to this writer) that Japan was not making an adequate contribution to the US–Japan military alliance. The apologetic tone of Japan's own senior defence staff in the Ikeda-Sato years was symptomatic of the failings of both the Japanese leadership and American civilian specialists handling relations with Japan. The commandant of Japan's National Defense College could write in a volume published in 1965 that 'we must admit it is impossible to arouse the sense of the need for national defence among the Japanese people by rational, logical persuasion. Perhaps we should wait for their emotions to return to normal as time passes by.'[18] The problem would appear to be one that, with hindsight, ought to have been tackled earlier, though there were most certainly arguments that suggested caution was the better approach.

On defence, as with trade questions, a firm national response to pleas for change from the United States had solidified in the 1960s. Overseas audiences were almost certain to be regaled with a set reply to suggestions on improving the Japanese SDF. Memories of the Pacific war, the atomic bombings, suspicions over the possible reemergence of an officer corps along earlier lines, residual difficulties of economic reconstruction, public apathy and lack of political bipartisanship were constantly evoked to explain away the meagerness of Japan's remilitarization in a region bristling with weaponry and mass conscript armies. The dilemma for the United States was an unenviable one, but the consequence of not pressing Japan too hard was that the spur to improvement went missing. Self-generated internal pressures were most unlikely, given the constant invocation of the national litany on the virtues of a small military establishment, to gain approval. If the United States failed to maintain its pressure and display sufficient concern then the SDF were likely to remain undermanned and underequipped against even the modest standards prescribed by the Japanese government.

It was not a question of Washington failing to become involved in Japanese security questions. It was there already by benefit of the existing military agreements, and the influence of the United States Armed Forces was pervasive in the realms of Japanese armament and strategy. What evolved, however, in the 1960s was an unwillingness to persuade Japan to adhere to or accelerate what had been supposedly agreed to in the May 1957 Basic National Defence Policy statement as approved by the National Defense Council[19] and the delayed Second Defence Build-up Plan (fiscal 1962–1966). The political and administrative realities of Japan were to leave the Ministry of Finance in the driving seat with strong powers over the actual expenditure levels attained by the SDF regardless of paper policies. Problems of the SDF's precise mission, procurement levels and morale abounded.[20]

Japanese defence objectives were decidedly slight and seemingly without much regard to the military balance of power in east Asia.[21] It was surely testing fate for senior Japanese defence commentators to state so confidently that there were no external threats to the Japanese archipelago when the People's Republic of China saw Japan as being under 'semi-military occupation'[22] and serving as an important American nuclear base.[23] Yet the deficiencies of Japan's remilitarization persisted. One naval authority would later note that the Second Defence Build-up plan achieved 'no qualitative gain in ships or aircraft at all, and the military mission was as open to doubt as ever'.[24] Ground troops used Second World War infantry weapons in the mid–1960s. No submarines were delivered before 1960, no hypothetical enemies were officially announced, and little was done to prepare the public for any appreciation of what role the SDF were expected to perform beyond its stand-by emergency tasks of flood control and firefighting. Success appears to have been measured solely by the bureaucratic criterion of how nearly funded allocation was expended in any designated fiscal period.

Japanese politicians might make bold claims on the role and effectiveness of the SDF in the 1960s but few took their words too seriously. The actual state of affairs with regard to the SDF was disturbingly less than Foreign Minister Aichi's remark that 'they constitute a very effective homeland defence' and played 'an important contribution to the keeping of the peace in East Asia'.[25]

It has since been suggested that the Maritime Self Defence Forces even following the Third Defence Build-up Plan (1967–71) could not prevent direct invasion of the Japanese islands, protect coastal shipping or blockade the three straits that are crucial to Japan's security. The MSF in 1971 was described as little better than it had been at its inception and remained 'a good minesweeping force'.[26]

The most convincing argument Japan's leaders could employ in favour of the maintenance of the US–Japan alliance in the 1950s was to note that national reconstruction was greatly assisted by American aid, procurement orders and trade. Whatever their ideological persuasion it was rare to find citizenry who would dispute the need to rebuild the Japanese economy as rapidly as possible. Differences over the organization of industry and the appropriate roles for the state and trades unions might be very considerable but recognition of the need for economic growth to make these various ends possible was

commonplace. There was an additional element of undisguised nationalism in this objective, since the idea of both catching-up with, and
then possibly overtaking, the West was highly attractive. (The statistical pitfalls of comparative national income did not matter a lot in the
1960s, since much was still to be achieved in gaining perceived parity
with first European and then American standards of wealth.) Evidence that the public, often irrespective of professed political orientation, was principally concerned with improvements to the standard of
living in the 1960s is substantial, though the inflationary and environ-
mental consequences of economic growth were certainly not ignored
among some of those polled.[27] This apparent eagerness for high
growth rates played into the hands of the LDP and its American ally.
The United States might not be a trustworthy partner in the opinion of
some in the field of defence but it was hard to opt for material
improvement and to simultaneously disparage the American
economy and the opportunities it presented for Japanese exporters.
'Economism', of course, has had its critics but, as one Japanese
observer pointed out in 1968, for a majority of the people economic
activities became the only legitimate national purpose. It was felt that
the 'economy-first' principle was permissible and suitable, because of
its 'non-political' and 'non-military' character, for a nation which was
punished for being overly political and military in the immediate
past.[28]

Prime Minister Ikeda gained both immense publicity and support
from pressing ahead with ambitious 'income-doubling' plans that had
their origins in schemes within the Economic Planning Agency during
the late 1950s.'[29] The LDP was not slow to appreciate the advantages
that could accrue from the further promotion of economic growth both
as a vote-winner and as a means of distracting attention from the
security issues that had recently plagued the nation. Considerable
increases in national income and awareness that Japan was achieving
faster growth rates than its major international competitors[30] shored
up the LDP and left it less vulnerable to attacks from its opponents on
defence issues. The public had other, more immediate, priorities than
the US–Japan security pact and the electorate generally endorsed the
conservatives' conduct in office. Election returns in the 1960s saw the
dashing of Socialist hopes for an eventual opening to the left; instead,
the JSP lost seats in a succession of general elections and the birth of a
multi-party political system became the new theme in the writings of
analysts and academics.[31]

Industrial growth in the 1960s was even more rapid than in the
post-treaty years. The basis for prosperity was firmly laid in the period

between Ikeda's much trumpeted 'income doubling' plans and the Nixon 'shocks' of 1971. Vast increases in steel production, automobile sales and the manufacture of household electronic goods were evidence of the beginnings of a mass consumer society. In each successive election between November 1960 and December 1969 the Socialists' total number of seats in the lower house of the Diet decreased while the LDP's vote remained remarkably stable and quite unchallenged by the returns of the opposition parties. The tumult of the 1960 crisis was swiftly replaced by a more introspective era that placed affluence above foreign affairs.

The process of deflection owed much to Ikeda and Sato Eisaku, his successor in November 1964. Both men played it safe over the US–Japan alliance. Ikeda moved with considerable and characteristic caution – so much so that he was scathingly described in private by one of his colleagues as 'the worst Prime Minister of the worst cabinet of the worst Government in the world' – to distance his nation from new commitments.[32] Indeed at his first meeting with President Kennedy the subject of defence was not even included in the official communiqué. Two complementary approaches appear to have formed Ikeda's thinking with regard to the United States. The new premier wished both to increase bilateral trade ties, while simultaneously avoiding (at least in public) any fresh defence arrangements.

The National Security Council approved new policy guidelines for US behaviour towards Japan in the summer of 1960. This was immediately prior to the cancellation of the president's visit, but the guidelines were not substantially altered as a result of this decision. Most of the policy objectives in Japan that were stated in 1960 applied in 1950 and would do so again in 1980. There was, as we have seen, insistence on attempting

(i)   to preserve 'the territorial and political integrity of Japan against Communist expansion or subversion';

(ii)   to ally Japan 'closely' to the United States and cooperate with the West;

(iii)   to ensure political stability along 'the principles of representative government';

(iv)   to support a 'prosperous, strong and self-supporting Japanese economy';

(v)   to encourage Japan 'to complement US and other Free World power in stabilizing the international power balance particularly in Asia' by contributing to 'the economic development of less developed nations of the Free World', exercising

107

'a constructive and moderating leadership in the Afro–Asian Bloc', 'strengthen its own defense against external aggression, and 'contribute further to the security of the Far East through the continued provision to US military forces of rights, bases and other facilities';

(vi)   to press Japan 'to participate more actively in the defense of Free World interests in the Far East'.[33]

To flesh out such policy generalizations was immensely more difficult, and the available documents are coy about how the National Security Council thought some of these items mights be attained. Portions of the more sensitive rulings remain classified. Still, enough is known to form an approximate idea of what the Eisenhower administration had in mind and the obvious contrast between what the United States intended and the secrecy of its partner's thinking need not be laboured. Making Eisenhower's copy of the NSC report (complete with his doodlings) available for public inspection is in itself a political statement that this outsider at least finds reassuring.

What the report termed 'major policy guidance' was simply divided into political and military sections. The political objectives appear to have incorporated long-established practices of supporting the LDP, without antagonizing the opposition parties and their domestic allies, but the military aspects are less clear cut. Since the new security pact had been signed on 19 January 1960 it was, inevitably, the central feature in the American discussion. The intent was to maintain within Japan US forces and facilities that were required by 'US security interests' and 'to demonstrate our determination to fulfill our treaty commitments in Japan and the Far East: but at a general level no higher than that mutually agreed upon by the United States and the Japanese Government'.[34] To assist in the defence of Japan, while encouraging Tokyo to build up its own military forces and defence-supporting industries, was the obvious goal, though there was less certainty within the NSC on how far Japan might be encouraged to think beyond its national boundaries. The majority view, supported by Eisenhower, appears to have been in favour of responding 'positively to, but ... not now stimulat[ing], initiatives by Japan to participate more actively in the defense of Free World interests in the Far East'.[35] The Joint Chiefs of Staff were said to have wished 'to make discreet efforts to induce Japan ultimately to extend the defense mission of the Japanese military forces beyond that of the defense of the immediate Japan area'.[36] In neither case, however, was there any willingness to try to persuade Japan to join collective defence pacts.

Once the sound and fury of the crisis in Tokyo over Eisenhower's visit had subsided, the National Security Council took up once again the question of an appropriate set of policies for Japan. The NSC meeting in November confirmed the earlier policy objectives for Japan verbatim. No specific reference to the security crisis or the dissension within the LDP was incorporated.

Japan escaped lightly from American attempts to persuade Tokyo to consider shifts in its international economic and political behaviour in the 1960s. Considerable pressure produced few substantial changes, while equally Japanese governments felt that they had had little success in persuading their counterparts that the United States might also shift from some of its established attitudes. No doubt the Japanese government kept its own counsel on occasion but even Prime Minister Ikeda could inform Pierre Salinger in the 'strongest terms' that US–Japan relations were still littered with inequalities. Ikeda cited the civil air agreement as an example of American intransigence and warned that an 'unfortunate degree of occupation mentality persisted on [the] part of some Americans'.[37] Attempts by some American diplomats in the first half of the decade to nudge their own government forward had only a limited effect and would thereafter be hindered by the escalation of the Vietnam war and differences over appropriate policy towards the People's Republic of China.

The State Department's measured verdict on relations between Tokyo and Washington during the Johnson presidency reflects this mixed record. American policy-makers could scarcely be unaware that Japan in 1969 was in economic terms at least the 'outstanding success story' of the region, yet there remained very considerable impatience with Japan's reluctance to confront its achievements and alter its cautious approach to foreign relations. Japan, the State Department commented, 'was a potential tower of strength for the Free World' but it 'was not yet playing its full constructive role in Asia or beyond'.[38] Similar phrases constantly reemerged in American press briefings and policy statements during the ensuring decades to leave audiences on both sides of the Pacific wondering if anything would ever alter; certainly in the 1960s little did. Secretary of Defense Robert McNamara might call for a new Japanese 'leadership role' in Asia and warn that the PRC was 'developing nuclear weapons which are not required to defend herself' but the Japanese state preferred to look the other way. It was virtually impossible to galvanize Japan into any substantial upgrading of its own military forces. Dean Rusk's observation to President Johnson that 'the US did not believe it should supply manpower to countries with adequate manpower reserves' make little impression on the LDP cabinets of the decade.[39]

One explanation for the failure of the Kennedy and Johnson administrations to persuade Japan was constant recall of the 1960 crisis. The position was also made more difficult for the United States because of the lack of presidential attention to the general subject of US–Japan relations. Things were rarely sufficiently vulnerable for issues involving Japan to gain the president's ear. Diplomats, of course, hope and work to avoid crises with their allies and aim to pass on to their successors a trouble-free agenda, yet the fact that Japan had little priority in the White House permitted the bureaucracy to run the show. It may appear irresponsible in some quarters but perhaps a 'containable' crisis every few years is an essential requirement for any healthy alliance partnership. Lack of this perverse ingredient would contribute massively to later troubles.

The question of personality differences between the sober, largely ex-bureaucrat, cabinet ministers of the Ikeda and Sato governments and the mixture of extended periods of indifference and then sudden attempts to impress during the Kennedy–Johnson years may also have damaged ties. President Kennedy was far from fascinated by the subject of US–Japan relations and what casual interest he may have obtained came largely through the informal promptings of Ambassador Reischauer and Attorney-General Bobby Kennedy. Proposals by some of his staff that the president should conduct a lengthy tour of the Asian-Pacific region later in his presidency were not apparently well received by senior White House aides and might not have been approved.[40]

Likewise, President Johnson, while he certainly maintained the tradition of high-level governmental exchanges inherited from the Eisenhower and Kennedy administrations, appears to have found negotiations with Japanese leaders a hit-and-miss affair. The handing round of ten-gallon hats to visiting Japanese ministers at formal dinners was not entirely in the Japanese tradition, though Johnson could successfully twist Prime Minister Sato's arm in private conversation and squeeze out of him commitments to south-east Asia that a more structured committee gathering would have been able to evade.[41]

The 1960s saw two contradictory forces at work in US–Japan relations. There was both an improvement at the highest levels of government and a clear lack of any substantial popular understanding between the two nations. The degree of increased official consultation was not necessarily all to the good. The knowledge that annual meetings are obligatory may leave the agenda packed merely to fill the greatly expanded available time; discussion frequency need not be correlated to intensity or necessarily lead to greater understanding. The American minutes of such cabinet-level occasions suggest that they were seen by many Japanese figures as an opportunity to criticize and by the Americans as a time to encourage. It was the Japanese government that spoke more frankly and defended its policies with greater vigour. MITI Minister Fukuda, for example, at the January 1964 US–Japan trade and economic summit could speak with extraordinary candour over the instincts of American industry 'at the slightest increase in Japanese imports' to raise 'a hue and cry for additional restrictive and discriminatory controls.'[42] Fukuda complained that Washington's 'Buy American' policy was incomprehensible to the Japanese public and then noted that 'in the majority of cases over the years the so-called voluntary restrictions on Japanese exports had in effect been forced on the Japanese against their will'.[43] Only lack of time apparently foreclosed further denunciations by Fukuda on this occasion, though it did not prevent his colleagues from returning to the fray. Secretary of Commerce Hodges responded diplomatically by saying that he would reserve comment until later, and that though 'he had been disturbed by the tone of the comments . . . he had liked the vigor with which they were presented'.[44]

Equally disturbing for American ears was Foreign Minister Ohira's response to Secretary Rusk's hopes that Japan would find itself able to make substantial tariff cuts in accord with GATT negotiations. Ohira, hardly regarded as an outspoken figure, warned that 'Japan has many problems peculiar to Japan' and insisted that 'we think it indispensable to continue with protective measures for quite some time to come'. While promising, in characteristically Japanese style, to 'maintain flexibility in a forward-looking manner' Ohira stressed the structural difficulties of the Japanese economy and the failure of the European Economic Community to end 'discriminatory treatment against our exports'. If the United States government had hoped that by taking Japan seriously it would be able speedily to alter entrenched Japanese views it was in for considerable disappointment.

Over the general field of trade and investment the Japanese authorities gave little ground during the decade. Even the State Department's own administrative history of the Johnson presidency was obliged to admit that 'progress on the issues was slow, but, in the context of historical Japanese concerns, it was significant and constituted a process of gradual erosion'.[45] Yet 'general but continuous pressure on Japan to (1) reduce the number of quantitative restrictions against imports and (2) modify its highly restrictive procedures affecting direct investment by foreigners' could hardly be said to have produced much fruit when the subject had to be listed repeatedly in every joint communiqué following the annual Joint United States–Japan Committee on Trade and Economic Affairs meetings and the prime ministerial visits of Sato to Washington in January 1965 and November 1967.[46] Trade liberalization to combat what the State Department authors described as 'the maze of restrictions maintained by Japan' was at best half-hearted and was no nearer solution at the end of the Johnson presidency. The United States government was obliged to officially notify Japan in the early summer of 1968 that 'unless Japan promptly removed illegal import restrictions the United States would take the issue up with the Contracting Parties of the General Agreement on Tariffs and Trade'.[47] A face-saving formula presented by the Japanese government was intended to avoid this new embarrassment.

Japanese attention to American requests for the dismantlement of barriers to foreign investment was equally dilatory. Japan might now possess the third largest economy in the world but it still prefered to recall the humiliations of the Meiji era when the Western merchant and banker had a hammerlock on a vulnerable and underdeveloped state. It would take a generation and more before some of the requests and exhortations of the Kennedy-Johnson years in the area of international economic cooperation began to sink in. Perhaps the American side had an exaggerated belief in the open trade system but the extraordinarily timid response of successive Japanese cabinets should be underlined. The State Department's predictions of June 1964 that the next decade would see Tokyo voluntarily assuming 'a greater share of Free World burdens and responsibilities' hardly transpired.[48] What was largely absent in the 1960s was any very effective American sanction against Japanese trade. The crude message that without the vital trade link with the United States the entire pro-American foundation of Japanese external relations might crumble was usually sufficient to prevent display of overt American displeasure. It was felt that 'Japan's internal policies, foreign policies and security alignment all depend in the last analysis on the orientation of the nation's economic relationships, or more simply, on where it can make a living. Throughout the postwar period this has been overwhelmingly with the Free World, principally with the US'.[49] To retain Japan's friendship there was not to be anything but the gentlest of comment and the politest of encouragement. The end of the decade saw little American thinking beyond the view of George Ball in July 1961 when he cabled from Tokyo during the textile dispute that 'there can be no solidity to

Japanese free world political relationships unless cemented by increasingly close and mutually advantageous economic ties'.[50] Frequently this resulted in Japan being only too quick to rehearse its own 'uniqueness' and the faults of its principal ally. Economic ties were unequal in precisely the opposite manner to US–Japan security links. Japan's powerful industrial sector steamed ahead without policy-makers taking much notice of repeated suggestions from the United States that new behaviour was now called for. It took American uni-lateralism in 1971 to force a belated shift in Japanese attitudes. It is difficult to deny that there had not indeed been a lengthy period of attempted persuasion beforehand; the shocks of the early 1970s should not have been such a rude awakening.

The view that during the Johnson presidency 'the position of Japan as a protégé of the United States began to change to one of equal partnership' is difficult to sustain.[51] Admittedly there were sub-stantial shifts in some areas of Japanese foreign policy, in part through American efforts, but in the critical fields of defence and economic affairs it is hard to discover much progress. Movement in less vital fields should not be permitted to brighten the picture exces-sively. Certainly Japan's accession to the Organization for Economic Cooperation and Development (OECD) in April 1964 as a full member was an event of importance which gave the lie to the argument that the OECD was an exclusively Eurocentric institution[52], but this was hardly followed by any speedy change in Japan's trading or financial behaviour. In the case of membership of the OECD and in the areas of foreign aid and Asian regionalism the hand of the American govern-ment was barely disguised. Probably the most impressive of these hesitant steps in Japan's gradual return to an Asia that it had des-poiled a generation earlier was Tokyo's predominant role in the estab-lishment of the Asian Development Bank in Manila in the autumn of 1966. Here was an instance of Japan contributing an equal share of the starting capital as the United States and having its role recognized through the appointment of a Japanese national to the post of ADB president, a tradition that has continued to date.

The issue of Japan's commitment, however, to the region should not be exaggerated. It was, as the State Department's internal history admitted, difficult for Japan to assume 'the full burden that the United States felt it capable of undertaking'.[53] The need for 'con-tinued assurances of general US support and long-term interest in Southeast Asia' and 'occasional US expressions of interest in specific undertakings' remained throughout our decade.[54] Foreign aid, par-ticularly in light of the strength of the Japanese economy, was small

113

and bureaucratic problems in Tokyo further reduced its potential effect.

The extent to which Japan had been open to American suggestion can be judged through commentary by senior members of the Johnson administration in the late 1960s. Revealingly the president, as reported by his aide Walt Rostow, asked for 'the things we want to get from Japan'.[55] Following the submission of separate memoranda from the secretaries of State, Defense and Treasury, Rostow suggested to Johnson in September 1967, on the eve of visits by Japanese ministers, that there might be a trade-off negotiated between Premier Sato's overriding interest in regaining Japanese sovereignty in the Ryukyus and Bonins in exchange for Japanese military and financial commitments that would buttress American goals in the Asian-Pacific region.[56] It was suggested to Johnson that in return for the Bonins and future arrangements over the Ryukyus Japan 'should commit itself to undertake:

> (1) Steps to balance our large outlays for military related expenditure in Japan – primarily by increasing Japanese purchases of US military equipment, Japanese purchases of long term US securities, and limits on Japanese short term borrowing in the US
> (2) A full sharing of costs of the Asian Development Bank on a 50–50 basis including the Special Fund (an increase in the pledge from $100 million to $200 million)
> (3) A Japanese share in some areas – such as Indonesia – larger than that of the US
> (4) A significant increase in Japanese economic assistance to South Viet-Nam, including enlarged private investment in such areas as small and medium industry.'[57]

The intention, in the opinion of the president's staff, was to remind the Japanese government that 'our huge outlays in Asia – in men, in economic aid and in security support – are a political liability for us; that many Americans get the impression that we are almost alone in helping others in Asia' – a fact that was surely difficult to deny and almost completely true of Japan's support for American action in Vietnam. The idea that the 'security, stability and progress of all of Asia are in our mutual interest' was a decidedly Americo-centric vision given that the Japanese government would offer only token gestures of support for the war in south-east Asia. The occasional ministerial message of appreciation was practically all that Washington got from Japan – aside from a large volume of abuse from those who detested the war in Vietnam.

6 SHOCKS: ECONOMIC AND DIPLOMATIC REORIENTATION

> Like Panama and NATO, Okinawa by its very nature needs to have a White House push.
>
> McGeorge Bundy to President Johnson, 23 May 1966

> Where the Okinawa negotiations exemplified high policy, the textile problem proved a case of low comedy, frustration, and near fiasco.
>
> Henry Kissinger

> China and Japan are neighbouring countries separated only by a strip of water . . .
>
> Joint Sino-Japanese statement, 29 September 1972

For Japan the return of Okinawa was the most pressing issue in foreign affairs once the 1960 security treaty had been approved and the US–Japan relationship put back on an even keel. The eventual restoration of the Ryukyus to Japanese sovereignty in May 1972 demonstrated that Washington and Tokyo could work together to overcome their differences through what Henry Kissinger would describe rather grandiosely later as 'foresight and statesmanship'. His assessment that '[o]n the surface we yielded in Okinawa; in reality we preserved the US–Japanese relationship'[1] must now be assessed and a verdict reached on which ally won more in a protracted diplomatic contest.

Okinawa proved to be a running sore to successive Japanese and American cabinets. The conservative governments of the 1960s were required to manoeuvre to gain concessions from the United States and contain domestic pressures for instant reversion on military terms that no American administration would be likely to admit. It was to be a long struggle that had its origins in memories of the high casualties that the Americans took in their capture of the Ryukyus in the late spring of 1945.[2] As with the response of German troops to concentrated Allied bombardment on the Western front in the First World War, it had proved immensely difficult to winkle out the Japanese from their entrenched positions. The battle for Okinawa and the sacrifices expended by both US marines and sailors in the period from

April to June 1945 inevitably influenced subsequent American attitudes. Furthermore, the decision to separate Okinawa from Japan
proper and to administer the Ryukyus through US military commanders only added to the tendency to regard the islands as American
territory that should be defended against allcomers. Under the terms
of the San Francisco peace treaty, Okinawa's future was left deliberately vague.[3] Objection to the presence of the United States and its
extensive military installations led to the adoption of a unanimous
resolution in the Diet on 2 June 1956 demanding the return of the
islands to Japan. The United States responded the following year by
replacing the military administration with a high commissioner and a
civilian team, though this was hardly likely in itself to satisfy growing
demands for reversion.[4] The return of the Amami islands (north of
Okinawa) in December 1953 and the later concessions by the Eisenhower administration were quite inadequate to contain the dissatisfaction increasingly voiced by the early 1960s.[5] In 1961, Prime Minister
Ikeda became the first leader of Japan to raise the issue of Okinawa
with the United States.[6]

President Kennedy spent little time in dealing with Japan. Much
was left to his ambassador and the State Department in an attempt to
improve relations following the débâcle of 1960. Ambassador Reischauer would recall later that his objective was to stress economic and
cultural ties with Japan in order to prevent the relationship from
appearing 'so overwhelming military, as it always did to the Japanese
public and without great popularity for that side'. Essentially what
Reischauer intended was 'an expansion', which coupled with the
pro-Americanism of the new Ikeda cabinet, led to the establishment of
'a kind of relationship, certainly at the governmental level, such as had
not existed before'.[7] The extent of the alterations to the alliance must
now be assessed. Here the temptation is merely to endorse Ambassador Reischauer's extensive reminiscences and imagine that an entirely
new position had been agreed upon by both sides. This may be
questionable for a number of reasons.

Far less changed in the direction of US–Japan relations than the
intentions of the embassy in Tokyo. Reischauer was able to improve,
for want of a better word, the image of the United States with some
sections of the Japanese public but it was hard going and it is not
apparent that his energy and personality converted many on the left.
Reischauer would say later that his appointment had been made 'to try
to set up a different feel and a different kind of dialogue'[8] and he
undoubtedly was able to present a more pleasing picture of the United
States to large Japanese audiences, yet it probably served to reinforce

the opinions of those already somewhat sympathetic towards his nation. Certainly visits by people such as Attorney General Bobby Kennedy and the regular cabinet level conferences were useful but the security relationship hardly altered in the 1960s and the beginnings of direct American involvement in the Vietnam war left Reischauer in a dilemma. He had the task then of defending something he disapproved of and over which he would eventually resign.

The hope that it would be possible 'to try to help communicate with those who were against the American–Japanese relationship and educate them to see the problem in a better way so they would not be so much against it' would have been an uphill struggle at the best of times and was made virtually impossible from the mid-1960s onwards by the three linked issues of the Vietnam War, the wish to regain Okinawa and the question of the renewal of the security treaty in 1970. On such military matters there was only so much that an ambassador could do, though it may be that Reischauer's links to Bobby Kennedy helped bring the Okinawa question to the attention of the administration's senior figures more speedily than otherwise would have been so. Okinawa was the first test case for the professed change of heart behind American policy towards Japan. It was complicated by US military reservations over the future of American bases on the archipelago and the Pentagon's determination to hang on to Okinawa at all costs. Reischauer was surely correct to note that

> if we lost our right to bases in Japan, it would probably be because we had not given up Okinawa. And if we got in this situation with the Japanese in which we no longer had bases in Japan, why then our bases in Okinawa wouldn't be worth a damn anyway because 960,000 Japanese there would make that an absolutely useless base because of hostile feelings ... it was either bases in Japan and Okinawa or neither.[9]

Yet, although it would take until the next decade before Okinawa was finally returned to Japan, an important start was made in these years. Okinawa, however, was seen in the American public's mind as a prize of war that had been won at great cost in the last months of the Pacific fighting and was, therefore, not a territory to be easily given up. Its strategic importance could hardly be in doubt. It was not for nothing that its American number plates displayed the slogan 'fortress of the Pacific'. Public opinion in the United States was as strongly opposed to leaving Okinawa as its Japanese counterpart was intent on regaining the southern islands. It was clearly difficult for the Kennedy and Johnson administrations to move too fast against these domestic objections. One shift was to alter the governing process on Okinawa

117

from what Reischauer termed 'a military dictatorship of a rather unenlightened type'[10] and to gain some appreciation of the potential dangers of holding on to Okinawa in the teeth of Japanese protest. But it was a hard slog to give ground to Japanese opinion and explain to the American Congress that it made sense to gradually alter one of the premises of postwar American military power in the Pacific.

Opposition from American High Commissioner General Paul Caraway reduced the prospects for change. Caraway objected to any Japanese aid contribution to what was, in effect, American territory and the difficulty of persuading him to appear more cooperative towards the islanders acted as a brake to change. Only after Caraway's replacement took office in 1964 did relations between the American military command and the local officials improve, though the high dependence on employment at the bases for the Okinawan people occasionally dampened down the movement for reversion among trades unionists. It was not until 1966 that an American statement was issued in Naha that publicly noted that a new future ought to be considered when the Japanese government would eventually take over responsibility for the area. Study groups in Washington were reactivated. Deadlines were now considered and the importance of security treaty questions in 1970 (when the existing pact would have to be either continued or terminated) were linked to the Okinawan issue. The question was now promoted to the head of the US–Japan agenda.

Yet aside from this valuable cranking initiated by first the Kennedy administration and then the further movement towards reversion under President Johnson it is difficult to see any other gains in the relationship. Indeed, the increased US military role in Vietnam threatened at times to undo the goodwill that existed between the two governments. However carefully one handles the evidence from this source, public opinion polls indicated fairly convincingly that during the 1960s there was relatively little positive support for the US–Japan military arrangements. In November 1966, for example, only 19 per cent of those asked whether the security treaty should be best revised, cancelled or continued after 1970 were prepared to endorse the maintenance of the existing pact and a mere 18 per cent thought that it was good for Japanese security to retain American bases in Japan.[11] The difficulties were certainly compounded by the Vietnam War but it seems somewhat unlikely that Reischauer and his successor as ambassador, Alexis Johnson, could have made any major dent in the opposition's following even if things had been quieter in the region.[12] The renewal of the security treaty would still have been there as an albatross around the neck of the embassy and the Ikeda and Sato governments. It was a highly divisive issue for the ruling LDP cabinets in the 1960s, even without the additional dissatisfaction of the situation in Okinawa and the use of the Ryukyus as an important staging and military command post for Vietnam.

Massive street demonstrations in the late 1960s kept the pot on the boil. Protests on a scale never before seen in Japan took place in the years from 1967 to 1969 that surprised even the organizers of this loose umbrella federation of groups that rallied under the slogan of 'oppose the war, oppose the treaty, return Okinawa'.[13] The crowds were larger than those that had taken to the streets of Tokyo in the spring of 1960 to fight the renewal of the security treaty and the fact that some elements were decidedly rougher in their approach to the police and SDF hardly enamoured the fringe leftists to the wider public. The political dangers of the United States attempting to hang on to Okinawa, while pursuing an unpopular war and knowing that it shortly had also to gain Japanese approval for the extension of the security treaty were clearly very considerable. Evidence of American governmental concern can be seen in debate at the National Security Council meetings in the Johnson presidency. By 1967 the subject of 'revision to Japan of the Ryukyus, Bonins and other Western Pacific islands' was being discussed with the recognition that Japan wished to 'begin moving toward settlement toward the Ryukyus and Bonin Islands issues'.[14] Such NSC meetings were held under the pressure of deadlines created by planned visits by members of the Japanese government where it would be obviously necessary for the Johnson administration to prepare concrete responses to both Foreign Minister Miki and Prime Minister Sato's advocacy. The president himself met with the Chief Executive of the Ryukyus in March 1967 when he 'expressed sympathetic interest in the desire of the Okinawans for more local autonomy'.[15] Japanese diplomacy was beginning to get results.

Evidence of the effectiveness of Japanese governmental representations to Washington was seen by the return of the Bonin Islands to Japanese administration on 26 June 1968. This important psychological move by the United States had been foreshadowed in advice to the president in the late summer of the previous year. Walt Rostow had recommended then that the United States should hand over the Bonins 'by mid-1968' and form a 'joint study group to consider ways in which administrative control over the Ryukyus can be returned to Japan' in exchange for a greater Japanese economic role in Asia,[16] while Secretary McNamara wanted to stress the need for Japan to 'move gradually to share the very heavy political and economic costs' of Pacific security.[17]

119

The war in Vietnam took second place in the Japanese public's mind to concern with the Okinawa question. Admittedly there were loud and well-organized demonstrations against the war and the White House was inundated with protest cards from Japanese eager to argue that the American bombing of north Vietnam should cease and 'that you stop using Japanese military bases in any forms [sic] for your war efforts in Vietnam',[18] but it was easier to gather support by calling for the return of the islands. Premier Sato was able eventually to defuse the crisis that he faced from domestic critics over Okinawa by his visits to Washington in the late 1960s.

It was the United States that gave more than it got over the Okinawa question. The Japanese government could hardly complain at the gains it made at the expense of the United States following from Prime Minister Sato's visit to Washington in the autumn of 1967. It was then that in a joint communiqué Sato had spoke of his 'belief' that the Okinawan problem could be solved by achieving 'an agreement', 'within a few years on a date satisfactory to them for the reversion of these islands'.[19] American press correspondents were quick to query whether this implied that Johnson had also endorsed the timetable and if the agreement to agree on a timetable might not be different from any eventual date for the return of Okinawa.[20] The arrangements for deciding United States policy appear somewhat haphazard if the available documents are a reliable guide. There was, however, little doubt that Japan's wish to regain Okinawa before public opinion ensnared Tokyo and Washington on links between the Ryukyus and the 1970 deadline for the US–Japan security pact greatly assisted the Japanese case. It is apparent from the State Department briefings prepared for President Johnson prior to Sato's visit in 1967 that Washington was only too well aware of this factor and 'we are prepared to work out arrangements and language within this framework to meet Sato's problems with his public opinion'.[21] The problem, of course, was as much Johnson's as Sato's. The United States, while not giving any firm undertaking over a precise date, had little choice but to negotiate if it wished to avoid any repetition of the 1960 crisis. It was now American policy to 'control pressures for Okinawan reversion until return of the islands can be accomplished consistent with the security interests of Japan and the United States'.[22] President Johnson was advised by Secretary Rusk that Sato expected 'a general understanding that [the] return of Okinawa will be feasible when Japan is able to assure effective American use of its bases there to fulfill its security commitments'.[23] The logjam was being broken and the piecemeal approach of both parties was clearly achieving results.

Johnson received advice on Okinawa from several sources. Ambassador Reischauer corresponded with, and spoke to, senior officials in the administration, while the president is known to have received memoranda from McGeorge Bundy in May 1966 that warned 'between now and 1968 the situation is sure to change' and that the present absence of comment by Japanese journalists and politicians in speaking up over the subject would soon alter.[24] Bundy asserted that '[w]e have about six months in which to frame a careful and forward-looking policy which will allow us to trade with the Japanese effectively.' Such negotiations, Bundy claimed, would permit the restoration of 'Japanese civil government in Okinawa while insuring explicit Japanese acceptance of whatever military rights we need there. The trick here is that we need nuclear rights in Okinawa and that it will be hard for the Japanese to grant them explicitly . . . Both the Okinawans and the Japanese will be pressing for full civil government, but as of 1966 it would be difficult for the authorities in Tokyo to admit that they were accepting nuclear weapons on Japanese soil by their own free choice.' Bundy pointed out that low-level talks between the State Department and the Pentagon were already in existence and that both would be obliged to cooperate 'on a new Okinawan policy in the coming months', when it would be useful if the presidential interest were made clear and progress reports called for.[25] It was, and they were.

Movements over Okinawa was a gradual process for both the United States and Japan. The meetings between President Nixon and Prime Minister Sato in November 1969 that produced the final agreement were essentially stage-managed to confirm what had been agreed earlier by emissaries from each side. The largest problem had long been over defining the exact conditions under which US military forces in Okinawa might operate in any post reversionary period. Presidential security advisor Henry Kissinger took up the question of Okinawa on an interagency basis immediately after Nixon was sworn into office in late January 1969. By March, Kissinger was able to write to Nixon that, along lines similar to those employed earlier by Ambassador Reischauer, 'our refusal to negotiate an accommodation could well lead as a practical matter to our losing the bases altogether'.[26] Kissinger and the State Department argued that 'the military and political risks of seeking to maintain the status quo outweighed the military cost of having somewhat less flexibility in operating the Okinawa bases under Japanese sovereignty'.[27] There was, in the opinion of Kissinger, considerable evidence that '[f]or once, the United States government was united on an issue'.[28] American relations with Japan were now seen as too important to be jeopardized by prevarication over the Okinawan question.

When negotiations, however, began between the US embassy in Tokyo and the government of Sato Eisaku, President Nixon had intended not to reveal his hand on the highly sensitive question of nuclear storage on Okinawa. Before making major concessions on this score the American diplomats hoped first to put Japan on the rack and screw out of its officials a deeper commitment to Asian affairs and an improvement in Japanese defence capabilities. This was indeed deemed necessary to many in Washington since it was noted that Japan in 1967 ranked 58th in any international comparison of per capita military expenditure[29] at a time when portions of Japan's military equipment was judged to be obsolete.[30] The wish to cooperate that undoubtedly existed between the two Pacific nations could hardly prevent setbacks to the talks but, in contrast to the security crisis of 1960, greater attention may have been paid to Japanese domestic critics.[31]

Five months of intense discussions now began. Twin diplomacy was soon at work with both formal talks and private presidential–prime ministerial dealings in operation simultaneously. Kissinger acted as the president's right-hand man in discussions with an aide of Premier Sato's in the hope that this might better prevent leaks to the press and the entanglement of unwanted bureaucratic interest. Nixon approved of this privileged method, instructing Kissinger that he should 'not fool around with the State Department'.[32] Both government leaders were wary: Nixon wanted some freedom to manoeuvre on the right to ship nuclear weapons to Okinawa in an emergency by employing the existing 'prior consultation system' of the US–Japan security treaty,[33] while Sato had to demonstrate to the Japanese electorate that Okinawa would shortly obtain exactly the same period rules as applied to the facesaving communiqué approved at the Nixon–Sato talks that Kissinger would later dryly describe as an invention that was 'as ingenious as it was empty'.[34]

The difficulties of working out the terms for Okinawan revision were quite complicated enough for even the most hardened of negotiators, but an additional factor next arose to further entangle US–Japan relations. The new controversy concerned textiles and the campaign promises of Richard Nixon in the previous year to do something to aid Southern textile areas fight off Japanese competition. Economic diplomacy was not Kissinger's *forte* (as even he recognized) but it was an important issue for his president and would shortly lead to what Nixon is reported to have angrily called 'the Jap betrayal'.[35]

The textiles affair has since entered the realm of mythology to be incorporated into textbook analyses of how not to conduct cross-cultural negotiations with Japan, but even at the time it was, to employ Kissinger's metaphor, an intricate political theatre worthy of *kabuki* that ended up in the darker world of Kafka.

> The textile saga was a long and sad one. No one issue during my three-year sojourn in Japan was more vexatious. It poisoned the atmosphere, far out of proportion to the issue's intrinsic worth ... more telegrams by far were written on the subject of textiles than on any other. Hundreds of hours were invested in seeking a resolution of this problem. It was an irrepressible topic ... All this, despite the fact that the Embassy was never involved in the actual negotiations.[36]

So wrote Armin Meyer shortly after leaving his post as US ambassador to Tokyo when reviewing a painful period of US–Japan relations.

The entire dismal episode may perhaps be best seen as only part of a wider series of difficulties involving US–Japan trade relations. It is hard to imagine that textiles alone could have created the extraordinary (and extraordinarily tedious) diplomatic disaster. Since others have been brave enough to chart the textile developments in minute detail we shall merely draw on their labours and place the affair in a wider context.[37] These authorities on the subject have concluded that virtually no one of either nationality, whether politician, bureaucrat or industrialist, gained much advantage from the convolutions; seemingly the sound and fury signified very little. Yet the textile diplomacy of 1969–1971 has a number of lessons for the Pacific relationship that suggest it was indeed a turning point in American thinking towards Japan. Once the textiles issue finally had been resolved the United States adopted more strenuous economic policies. The eventual dictated settlement of October 1971 was a foretaste of things to come. Ambassador Meyer's fear that 'the "get tough" enthusiasts in the White House might prescribe such brutal tactics as standard operating procedure in dealing with the Japanese'[38] was later often proved to be correct. From the early 1970s to the present the importance attached to dealing with trade disputes can hardly be doubted. The subject remains at the forefront of the relationship. What the first post-San Francisco generation saw as largely irrelevant has since become increasingly visible and important; the 'low politics' of trade now rival the 'high politics' of bases and military cooperation.

The textile affair was a watershed in this switch from strategic issues to more mundane diplomacy. It reflected the beginnings of American concern that its industrial strength was under serious challenge from its Pacific protégé and the ability of sectoral interests within the United States to use their influence to alter the previously open trading arrangements. The problems were compounded by the belief that the US had permitted the opening of its markets, while waiting (too patiently in the view of many) for Japan to reciprocate. The textile dispute was to be rapidly followed by a host of other trade problems.[39]

President Nixon's determination to deliver on his 1968 campaign pledge to assist textile areas of the United States was the immediate cause of the troubles.[40] Yet textile differences between the US and Asian manufacturers certainly precede the Nixon administration's efforts and there was already a considerable history of strained talks and mutual suspicion. Nixon's handling of the textile affair needs to be placed within this context and his disappointment at the inability of Prime Minister Sato to fulfil his supposed promises made at the White House in November 1969 to limit Japanese exports. The president was surely more sinned against than sinning over the textile issue. He pressed Japan to accept voluntary import quotas in specified categories but the Sato cabinet made little attempt to compromise. The strengths of the Osaka textile groups in rejecting the USA case and their support within MITI severely weakened the credibility of the Japanese government in the eyes of Washington. What began as a relatively minor debate soon ran the risk of emerging as a well-publicized international issue that could impair progress over the Okinawa question.[41]

The Nixon–Sato 'agreement' for resolving the textile issue did not take long to start unravelling. Too many groups within the Japanese establishment, particularly allies of the textile industry in the Ministry of International Trade and Industry and sympathetic voices inside the media, continued to fight to prevent any implementation by the prime minister. The whole business was complicated by Sato's unwillingness to reveal the details of his 'agreement' with Nixon that had been worked out at the November 1969 talks, although suspicions were high within the Japanese bureaucracy and textile organizations that something had in fact been devised during the White House 'summit'. Juggling ministers and offering encouraging but characteristically vague words of encouragement to the Japanese embassy in Washington and to his own LDP members could not get Sato off the hook.

Despite private talks and secret couriers the United States and Japan floundered. Textile diplomacy became a confusing area of proposals and counter-proposals with schemes from American sources to institute quotas and Japanese insistence that its industry was far less damaging to its Pacific partner than the American industry's representatives claimed. The failure of official level talks was finally confirmed by the inability of MITI Minister Miyazawa Kiichi and US Secretary of Commerce Maurice Stans to reach any formal agreement in June 1970. Many within Japan were delighted with this outcome. The Asahi Shimbun went so far as to claim:

> The US–Japanese textile negotiations turned out to be the first instance in which Japan rejected a US demand, and could be considered the first example of 'independent foreign policy' in the postwar Japanese history of economic diplomacy ... The fact that Japan has managed to follow through with such an independent posture has an epoch-making significance as the cornerstone of its economic diplomacy of the 1970s.[42]

Sato spoke with mixed feelings in his farewell address to the Diet in June 1972 of having long regarded 'the maintenance and the development of US–Japan ties as the great issue of our foreign affairs into which I poured both heart and soul'.[43] He noted next that 'nothing must be allowed to jeopardize Japan–US relations' both because of the dangers this would cause to the two nations involved and for the repercussions that this 'fatal blunder' would have on 'international order'.[44] Sato, after pausing to pay appropriate respect to Yoshida Shigeru, his former political mentor, stressed that he had followed the direction marked out by Yoshida and that as retiring premier he trusted that the new generation would realize that 'without Japan–US friendship, there can be no prosperity for Japan and no peace for Asia.'[45]

The private views of politicians and diplomats on both sides of the Pacific, however, were very different. Sato's overoptimistic vision of US–Japan relations disguised considerable reservations on the part of the Japanese establishment. Recollections of the series of differences between Tokyo and Washington in the early 1970s were to be swiftly recalled when tempers were once again frayed over the ensuing decade.

The issue of trade friction, on a sufficiently limited scale that today must appear the height of triviality, between Japanese textile manufacturers and the Nixon administration was the initial cause of much unpleasantness. The apparent impossibility of compromise led to the escalation of what observers would later term the 'textile wrangle' and its subsequent entanglement with wider political affairs in the Pacific relationship. From the outset Nixon felt that he had received a firm commitment from Sato in November 1969 to reduce Japanese synthetic textile exports to the United States at the moment when Nixon had pledged his nation to the return of Okinawa in 1972. The exact (or inexact) pledge is not known. Nixon, perhaps not unreasonably, felt that Sato had given his word to temper Japanese exports that were hurting portions of Nixon's southern constituency. The result was much clearer than the rival interpretations of the agreement. It has been further maintained that President Nixon, having taken the unpopular decision immediately after he assumed office to return Okinawa, greatly resented Japan's behaviour over the textiles issue and, therefore, chose not to inform Sato in advance of the Nixon–Kissinger China initiative.[46]

1971 was the year of multiple embarrassments for the Sato cabinet. Nixon's diplomatic 'revolution' with regard to the People's Republic of China hurt the Japanese government and weakened popular respect for the United States. It put the Japanese cabinet at a severe domestic disadvantage because of continuing resentment over what Kissinger in his memoirs rightly termed 'the textile fiasco'. The success over the Okinawa issue had not been repaid by any easy arrangements over reducing the exportation of Japanese textiles. The difficulties over textile diplomacy generated labyrinthine negotiations that at times were not far short of the absurd with secret envoys from Tokyo, puerile code names and the intervention of unauthorized figures to further muddy the waters.

US–Japan relations were subjected in the summer and autumn of 1971 to a series of buffetings that tested the foundations of the entire structure. The strains, however, were overcome and the two states were able, at least on the surface, to confound their critics and move forward quickly to the point by the mid-1970s when American commentators would increasingly suggest that 'Japan was America's most important single ally'. Yet it would be illusionary to imagine that much did not alter as a result of the so-called triple Nixon 'shocks' of 1971. The anger on both sides of the Pacific was not merely theatrical; the consequences were far from quickly forgotten or discounted.

Part of the explanation for the long months of tension reflected a failure in the relationship during the previous decade. The 1960s had been years of deliberate quietism as the United States worked studiously to avoid any recurrence of the 1960 crisis. In this Washington and Tokyo had largely succeeded, but only at the cost of ignoring the considerable weakening of relative American strength by the early 1970s and the consequent need for a more equitable relationship. The unwillingness of either government to confront the need for a radical reassessment of the respected roles through what would soon become known as 'burden-sharing' was to prove almost as great a danger to the partnership as the earlier security crisis had been. In successfully avoiding one problem both governments found themselves facing at least three new ones by 1971.

No sooner had the Okinawa question been settled than fresh issues emerged. Congratulatory talk of the ending of Japan's post-war era and the beginning of a new chapter in US–Japanese relations was quickly replaced by very considerable anger on both sides of the Pacific. Within a few brief weeks of the euphoria over the reversion of the Ryukyus Japan received what its media instantly termed the first two of the Nixon 'shocks'.

For Japan, the anger at President Nixon's announcement on 15 July 1971 that the administration was talking to the People's Republic of China and his New Economic Policy of exactly a month later acted as a double punch to the body politic. Even true-blue supporters of the US–Japan relationship were stunned. The Japanese criticism first of the China move and then of the NEP had two aspects. First, there was concern over the nature of American policy shifts, but perhaps equally importantly there was open talk of betrayal and an inexcusable lack of prior consultation by Washington. Some of these views were shared by important members of the Nixon administration at the time and others would soon be prepared to admit that a great deal of unnecessary damage could have been prevented if Washington had been more attentive to prior warnings from its Japanese specialists.

President Nixon, however, thought otherwise. He remains unrepentant over not informing the Japanese prime minister in advance of his intended diplomatic revolution. Nixon, speaking of his visit to Beijing in 1972 from the perspective of the brutal events of Tiananmen Square in 1989, saw the Sino-Soviet split as an obvious advantage to the US that had to be explored and secondly that 'even if there had been no Soviet threat, it was essential for America to have relations with a government that was a member of the nuclear club'.[47] He continued:

> Today a strong, stable China is as vital as ever to the security interests of the United States and to peace in the Pacific. A weak, fractured China would leave the Soviet Union as the dominant military power in Asia, and Japan as the dominant economic power. It is imperative that Sino-American relations remain strong so the United States can help maintain the balance between China, Japan and the Soviet Union.

This clear lack of sympathy for Japan's predicament was probably worsened by the manner in which Tokyo had long prevaricated over trade issues and its relatively feeble military contribution to the

American strategic ledger. Japan seemingly had little reason to expect any special treatment from President Nixon.

President Nixon next attempted to regroup his forces and press Japan once again by designating new officials to handle his textile diplomacy. Presidential assistants Peter Flanigan and Henry Kissinger were given the unenviable task of dealing with the issue. Kissinger, admitting later that his 'ignorance of the subject was encyclopedic', had been thrown earlier into the textile waters without the slightest ability to swim. He recalled in his memoirs that 'Nixon told me in no uncertain terms that he meant to have a textile agreement and that as a Presidential Assistant I was to contribute to the objective'. The president also regarded Sato's instigation of secret intermediaries an improvement on the earlier bureaucratic route that had failed so completely, saying that Sato and Kissinger should develop such approaches and try not to 'fool around with the State Department.' Yet Sato's inability to fulfil his commitments made Kissinger's tasks almost impossible. With ignorance of the initial Sato-Nixon White House agreement among bureaucrats in Tokyo and far too many Congressional and even private individuals involved on the American side, the problem was soon intractable.[48] Diplomacy gradually failed over the next two years. The process became almost comic. Kissinger, writing after the event with probably more gusto than during the dreary round of negotiations on textile categories and duration agreements, could refer to Premier Sato trying to demonstrate his commitment by saying farewell to the president at the White House in October 1970 and then quickly reappearing to talk yet again to Kissinger at his office in order to go over exactly the same ground. At times it appeared that an agreement, acceptable to both governments and their constituents, was within reach, yet nothing ever quite gelled.

Kissinger claims that Sato did all could to resolve the US–Japan differences,[49] but he was hardly well served in Tokyo by some of his fellow LDP members, who disliked American schemes to restrain trade. The eventual outcome was a decision of the Nixon administration to deal with the textile sore unilaterally. After White House embarrassment on a large scale in the spring of 1971 when Congressman Wilbur Mills had persuaded the Japanese textile industry to voluntarily offer concessions that Nixon angrily rejected, he appointed David Kennedy to handle the problem. Suddenly the issue was settled and very much along American lines. There was indeed a capitulation by the Japanese cabinet at a time when Tokyo was already reeling from the first two Nixon 'shocks'.

Taking advantage of Japanese disarray at the economic and foreign policy changes of the Nixon administration and the rivalries within what was widely seen to be the final Sato cabinet, the White House pressed for Japanese surrender. It got it by what the Washington Post termed 'the crudest of coercion', through forcing Japan's new Minister of International Trade and Industry Tanaka Kakuei to accept an import agreement or face a unilateral quota system. The visible fist behind the eventual Japanese submission was Nixon's preparedness to employ Trading with the Enemy legislation devised originally in October 1917. Secretary of Commerce Peter Peterson, for all his distaste at having to organize such a legislative programme, carried out his instructions, while the American negotiators in Tokyo talked mercilessly at length with Tanaka.[50]

The outcome to the textile issue was the result of American pressure and a totally new spirit of realism from those few in the Japanese establishment, led by Tanaka, who could see that the writing was on the wall. Tanaka, unlike his predecessors as MITI minister or his prevaricating prime minister, moved quickly to adjust Japan's position. Tanaka, alone, was prepared to brave the hostility of the textile lobby by going to the cabinet and gaining approval for relief funds to assist the beleaguered Osaka firms. If the dreary textile story shows any one Japanese figure emerging with much credit it is surely Tanaka Kakuei. He demonstrated consummate political skill in galvanizing a hesitant and divided government, and his role undoubtedly prevented any further deterioration in US–Japan relations. His ability to reckon with what had to be done and then to knit together the essential bureaucratic agreement without which no Japanese minister can rule effectively was a rare example of initiative and management.[51] His performance helped propel him to the premiership shortly afterwards.

The agreement of 15 October 1971 saved the day for both sides. It most certainly was a necessary prize for the Nixon administration after years of effort and little to show for its endeavours and it was equally necessary for the Sato cabinet since the issue had dragged on for far too long and was fouling the entire alliance to Japan's detriment. The textiles saga ended only when gentle (and not so gentle) threats finally convinced some within the Japanese government that enough was enough.

What is extraordinary is that it took so very long for Washington to win the battle. It was only after it became clear that the US would unilaterally insist on quotas if Tokyo refused to give ground and the return of Okinawa might be delayed that Tanaka moved to clear the well-entrenched domestic obstacles.[52] Those who argue that the 'textile wrangle of 1969–71 was clearly an unnecessary and wasteful exercise, even with respect to the narrow goal of textile trade regulation'[53] may be weighing responsibility for the debacle a little too evenly. Prime Minister Sato's inability to explain exactly his position to his appointed representatives was an impossible handicap for the Japanese side. The result strangely was to strengthen, at least temporarily, US–Japan ties and to demonstrate that the United States would no longer accept the dilatoriness of the past in trade negotiations. Once again, as had happened in the 1960s after the security crisis, the textile issue was followed by a period of considerably improved relations. Commentators, when reviewing the economic strains of the 1970s, would conclude later that, for all the noise and protestations, '[i]n the end, things seemed to work themselves out.'[54] Certainly the issue of what was increasingly termed 'trade friction' was forcing itself to the head of the US–Japan agenda but the 1970s were to be the last years before trade and financial questions threatened to overturn the entire postwar Pacific edifice.

On 16 July 1971, US Ambassador Armin Meyer was having his hair cut, while listening to the local American military radio station. The Far East Network, interrupting its normal programming, was about to carry a live broadcast from President Nixon in Washington. The next three and a half minutes were to have 'seismic impact' on Japan[55] and indeed the entire international order. Meyer '[q]uickly dispensing with the barber' scrambled to get information and instructions from Washington and Nixon's Pacific retreat at San Clemente, once Nixon had calmly announced that the United States was set on normalizing relations with the People's Republic of China.

It was not merely the American ambassador to Tokyo who had egg on his face. President Nixon's determination to prevent potentially highly damaging leaks over his preliminary soundings with Beijing had left virtually the entire US bureaucracy in the dark. Yet, as Kissinger pointed out later, '[t]he principal sour note came from Japan, whose Prime Minister Eisaku Sato had been a staunch friend of the United States. It was particularly painful to embarrass a man who had done so much to cement the friendship between our two countries.'[56] It may have been painful but for Kissinger and Nixon it was deemed necessary. While Nixon's moves towards the PRC were greeted with applause in many capitals, they left Sato in an almost impossible position. The long-held Japanese fear of an American president recognizing the PRC before Tokyo had received more than the barest of hints as to this eventuality had finally taken place. Nixon and Kissinger's global concerns were deemed too important to be squandered by protest from Tokyo. The president had had the courage to disown his past stridency against Beijing and seize the moment. As one of Kissinger's fiercest critics admitted in 1977: 'Détente with Moscow at once encouraged and balanced détente with Peking. It was a delicate calculus, involving two sets of leaders with their own volatile oligarchic politics, military pressures, domestic dissent, and not least an instinctive xenophobia bred of war and more than two decades of acrimony.'[57]

This deftness, however, led to a temporary rift with Japan where public opinion felt that the nation had been penalized for its two decades of loyalty (or subservience) to Washington. There had, however, been both public and private hints prior to July 1971 of this diplomatic revolution and the Japanese media was being less than honest in immediately labelling the Nixon move a total 'shock'.

Yet, the statement that Nixon's new relationship with the People's Republic of China 'will not be at the expense of our old friends'[58] was hardly of much comfort to the Japanese government at that moment. Sato's cabinet felt badly let down, and, worse still, the entire China question was certain to be subject to intra-factional disputes over the appropriate Japanese response to Nixon's moves and how to handle future relations with what was likely to be the rump state of Taiwan.[59] The scramble within and between Japan's political parties to win the race to Beijing was on, and the pace quickly proved deadly.

The principal casualty was Prime Minister Sato himself. Having benefited from the closeness of his ties to Washington, chiefly to bring about the reversion of Okinawa, it was inevitable that the premier would be subject to vehement criticism over the embarrassment that his nation now faced.[60] Sato's past record of speaking up in favour of Taiwan further damaged his standing, since it had long been apparent that the People's Republic of China would want no truck with him. The old wartime slogans on not missing the bus to China were now once again revived with the intent of encouraging all and sundry to make haste to Beijing. This extraordinary China boom would have no room for Sato as either driver or even humble backseat passenger.

The winner in the LDP factional stakes was Tanaka Kakuei. His tactical skills and considerable financial resources enabled him to trounce his rivals and assume the premiership in July 1972. Tanaka, by withdrawing himself and his followers from the Sato faction, was able to build bridges to Ohira Masayoshi's supporters and defeat his arch-rival Fukuda Takeo. A new China policy quickly emerged once the bitter party battles were over. In the making of this approach to the PRC the United States could hardly complain. President Nixon had

himself visited Beijing in February 1972 and constructed the beginnings of a dialogue that would eventually lead to the normalization of
relations. In the course of Nixon's meetings with Chou En-lai the
president had noted:

> The United States can get out of Japanese waters, but others will still
> fish there. If we were to leave Japan naked and defenseless, they
> would have to turn to others for help or build the capability to defend
> themselves. If we had no defense arrangement with Japan, we would
> have no influence where they were concerned.[61]

Clearly Nixon felt there would be little or no long-term difficulties to
the United States dominating links with Japan and indeed the final
communiqué spoke of America's wish for the continuation of these
bonds, despite Chinese insistence that Japanese militarism was to be
deplored and neutralism encouraged.[62]

For all the complaints issuing from Tokyo, Nixon was soon proved
correct. The Tanaka cabinet simply went in to China through the door
left ajar by the United States. Of course, the ditching of Taiwan was
uncomfortable to many in both capitals but it can hardly be said to
have done much but delay what had become inevitable. Once the
elderly leadership of the PRC had indicated that it wished to see a
fresh relationship and the American administration could use the
advantage of being able to court (and be courted) by both Beijing and
Moscow, following the worsening of Sino-Soviet ties, the machi-
nations of international politics suggested only one outcome. Taiwan
was indeed sacrificed, leaving some of its former supporters with
guilty consciences.

By July 1972, the new Tanaka cabinet was proclaiming that 'the days
are over for Japan to follow in the footsteps of the United States'[63] and
extensive negotiations began to secure the normalization of relations
between Japan and the PRC. On 25 September Tanaka was in Beijing.
The nine-point Tanaka-Chou En-lai joint statement was signed four
days later to be met with enormous acclaim in Japan.[64] Public opinion
was overwhelmingly in favour of the Sino-Japanese rapprochement,
though elements within the LDP and the Japanese Communist Party
distanced themselves from the celebrations. Pro-Taiwan LDP
members and pro-Soviet JCP figures remained conspicuously absent
from the delighted reception committees that assembled to greet
Tanaka and his foreign minister Ohira Masayoshi on their return to
Tokyo.

The speed and confidence with which Tanaka drove the China bus
was impressive. His success over solving the textile imbroglio was

now repeated. The close working relationship with Ohira, the dampening down of the pro-Taiwan fires within the LDP, and the tactical cooperation with the Socialists all contributed to the sudden and successful overtures to Beijing. For once Japanese foreign policy was generally united and far-sighted; yet part of the applause should have been reserved for the United States. Those who thought the Japanese government was taking a rare gamble and demonstrating national initiative may have overlooked how much of Japan's goal had been reached by following in Washington's footsteps and the degree of apparent US–Japan consultation that preceded Mr Tanaka's visit to the PRC.

Ohira was to note later that Japan's actions were in fact conditional, first, on tacit approval from the United States and then on Beijing's preparedness to accept the 'international order established in San Francisco that pivoted on the Japan–US Security Treaty.'[65] The Tanaka cabinet moved towards normalization with the PRC only after American–Japanese talks in Hawaii had ensured that Nixon and Secretary Rogers had 'expressed their appreciation of our support and wished us success on our approach to China'.[66] The suggestion that Japan had now made its entry onto the global diplomatic stage was trumpeted from all quarters in Tokyo but the degree to which the United States had reason to be satisfied with the outcome was rarely considered amidst the self-congratulatory speeches. Washington was at last relieved to see Japan playing a larger role in international affairs and could feel reasonably confident that Japan's conservatives would accept that this was best realized under the existing Pacific relationship.

It is difficult to accept the view that Japan had suddenly stood up and shown its true unilateral colours.[67] Japan was still the conformist ally of the United States, while it was the PRC that had been obliged to retreat the furthest. Its foreign minister's insistence that the Sato cabinet 'stops tailing after the United States' before normalization could be concluded was quietly forgotten.[68] The view that Japan 'is politically following the US anti-Chinese policy, while economically it wants to reap gains from Sino-Japanese trade . . . is self-contradictory' had to be jettisoned by Beijing.[69] Far less had in fact changed for Japan. Its foreign policy certainly now had new dimensions and its voice would be heard more frequently but, as one observer noted in 1976, the 'absence of diplomatic relations with the People's Republic of China (PRC) until 1972 probably cost Japan very little in economic terms, just as its diplomatic relations with Peking since 1972 have hardly affected economic relations with Taiwan.'[70] The familiar twin

Japanese external objectives of economic security and military links to Washington were still firmly in place once the excitement and noise had subsided.

As in earlier crises, the United States moved next to shift the relationship back to a firmer base. Ambassador Meyer worked diligently to repair the damage and would later suggest that American faults were matched by 'overreaction in Japan'.[71] Evidence at the public level of measures taken to stress the amicability of US–Japan ties included President Nixon's meeting with the Emperor at a USAF base outside Anchorage in August 1971 and the more important Nixon-Sato summit at San Clemente in January 1972. What Japan found difficult to ignore was the growing closeness of American-Chinese ties and a fear that the US–Japan partnership would be weakened as Washington developed a triangular relationship in east Asia.[72] The suspicion grew within the LDP and bureaucracy that Tokyo might well be relegated to the sidelines as Sino-American political and economic consultations developed in intensity. These fears could hardly be allayed when American actions were seen by third parties as in danger of collision. André Malraux, for example, suggested to Nixon that, in Kissinger's words, '[w]hat mattered was our Pacific policy. If Japan ceased believing in our nuclear protection, it would move toward the Soviet Union. If we could keep Japan tied to us, this might accelerate the need of the Soviet Union and even of China to attend to the satisfaction of their populations. Somewhere down the road, Malraux warned, maybe as early as within two years, our Chinese and Japanese policies would begin to conflict and require careful management.'[73]

One response by Japan to closer Sino–American ties was to conduct its own talks with Moscow. Foreign Minister Andrei Gromyko visited Tokyo in January 1972 to restart what had long been an uncomfortable relationship. Ambassador Meyer joked to officials from the Soviet embassy and Japanese Ministry of Foreign Affairs that the final communiqué on the Gromyko visit ought to have incorporated the passage: 'Both parties wish to express their appreciation to the President of the United States for having made this resumption of Ministerial discussions possible.'[74] Clearly, the American government felt sufficiently confident of its stout links with Japan not to be overly concerned with Soviet approaches that were widely seen as Moscow's belated response to the possibility of a Sino-American-Japanese front. The Soviet press might begin after 1972 to stress the need for 'a new climate in Soviet–Japanese relations' and 'an intensification of contacts in all spheres, including the political sphere'[75] but there was to be precious little progress in the ensuing decade. One dramatic failing of the Soviet Union was its inability, after a great deal of public pressure, to persuade Japan to drop all reference to the phrase 'hegemony in the Asian-Pacific region' in the eventual Sino-Japanese peace treaty of August 1978.[76] Moscow's inability to persuade Japan to erase what was known everywhere to be none-too-subtle Chinese code language for criticism of the Soviet Union symbolized how fragile Soviet–Japanese relations remained.

One useful piece of political symbolism was the visit by President Ford to Japan in November 1974. Before his resignation Richard Nixon had accepted an invitation from the Japanese government to be the first ever American head of state to go to Tokyo but the Watergate scandal and Nixon's long-drawn-out fight to save his administration made this impossible. Ford discounted domestic objections and decided 'it was about time' that an American president came to Japan. It was, of course, more than time and his hosts would hardly have been pleased to learn that Ford later described the visit as 'more ceremonial than substantive – I would deal with weightier matters when I continued on to South Korea and Vladivostok', although Ford did add that he 'looked forward to a visit that would symbolize the special relationship that existed between our two countries'.[77] After talks with Prime Minister Tanaka, who was concerned that the United States 'Congress or Executive Branch might impose new quotas upon a variety of Japanese goods', Ford saw Kyoto and then flew on to Seoul.[78]

By the mid-1970s US–Japan ties appeared to have regained an element of balance. American scholars could agree that they were witnessing 'a time of significant transition, but the question is how great the changes will be and in what direction they will lead'.[79] Many commentators, at least on the American side, were beginning to sense that the worst was behind them. In part this was coming about by default. Reischauer's 'cautious optimism' was based on the lack of alternatives to the Pacific partnership. He predicted that 'American and Japanese concepts of world order, international economic relations, and a desirable domestic social and political system are almost certain to remain much more compatible with each other than with the comparable ideologies of either China or the Soviet Union.' The former ambassador suggested that 'even if Japan and the United States should drift apart for other reasons, neither is likely to develop a relationship with China or the Soviet Union that could be a substitute for their relationship with each other'.[80]

Undoubtedly, the eventual ending of American involvement in the

Vietnam war and the continuing Sino-Soviet disputes acted to bring Washington and Tokyo together once again. Japanese domestic scepticism over the direction of American foreign policy was greatly reduced by the retreat from south-east Asia in particular, though Washington's 'loss of prestige' by such disengagement, 'signs of decline' in American international economic leadership, and 'rifts . . . at home in the cohesiveness of American society'[81] were underlined in print even by its friends within Japan. The ambivalence of much Japanese thinking on the United States was growing. On the one hand sympathetic observers such as Ohira Masayoshi would note in the 1970s that 'America did much to help the world after the Pacific war, but she seems to have lost a great deal in the process', while still seeing the US as the nation with 'the strongest influence in the world and the heaviest responsibilities'.[82] Japan had in addition to begin to reckon with a new impatience from the United States over the hesitancy and incoherence of its foreign policies. As one academic noted by mid-decade, 'as Americans become accustomed to thinking of Japan as a powerful international actor, there may be new expectations for Japanese support of US policies in return for the years that the United States assisted Japan.'[83] There was indeed to be not only growing encouragement for Japan to assert itself in company with the West but also increasingly shrill comment when these hopes were not realized.

During the years of the Carter administration, however, efforts to stress the cordiality of US–Japan relations were generally successful.[84] Bilateral ties improved, although the two obvious issues of contention remained the question of growing trade imbalances and the debate over Japan's contribution to Western security interests in the Asian-Pacific region. In neither case was much accomplished to the satisfaction of the administration but, as so often in the past, disagreements were not pressed to the point of causing any permanent dislocation. Once again the supposedly 'weaker' partner was able to benefit by the United States' clear unwillingness to contemplate action that could lead to a serious rift in the relationship.

The frustrations, however, that this self-checking mechanism engendered amongst some within the Carter administration would on occasion spill out into the public domain. Secretary of Defense Harold Brown certainly pulled no punches in December 1980, for example, when he lectured Tokyo on the feebleness of its budgetary efforts to meet what Carter saw as the common danger of a great Soviet military threat within the region. Brown warned that Japan's miniscule increase in defence expenditure 'is so modest that it conveys a sense of complacency which simply is not justified by the facts. It falls seriously short, whether measured by the security situation, by the discussions held between senior officials of our two governments over the last year, or by considerations of equitable burden-sharing.'[85]

7 TROUBLES: DEFENCE AND TRADE ISSUES TODAY

The Japan-US economic-security relationship is without parallel in history.

Lee Kuan Yew, 11 November 1987

As long as Japan remains a merchant-cum-industrialist, we must always defer to the United States. We have to swallow our pride, accept insults and not argue back. Otherwise, we may lose the American market.

If that is too high a price to pay, we have to raise our sights and become a leader. We would need our own ideology, independent defence and economic policies, and leaders who can perform on the world stage.

Amaya Naohira, *Tokyo Shimbun*, 24 June 1987

The important thing for Japan is to win for itself the power to say 'No' based on a position representing its people. In this context, it is essential for Japan to free itself from the yoke of the Japan–US Security Treaty and to win economic independence.

Murakami Harumitsu, Japan Communist Party, December 1990

'... a real danger exists for strains and tensions in the bilateral relationship to be exacerbated in this decade, unless concerted efforts are made to recognize problems, cooperate in solving them, and isolate those that are not amenable to short-term solutions'.[1] So warned Gerald Curtis in the autumn of 1980 as commentators began the predictable ritual of predicting how events might evolve in the decade ahead. Many of the anxieties voiced at the start of the 1980s would be amply fulfilled in the ensuing years without, however, the advent of the catastrophe that some foresaw and others would have welcomed.

It was to prove a decade of tensions, abuse, congratulatory rhetoric and frequent change without the final emergence of any clear pattern. The doomsters and the publicists for what was held by some to be 'the most important bilateral relationship in the world – bar none'[2] both got it wrong, since the continuities in 1990 were to prove as remarkable as all the widely-noted transformations. At the end of the decade it was still difficult to discern the hoped for alteration in Japanese foreign policy. The expectation that Tokyo would be willing and able to act as a major power in concert with Washington in a wide range of political, military as well as economic areas was simply unfounded. Japan by 1990 was most certainly recognized as a global player but rarely behaved as a global leader.[3]

It took no great wisdom for most forecasters at the beginning of the 1980s to suggest, in the words of former US ambassador to Japan Robert Ingersoll, that the 'one major issue that remains in the forefront, and probably will for the foreseeable future, is the trade relations between our two countries'.[4] Ingersoll also warned that since he saw 'the United States and Japan as being industrial competitors for the foreseeable future ... We are bound to be competitive and bound to have frictions'. Ingersoll, who acknowledged that trade issues took up the bulk of his time when in Japan from 1972 to 1973, could only hope that 'the confrontations of our trade relations could be kept within bounds and would not seriously jeopardize our close political ties'.[5]

It was the objective of the Reagan administrations to maintain the alliance, while having to reckon with a domestic tidal wave of criticism of Japan's trading behaviour. Mr Reagan's policies towards Japan were a balance between encouraging Japan to move closer to the centre of international affairs and being obliged to chastise Tokyo for not behaving in the economic arena in a more liberal and transparent manner. For most of his presidency Ronald Reagan worked to persuade Japan to contribute more to American and Western policy objectives and appears to have felt that Japan could be best enticed forward by honeyed words rather than threats of reprisals. Yet the public avowals of US–Japan friendship were almost too frequent for comfort and must have led many waiverers to ask themselves if there was not at bottom something fundamentally unstable with a relationship that seemed to require such continuous and plentiful dosages of saccharine. There was also a danger that the Japanese elites would listen to the message and feel that such American professions of good will required in return little further action from the Japanese side. The long and, in some ways, successful tenure of Ambassador Mansfield, tended to reassure Japan that, despite the obvious difficulties aired so frequently in public, all would work itself out and that the nation could still count on American benevolence. Ambassador Mansfield's age and personality appealed to Japanese audiences but his listeners on occasion may have been misled by the avuncular image. Statements that, for example, the United States and Japan 'are now true global partners' in an article entitled 'A Shared Destiny'[6] risked giving the impression that all was well with the relationship.

President Reagan's global foreign policy objectives stood in contrast to those of his predecessor. Reagan took office determined to rebuild American defences and to confront the 'challenges' of the Soviet Union. His administration was committed to expanding American power and influence. This, as one senior State Department official noted in June 1981, 'will require that we take better advantage of our political, economic and other assets – and those of our allies'.[7] Critics, however, were quick to claim that there was something familiar about a new president distancing himself from his predecessor, and defended Carter from some of the attacks made on his record. Reagan's policies were probably less clearly differentiated from those of Carter's last years at least than the new president's spokesmen suggested. Over policies towards Japan many of the American goals during the two Reagan administrations differed more in public tone than basic policy direction. During the Reagan years US–Japan relations became gradually both closer and more confrontational without seriously deviating from the premises that the new administration inherited.

What the United States hoped for from Japan was a considerably increased contribution to assisting the United States in its goals; what Japan wished for from the United States was reassurance over American leadership and competence. Similar questions were also being asked in Western European capitals but in 1980 the American public was only beginning to get used to such criticism from its principal Asian ally. Commentators, such as George Ball, warned in a special issue of *Foreign Affairs* on 'America and the World 1980' that

> Japanese–American relations are vulnerable not only to a resurgent protectionism but to resentment flowing from the disparity in military expenditures. At a time when the United States is reluctantly increasing its defense appropriations while trying in other areas to trim the national budget, it will hardly pass unnoticed that Japan, in spite of its spectacular economic success, is spending not much more than one percent of its gross national product on defense as against something in excess of six percent for the United States. Should it continue to have a free ride while American industry suffers its intensive competition? That is a rhetorical question tailor-made for demagogues.[8]

Ball's fears need to be placed in context. Reagan, it was pointed out in the same issue of *Foreign Affairs*, was fortunate in taking over

140

'US-Japanese ties that are stronger, and more free of tensions, than they have been in years. That may be one of the Carter Administration's most overlooked accomplishments in Asia; it is also to a large extent the personal accomplishment of Ambassador Mike Mansfield, who has quietly and effectively used the respect he commands both in Tokyo and on Capitol Hill to take the sting out of the disputes between the two nations.'[9] Andrew Nagorski also suggested that provided 'Reagan resists pressures to opt for protectionist solutions, further progress can clearly be made in strengthening bilateral ties. Japan is America's most stable and reliable ally in Asia: the new Administration should be careful not to make the mistake of Nixon and Kissinger of taking those ties for granted'.[10] Much then existed to make a substantial change in the Pacific relationship possible, but it would be a slight on the incoming administration's record to imagine that serious alterations would be easily obtained and endurable.[11]

Many of the changes in the US–Japan relationship during the 1980s were the work of officials answerable to Reagan and Prime Minister Nakasone Yasuhiro. But before Nakasone gained office there was Suzuki. Mr Suzuki, for all the barbs directed at his short tenure, went some way to breaking the ground for the shifts associated in the public's memory with Nakasone. Suzuki matters for two reasons. It was during his two and a half years as a rather uneasy head of government that constructive, formal trade restraints were drawn up between Tokyo and Washington and a considerable widening of Japan's security policies took place. Both actions prepared the Japanese electorate for some of the more publicized and personalized moves by Nakasone.

Changes in trading policies were highlighted by the reluctant agreement of the Japanese car industry in April 1981 to accept a 'voluntary' arrangement restricting the volume of annual export shipments to the United States. Once signed, it remained in force throughout the decade. The yearly total of 1,680,000 cars was resented by companies in Nagoya as an unfair trade restraint and equally criticized by spokesmen from Detroit as too liberal, when, as Congressman Hillis argued in 1983, '[w]e cannot be expected to successfully compete in a very tough trade market if we are playing with a whiffle ball and they are playing with a hard ball.'[12] The fact that the Suzuki cabinet was prepared to risk domestic attack and still consent to what MITI called 'very temporary and exceptional measures in order to maintain the free trade system and to develop further the good economic relations between Japan and the United States' is indicative of the deterioration in the overall relationship.[13] It was

141

hardly coincidental that the car agreement was reached between US Trade Representative William Brock and MITI Minister Tanaka Roku-suke on 1 May 1981 and that summit talks began in Washington between Prime Minister Suzuki and President Reagan a week later.

Since both leaders were newcomers, their advisors may have anticipated nothing more than a succession of general talks and an anodyne communiqué. Events proved the reverse, however, when Prime Minister Suzuki spoke to the Japanese press after the summit. Suzuki's denial of much of the official joint communiqué's statement on sharing illustrated all too graphically the distance that remained between what the United States hoped Japan might contribute to the security of the Asian-Pacific region and what Japanese public opinion was prepared to accept. Suzuki turned a series of somersaults that left him virtually disowning what he had just agreed with Reagan and led directly to the resignation of his foreign minister shortly afterwards. It was an extraordinarily inept performance by Suzuki.[14] He apparently reckoned that Japan could continue to have it both ways and promises made in Washington might be reinterpreted in Tokyo to reassure domestic audiences that nothing had changed. But they had, and it was presumably an acute sensitivity to the probable reactions of the electorate that led Suzuki to stumble so badly. The joint communiqué of 8 May referred in its first paragraph to Suzuki and Reagan 'recognizing that the alliance between Japan and the United States is built upon shared values of democracy and liberty'[15] and to some in Japan the reference to an alliance with military implications was deeply disturbing. Suzuki compounded the problem, however, by reassuring the Japanese journalists covering his visit that '[t]he idea of a military alliance is not contained in the joint communique'.[16] Worse followed when Suzuki contradicted the final paragraph of the joint communiqué, which had stated that Japan 'will seek to make even greater efforts for improving its defense capabilities in Japanese territories and in surrounding sea and airspace'. The prime minister, answering questions on the widely reported issue of Japan assuming eventual responsibility for the defence of sea lanes up to 1,000 nautical miles from Yokohama, virtually denied the entire concept. Since the US administration had been publicly encouraging a greater naval role for Japan, particularly in the light of having ordered units of the Seventh Fleet to the Gulf and Indian Ocean under pressure from the Iranian crisis and the Soviet invasion of Afghanistan in December 1979, this was unhelpful. It certainly made nonsense of talk within the joint communiqué that 'all Western industrialized democracies ... have a shared recognition of the various political, military and economic problems of the world and to cope with them in a consistent manner in order comprehensively to provide for the security of the West as a whole'.[17]

Despite Suzuki's *faux pas*, Japan was committed to modernizing its defence posture. The following July the National Defence Council approved a new defence plan for the period 1983–1987. This drew critical comments from newspapers such as the *Asahi Shimbun*, where editorials warned that 'Japan is being pulled down the road toward becoming a "military power"' and argued that the trend deserved to be arrested, even though the Suzuki cabinet held that the demands of the United States had to be answered.[18] The paper pointedly noted how '[f]or some time now, Prime Minister Suzuki has been proclaiming that Japan stands for the principles of peace, refuses to become a military power and intends to pursue disarmament and peace. If he meant what he said, another form of cooperation must be found, no matter how difficult it may be.'[19] Suzuki's attempts to straddle between constant US pressure for extensive rearmament and the wariness of much of Japanese public opinion was best illustrated in his comprehensive security concept. The premier argued that Japan 'must not see security from the defensive aspect alone' and warned against neglecting diplomatic and economic security in any new emphasis on a defence role.[20]

Much of the tentative nature of the Japanese moves towards accommodating the United States altered once Nakasone Yasuhiro finally achieved his long-held ambition of scrambling to the top of Japan's greasy pole of politics. Foreign policy now received a much higher priority and instantly became a more public issue. This was to result in considerable shifts in the overall relationship that were hard for many within Japan to accept. It was partly the consequence of Nakasone's personality and drive but also a recognition that American impatience at Tokyo's political and economic behaviour was growing apace. Self-criticism and policy changes were now the order of the day. Nakasone spoke his mind. He calculated that he would have more prospect of gaining his goals if he lept over his more cautious colleagues within the LDP and bureaucracy by grabbing public attention. In his remarks at his inaugural press conference the new premier stated candidly that '[o]ver the past years Japan has obtained its defence on the cheap, as compared with Western European countries and the US. Considering those countries' defence efforts in the past, it can hardly be said that Japan has made strong and sufficient efforts.'[21] The State Department's reaction to hearing a Japanese prime minister say publicly that the 'level of Japan's defence efforts has been such that it has deserved the criticism it received' and 'Japan must cooperate, albeit within certain limitations, with the US and Western European nations and help maintain the unity of the free world' may be imagined. Suddenly Japan appeared light years away from the hesitancy of the Suzuki period.

Both Nakasone's style and substance were welcome news to the Reagan administration. Not without some justification was Nakasone able to boast after his years at the helm that '[b]efore I became prime minister, Japan was involved in international economic affairs. After I became prime minister, Japan became committed to world political affairs'.[22] It was over his bid to raise Japan's international status that Nakasone took the greatest pains. In many of his moves to arouse the Japanese public and invigorate the political and bureaucratic elites Nakasone was encouraged by the US government. As before, the central issues remained the question of further liberalization of the Japanese market to facilitate foreign access, which in turn it was hoped might begin to shrink an embarrassingly large trade surplus, and greater attention to strengthening Japan's defences.

Nakasone's visit to Washington in January 1983 marked the first of a series of occasions when both leaders could demonstrate their common goals. The tone of public remarks by Nakasone and Reagan was consistently positive as both sides appreciated how television news reports were gradually bringing home to audiences on both sides of the Pacific that their two nations were more than merely trade adversaries from alien societies. This educational process proved to be the most enduring result of the Reagan-Nakasone or 'Ron-Yasu' relationship as the media quickly labelled their personal friendship. It was, of course, no more than a start at repairing what the British ambassador to Tokyo during this period would shortly afterwards term the 'horrendous' communications gap caused by the lack of bilingual politicians and the differences in cultural behaviour.[23] The fact, however, that President Reagan was prepared to travel to Japan in November 1983 did contribute to cementing ties between the United States and Japan during a period when others in Washington were demanding retaliatory measures against Japanese exports. Yet for all the official promises and publications by both sides it may be that the two leaders were only able at best to delay what rapidly became a torrent of criticism and counter-charges.

Opinion polls in the United States were one crude but important indication of the difficulties that the Reagan administration faced in wishing to enlist Japan as a fully-paid up member of the Western camp, while simultaneously being obliged to take note of growing trade friction.[24] Congressional voices also were strident. By 1985 even Ambassador Mansfield was obliged to caution the Nakasone cabinet that the Reagan administration possessed 'weakening ability to fight growing protectionism in Congress'.[25] By mid-decade some of the earlier optimism of the Reagan-Nakasone personal-style diplomacy had lost its bloom. The Japanese media made great play of reporting statements by Senator Danforth, who argued that the latest in a series of market-opening measures announced in rapid succession would be regarded with suspicion. He warned that '[t]he problem of Japanese trade barriers will not be solved by a single Nakasone speech, announcement or package of promises. The only thing that counts is results. Evidence of real market opening by Japan will have to be new sales of competitive American products.'[26]

The Reagan administration found itself by 1985 having to pay greater heed to the critics of Japan. When, for example, Secretary of State George Shultz spoke at Princeton in the spring on international economic problems he had to admit that 'Japan is a special case. The 37,000 million-dollar US trade deficit with Japan, as we all know, is a source of intense friction in our bilateral relationship and the cause of much of the growing demand for protectionism in this country.'[27] Shultz's solution for this political problem was for the Japanese to 'reduce their trade surplus with the world by pursuing policies to offset the impact of their high savings rate.' He told his academic audience that Japan's 'high saving means low consumption. The excess of production over private and public consumption is not being used in domestic investment. It therefore appears as net exports. Or, to put it another way, under current conditions Japan relies on a large excess of exports over imports to maintain full employment.'[28] The Reagan administration hoped Nakasone might do much more in both the financial and trade fields but there was widespread scepticism within the United States that could hardly be altered by Japan's piecemeal and dilatory actions. Shultz noted that 'the Japanese Government's package of measures to lower trade barriers and encourage imports' were 'a laudable and encouraging beginning' but he quickly added '[m]ore specifics must come.'[29] Yet little more was forthcoming from Japan for two reasons. First, many influential figures in Japan disputed the American insistence that its ally was an 'unfair' trading nation and secondly Japanese public opinion was no longer as defensive or apologetic about responding to the charges of the United States. The meekness of the past was increasingly over and Japan felt it was more than time for the United States to put its own house in order. Japanese speakers now reminded international onlookers that in 1985 'Japan's handicap is almost identical to that of the United States and is even lower than those of the European countries'.[30] As the vice president of Matsushita Electric Industrial Co. maintained, 'Japan is now playing the game with a negative handicap in the form of voluntary restrictions. It does not stand to reason that the Americans should blame Japan for being unfair without knowing these facts. It is amazing that so many Americans are telling the story on the old facts of days gone by.'[31] It was a theme that senior Japanese politicians were quick to echo. Miyazawa Kiichi, then chairman of the LDP's Executive Board and the most experienced figure involved in US-Japan dealings by 1985, rebutted the 'free rider' accusation by arguing that Japan had gained its status as the second largest economic nation 'as a result of pursuing free trade and liberalization'.[32] He noted that only a few items remained on his nation's import restriction list and that '[i]n terms of other advanced nations, Japan is in no position to feel any sense of reticence about this . . .'[33] Miyazawa argued also that societal differences made absolute reciprocity an impossibility. He conceded that the political pressures on Japan to further open its markets had to be accepted, but the difficulties of evaluating what constituted fair dealings were immense. He stressed that 'Japan is not a Judeo-Christian culture . . . We have our own culture and we are trying to contribute to the world culture at large.'

By the mid-1980s, the economic relationship between Japan and the United States had become a story of almost continuous strife, at least if judged from press accounts. The anger from entire sectors of American industry was increasingly difficult for the US administration to contain. A succession of Japanese voluntary trade restraint agreements were necessary to prevent further dislocations. In the winter of 1984, there were steel negotiations that ended with Japan agreeing to limit its share of the American market to 5.85 per cent from the following year and in March 1985 the Japanese government extended the car export restraint programme for yet another year at the level now of 2,300,000 units. It was only by such actions that worse political consequences were avoided in the light of unanimous Senate resolutions that called on President Reagan to adopt retaliatory measures against Tokyo.

Nakasone had two cards to play in response to repeated claims that Japan largely by subterfuge and unholy government-business linkages had unfairly racked up a trade surplus with the United States of over $50 billion by 1986. The first and ultimately self-defeating ploy was to announce to a sceptical world that Japan would cut tariffs, introduce greater transparency into its domestic economy and generally behave as others had long sought. The scheme failed because Nakasone made too great a show of these supposedly far-reaching measures and was then unable to demonstrate the intended effect. Year by year the surplus grew – not only with the USA but also with virtually all of Japan's trading partners with the exception of its middle east oil producers. The European Community was quite as vocal as the United States in demanding reform of Japan but for most of the decade Brussels was not taken seriously by Tokyo. Remarks by Leslie Fielding, the EC's Director-General for External Affairs, in June 1985 that 'on specific requests for major market-opening for agricultural and industrial products to Japan, there has been almost no progress . . .' left the Japanese government unmoved. Fielding's question, however, over 'Is Japan determined to follow an import substitution policy where it is not fully competitive while at the same time wanting to export where it is competitive?' echoed numerous asides from American negotiators.[34] The warning that 'there is a storm coming. People do not concentrate their minds soon enough'[35] could be found in editorials and speeches throughout the industrialized world, yet movement was desperately slow.

Nakasone too was disappointed by the resistance from within his own party and the entrenched bureaucracy. Working to a different calendar these individuals knew that sooner or later the prime minister would have to leave office and that his successors might be more inclined to appreciate their conventional approach to trade issues. Nakasone's tactics of appealing over the heads of Japan's ruling elites became in time a less successful ploy as counter-strategies were devised to check the prime minister and restrict his independence. Nakasone's talk of acting in a 'presidential' manner was rarely accomplished for all his claims. The fact that Nakasone's factional base within the Liberal Democratic Party was relatively weak was a further impediment that he could hardly ignore as his term in office lengthened.[36]

The second strategy that Nakasone used was to announce boldly to allcomers that Japan was at last a committed ally of the United States and the West at a time when there appeared to be a second Cold War in operation. This political stance by Japan gained Nakasone considerable respect and undoubtedly contributed to the Reagan administration's willingness to overlook, where domestically possible, signs of trading misbehaviour. Such American indulgence in turn acted, as intended, to buttress the prime minister's position and left many within Japan confident that Nakasone knew best how to cope with American pressure. It was in foreign policy that Nakasone sought to shine under the conveniently rousing but vague slogan of obtaining 'a final settlement of postwar politics'.[37] In the sporting metaphors beloved of Anglo-Saxon states, Nakasone told Reagan at the 1983 Williamburg summit: '"You be the pitcher, I'll be the catcher".' Yet Nakasone also cautioned Reagan '"once in a while, the pitcher must listen to the catcher's good advice."'[38] In retirement Nakasone noted that this was 'the kind of relationship I have in mind. This is the relationship I believe will continue for the foreseeable future.'[39]

It was in the strengthening of the US–Japan security relationship that Nakasone best impressed the United States government. What mattered more than specific improvement in weapon systems and joint force exercises in the region was the sight of a Japanese politician who might actually believe his prepared statements on Pacific cooperation. Nakasone looked the part and said clearly that his state had obligations that it ought to uphold. Unfortunately for Nakasone, his efforts, while appreciated in the US for beginning to redress the defence imbalance, were certain to bring criticism at home. This did not prevent the premier from, for example, breaking the psychologically important 'taboo' on limiting defence expenditure to less than 1 per cent of GNP in fiscal 1987, but it left Nakasone with fewer concrete successes that he had hoped for. He could commit Japan to participating in President Reagan's Strategic Defense Initiative (SDI) and saw the virtues of strategic aid as a means whereby Tokyo began to employ financial assistance to bolster the well-being of countries, particularly in south-east Asia but also in the middle east, that were friendly to the West but the broad framework of Japan's defence thinking was largely untouched.[40] Domestic constraints could hardly be ignored, even by a prime minister who was able to win a sweeping electoral victory in July 1986, with the result that Nakasone's 'educational' efforts in military matters had always to be countered by statements that his government 'will continue to uphold the principle of self-reliant defence ... Japan will not become a military power that would pose threats to other nations', and that 'the policy of civilian control will be firmly maintained.'[41]

While Reagan and Nakasone stressed the shared political values and the strategic links between Washington and Tokyo, neither leader was able for a moment to imagine that this new attention to defence affairs would do much to stem the trade criticism. The introduction of F-16 fighters at Misawa or the eventual decision by Japan that its next-generation support fighter would be a joint US–Japanese project made little impression on Congress. Where Nakasone was able to demonstrate his skill was in sponsoring and then supporting the shift to a more domestically-oriented economic system. The Maekawa report of 7 April 1986 quickly became a symbol of Nakasone's new thinking and a talisman for change. Economists might disagree as to the wisdom of Maekawa's recommendations but the fact that it proposed what critics abroad had long been advocating and it was published on the eve of Nakasone's annual visit to the United States certainly helped the Japanese government.[42] As with the supposedly radical nature of defence changes under Nakasone, the economic movement away from industrial self-sufficiency had been growing throughout the 1980s, yet Nakasone's penchant for dramatization (he liked to think that his speeches on economic themes would be clear to all with a high school education) gave his country a new national objective. It was now a case of import or die.[43]

Little, however, of Nakasone's message won immediate approval within Japanese society. The prime minister might continue to insist that 'maintaining the unshakable trust and developing the alliance with the United States is most important not only for relations between Japan and the United States but also for peace and prosperity in the Asia-Pacific region and the entire world'[44] yet the phrases were shopworn. Special interest groups, notably agriculture, small industries, the multi-layered distribution system and the construction companies, expected the LDP to make haste slowly in offering concessions to the United States. Any shrinkage of Japan's trade surplus with the United States would have to be at the expense of some of the government's most loyal supporters and important campaign contributors. Specific figures that might commit Japan to annual reduction in its trading position were carefully avoided and it remained the case that public opinion felt the upsurge of American criticism to be largely sour grapes. The skill with which entire sectors of the economy were able to survive and, indeed, prosper after the Plaza agreement of the finance ministers of the Group of Five worked to push down the value of the dollar against the yen in September 1985 evoked widespread national pride. Large-scale appreciation of the yen led to little immediate change in Japan's trade surplus with the United States.[45] The US Commerce Department had to announce in January 1987 that the American trade deficit with Japan for 1986 was a record $58.6 billion.

A somewhat disappointed Nakasone finally left office in November 1987. He would be remembered both for his obvious enthusiasm over improving US–Japan ties and for the gulf that remained between his laudable intentions and the end results. Unlike many of his predecessors Nakasone appreciated the urgency of explaining the realities of

Japan's predicament to the electorate but it has to be said that few paid him overmuch attention when he lectured on Japan's new responsibilities. His term had seemed only a partial improvement on the position when he gained office. Then, in Ezra Vogel's view 'the dominant question in Japanese national policy has been how to use the world order for the benefit of Japan. There has been only a narrow circle of officials concerned with the question of what Japan should do to help maintain and strengthen the international world order.'[46] In the years since Nakasone stepped down, it is still far from clear if national thinking has made much further progress.

At the very least it can be said that Nakasone worked well with President Reagan to enable the US–Japan relationship to cope with its many critics. Some of Nakasone's remarks at times weakened that alliance[47] but his attention to foreign policy issues was in itself reassuring to Washington. In return Japan was fortunate to have the support of President Reagan, particularly in his insistence on the need to preserve the free-trade system wherever domestically possible, and the presence of Ambassador Mansfield to act as a calm spokesman for both sides. Yet by preventing Congressional attacks on Japan from getting out of hand and with an embassy in Tokyo that had appeared overly sympathetic to Japanese interests there remained the continual danger that at some future date American policy toward Japan might take a different course. The 1980s did no more than 'contain' many of the problems that face the Pacific relationship. This in itself was a considerable achievement given the criticism – amounting at times to virtual hostility – that grew during the decade, but it was hardly reassuring.[48]

None of Mr Nakasone's successors has given much evidence of being prepared to go beyond the cautious changes that began immediately before Nakasone gained power and were then consolidated and in some cases strengthened during his years at the centre. Given that the worst had not happened during the two Reagan terms, it was doubtless comforting for Japan's ruling party to assume that the past remained a convenient rule of thumb for conducting its Pacific diplomacy until the twenty-first century. Yet Reagan's attempts to gently edge Japan forward met with only mixed results on both the trade and security fronts as the former president indirectly acknowledged when he returned to Tokyo in October 1989. Speaking as a known friend of Japan of long standing he warned on his arrival that 'Japan has a responsibility for more than its own success'.[49] The Maekawa report indicated to some within Japan that greater attention might be placed on improving Japan's social infrastructure, housing standards in urban areas still often suggest a developing rather than an advanced economy, but it was far from clear by 1990 that the switch to domestic consumption would necessarily benefit American exporters or service industries. The trade gap remained stubbornly large. The Reagan administration's record on trade negotiations was decidedly mixed. Improvements over agricultural imports (rice yet again a notable exception) and the relaxation of governmental regulations in what were known as the MOSS (market-oriented sector selective) negotiations were welcome news in Washington.[50] Progress, however, was frequently slow; in the case of lengthy debates over the trivial question of Japan finally deigning to import metal baseball bats, it was farcical.

The Bush administration appears to be continuing to adopt much of the same approach that President Reagan and his advisors employed when talking with Japan. Undoubtedly the most public piece of evidence of US–Japan cooperation was the conclusion of the Structural Impediments Initiative (SII) negotiations over trade barriers in June 1990. Bush described the agreement as 'an important framework in which the underlying causes of trade imbalances can be removed.'[51] He also committed his nation to a new concept of trade and financial reciprocity in its dealings with Tokyo. Bush agreed that in return for very substantial undertakings by Japan both to eliminate structural trade barriers and a remarkable pledge to double government expenditure on public work projects over the next decade, he would attempt to lower the federal deficit and boost savings. This, in the opinion of Deputy Foreign Minister Watanabe Koji, was 'probably unprecedented in history: a series of actions constituting interference – in the classic sense of the term – in each other's domestic affairs.'[52] It remains to be seen, however, if the external imbalances can be substantially reduced and the goals of 'more efficient, open and competitive markets ... sustained economic growth and enhance[ment of] the quality of life in both Japan and the United States' can be realized.'[53] The SII agreement came only after months of discussion and personal, last-ditch interventions by both Bush and Kaifu. For Japan the stress was on explaining the concessions made to the United States as being in the interests of Japanese society as a whole. This novel approach cut little ice. The public saw SII as yet another in the endless series of forced changes brought about through the need to maintain reasonable relations with Washington. Prime Minister Kaifu argued that the agreement promoted the 'global partnership' of Japan and the United States, but acknowledged that he was 'well aware that the implementation of the Japanese measures contained in the final report may

151

encounter difficulties and the process may be painful.'[54] He claimed that 'these measures are intended to achieve a major reform of the Japanese economy in the consumers' best interests.'[55]

No sooner had the SII arrangements been completed than a new crisis arose to impose fresh strains on the alliance. For once the issue was neither an economic question nor an Asian one. It was instead a severe challenge to the rhetoric of global partnership that had been evoked during the 1980s to describe the degree of commitment by Washington and Tokyo to joint cooperation. It was to be a test in the middle east that Japan patently failed.[56]

The Gulf crisis that began with the Iraqi invasion of Kuwait in August 1990 demonstrated all too clearly the limitations of Japanese foreign policy and the emptiness of some of its claims to being regarded as a full partner of the United States. The slow, indecisive and ultimately weak efforts by the Kaifu cabinet to play a responsible role in connection with the United States were a disappointment to many of Japan's friends abroad. Despite some efforts by a reportedly reluctant prime minister it was not possible for the government to provide anything beyond financial assistance to the American-led campaign to dislodge the Iraqis from Kuwait. Kaifu, the leader of the smallest and most pacifist of the LDP's factions, attempted to gather support for a Japanese contribution to a Gulf peace-keeping force to be authorized under the United Nations but failed to sway a sceptical public that this would be in the nations' best interest. Concern that the despatch of unarmed Self-Defence Force personnel to duty in the middle east would contravene the 1947 Constitution and might be the harbinger of a return to militarism ended the Bush administration's hopes that Japan could find it possible to play an active role. Mr Kaifu might talk of events in the autumn of 1990 as 'the most severe trial we have faced since the end of the war'[57] but public opinion was far from convinced that this was necessarily the case.[58]

The domestic opposition to what many felt could lead to the undermining of the postwar Constitution scuppered Washington's expectations that a more confident and richer Japan would recognize both its responsibilities and appreciate the need to help the United States-led coalition. Despite siding with Washington over condemning Iraqi aggression and imposing UN sanctions on Baghdad it proved impossible for the Japanese government to gain approval for its original scheme of sending personnel to the Gulf as back-up units. Kaifu's indecision over what might be an appropriate Japanese response hurt him politically as he appeared to waiver between his own cautious position and the more pro-American views of the LDP's

Secretary General Ozawa Ichiro. Ozawa argued that Self-Defence Forces could and indeed should be sent to the Gulf to support the United States. He maintained in November that Article 9 of the Constitution need not be seen as blocking Japanese cooperation with UN resolutions. Ozawa insisted that 'cooperation with UN peace efforts does not constitute an exercise of the right to collective defense banned under the Constitution.'[59] Others disagreed with this position, although Prime Minister Kaifu told the Diet in late October that Foreign Minister Okazaki had indeed stated that Japan would carry out all UN duties prior to being admitted to that body in 1956.[60]

Yet even if there were strict constitutional limitations on Japan's freedom to act, it was clear that the Japanese government was unprepared for even a minimal role in the region. It proved impossible to organize volunteers or persuade Japanese shipping lines and carriers that slight risks might have to be endured in order to ferry or air-lift in Japanese medical personnel to assist if war should break out. The impression that Japanese society was taking refuge behind its Constitution and leaving all questions of international order and justice to others was inescapable. Tokyo's bid to gain permanent membership of the United Nations' Security Council was promptly and rightly set back a decade. A state that could offer nothing but financial support in a global crisis clearly had no claim to the inner sanctum. Concern only over Japan's own plentiful fuel reserves[61] and calculations on how a prolonged war might disrupt the Japanese economy demonstrate the distance that Japan still has to travel before its voice will be heard overseas.

Once all Japanese hostages had been released the crisis was widely interpreted within Japan as being largely over. Kaifu might speak in the Diet of how his nation needed to remember that it was one that had 'most benefited from international peace'[62] and that a contribution 'to efforts to keep world peace is a natural and inevitable cost arising from Japan's international position' but the message was barely heard. All too frequently the public and its political leaders claimed that legal impediments[63] and memories of how Japanese militarists had gradually edged its way to the centre of power in the 1930s precluded any but economic assistance in support of economic and UN actions. The suggestions that the Self-Defence Forces and their masters could not be trusted after more than four postwar decades of civilian control was a serious indictment of the maturity of Japanese democracy.

The restraints of public opinion clearly limit the extent of Japanese defence cooperation and leave the US government with little foreseeable prospect of being able to alter Japanese views on alliance policy.

153

Not even a seemingly innocuous bill, carefully titled 'The UN Peace Cooperation Measure', could win approval from LDP Dietmen in the autumn of 1990 when the lives of Japanese citizens and the nation's economic fortunes were at risk in the Gulf region,[64] yet paradoxically it still remains possible for the same government to press ahead with very considerable annual defence expenditures at a time when public opinion in the West is anticipating a 'peace dividend'. Within weeks of admitting that unarmed SDF personnel would not be sent to the middle east on any non-combatant mission, the Kaifu cabinet published a new five-year Defence Buildup Programme that indicated some reduction in weapon procurements in the later years of the plan but no clear linkage between outlays and shifts in international relations.[65] As in the past decade, the Japanese government had committed itself to substantial increases in expenditure on defence and foreign aid[66] in line with policies adopted during the 1980s but without any revision of the legal restraints on military cooperation. Yet again memories of the Pacific war and strict interpretations of the 1947 Constitution prevented action even after what had become a full-scale conflict in the Gulf. By the time that the lower house of the Japanese Diet had belatedly approved the government's financial support programme for the Gulf region, the war had already ended.

154

8 FUTURE: RELATIONS TO THE TWENTY-FIRST CENTURY

> The Treaty before us is a step toward breaking the vicious cycle of war
> – victory – peace – war.
>> John Foster Dulles, speech at San Francisco, 5 September 1951

> An Alliance can only mature or decay.
>> Sir Anthony Eden, *Foreign Affairs*, January 1961

> . . . in some 10–20 years or a little more, the USSR will turn from an
> advanced country into a developing one, while the USA in approxi-
> mately the same period will become virtually a semicolonial country,
> dependent on Japan, West Germany and, in due time, maybe even
> South Korean and Swiss capital . . .
>> Georgi Arbatov, *Moscow News Weekly*, No. 17, 1988

> By the year 2000 . . . Japan's gross national product will nearly double
> in dollar terms and amount to 80% to 85% of the US GNP after
> inflation is discounted. This would bring Japan's per capita GNP to a
> level about 50% above the United States.
>> *Los Angeles Times*, 30 April 1990, quoting the views of Kenneth
>> Courtis

The postwar Washington–Tokyo relationship has been a qualified
success. Its development since the occupation has shifted from stark
inequality to approximate economic parity and onto more recent
tentative beginnings of shared political partnership that will persist, at
the very least, until the next century. The evolution of the relationship
has not been easy, but the bonds remain. Much has gone right, though
few of those present at the creation could have had more than an
inkling of subsequent progress in the ties between the United States
and Japan. There has been nothing inevitable about the past four and
more decades and things could yet come unstuck. It was an act of both
courage and brutal realism for the United States to adopt Japan as its
ward in the years immediately after the bloodshed and bitterness of
the Pacific war. The initiative was clearly the United States' and its
officials understandably have remained more prepared to recall the

155

past and assume the right to take the lead that was once theirs by default. Yet times are changing, and the reemergence of Japan as a great power, though on this occasion only (so far) largely in the financial and economic arena, will require very considerable adjustments by both partners. In addition, the state of these bilateral ties now has major consequences for other nations concerned for the security of the Asian-Pacific region and the health of the global economy. If the United States and Japan cooperate effectively, then other states can either breathe more freely or grow increasingly despondent, depending on their ideological persuasion.

Those who portray the United States as having been reluctant to assume international responsibilities following the collapse of the grand alliance at the end of the Second World War may have overlooked Washington's enthusiasm and professionalism in occupying and transforming post-surrender Japan. This venture was no mere reluctant improvisation or temporary holding operation. American troops have remained stationed in Japan in greater or less strength since the first planes disgorged their wary units in the summer of 1945. Japan, of course, is no longer the prize of war or the quasi-independent state of the years following San Francisco, but now the necessary partner for the United States in the Asian-Pacific region. It ought, however, to be stressed that Japan's reemergence as a great power was a gradual process and that the Pacific alliance played a substantial role in this development. The process (fortunately, for some) is hardly capable of quantification, but it is assumed that the United States' provision of economic assistance, a free-trade system and the maintenance of its security arrangements with Tokyo contributed substantially to easing Japan's way back.

The United States was generally solicitous of Japan's predicament until the early 1970s. President Eisenhower, for example, repeatedly instructed the National Security Council to consider the consequences for the United States of chastising Japan. He maintained that even a nation of America's preeminence would be highly vulnerable without allies in Europe and Asia, much as Dulles had informed the Governors' Conference in October 1951 that 'we must admit that Japan was formidable when it fought alone in Asia and, if its manpower and industrial resources could be joined with those of China and exploited by Soviet Russia, the total combination could be extremely unpleasant'.[1] Japan, therefore, was accorded a generosity that bred resentment elsewhere among America's allies. Other contenders for American aid and support were unable always to offend Washington over this new befriendment, though hardly a voice could be found in

Asia to support Dulles' position that 'the Community of free nations needs Japan'. European suspicions on the trade front were equally deep-rooted and consequently it was not to be until the 1960s that Japan gained full equality in GATT and membership of the OECD.

Japan's views on the United States were highly pragmatic. While its leaders felt obliged to express support for democratic ideals and the solidarity of the West, the reality of Japanese postwar foreign policy was dissimilar. Tokyo was linked to Washington but the connections were seen in different perspectives when examined from Japan. What was lacking was any substantial willingness to commit Japan to active alignment with the United States. Japan was both technically an ally of the Americans, by virtue of the San Francisco system, and at times a nonparticipant in the Cold War. Japan tried to have the best of both worlds. It saw, or at least most of its conservative cabinets and senior bureaucracy generally did, the necessity for American protection and it spoke out in favour of other American ideals in the shape of an open society at home and open international trading arrangements for the import and export of manufactured goods and financial services. The United States rarely felt that Japan up to the 1970s was quite the nation that its leaders proclaimed, but successive administrations felt it better to let sleeping dogs lie. Japan was hardly perfect in its political and trading behaviour, yet it was linked to the United States by important defence and alliance arrangements that took precedence over other failings. Until President Nixon decided that enough was enough, Japan was largely left alone to cultivate its own garden. Provided the military alliance remained *in situ* much else had been excused and freer trade was shelved.

Japan simply was not at the forefront of either presidential or public interest in the two decades from the San Francisco settlements to the Nixon 'shocks'. The evidence suggests that the relationship was handled largely by bureaucrats to the extent that, in similar fashion as the earlier Anglo-Japanese alliance, the links can be described as essentially secretarial.[2] Japan could only benefit from this style of partnership. The alliance was managed on both sides by small numbers of military and civilian figures. Even the 1960 crisis that went some way to questioning the premises of the previous era generated little sustained attention in the United States. The White House apparently received almost no mail from the public at large over the cancellation of Eisenhower's planned visit to Japan.[3] At the moment of greatest despondency, there was little likelihood of the United States altering its basic stance with regard to its Japan policies. The opposition in Tokyo would have been downhearted to learn that at this

157

juncture the American ambassador could cable the president to assure him that '[w]e will get the treaty through and in due course the Japanese situation straightened out'.[4]

The State Department was ever conscious of the domestic political restraints operating in post-treaty Japan. General Ridgway felt that short of battling the Soviet Union his most important challenge would be to persuade his own forces to act circumspectly.[5] Sebald urges that if, much against his advice, the United States were to insist on retaining its bases in Japan, then 'detailed indoctrination of the American Armed forces stationed in Japan' was called for[6], while Dulles told Truman that MacArthur 'had won many victories, but the greatest of all would be if he succeeded in getting the colonels out of the Japanese villas'.[7] It was little wonder that when Ambassador Reischauer assumed his post in 1960 he judged the Japanese public's predominant image of his nation to be of its military brass.

Yet by the early 1970s the Japanese vision of the United States had begun to shift. The question of gradual rearmament, under the constant pressure of Washington, now took second place to concern over economic and financial issues. President Nixon's 'New Economic Order' measures of August 1971 serve as a convenient signpost in this clear switch in Japanese attention. Increasing affluence and the question of Japan's new responsibilities to ensure the maintenance of an open international economic system replaced the earlier obsession with security questions. The present relatively calm debate over defence has been replaced by major differences that are more serious than the Japanese term 'trade friction' implies, though still not yet approaching the popular American depiction of 'trade wars'.[8] Unfortunately, as the defence ties have grown closer there has been a corresponding divergence over economic matters that have accumulated by 1990 to leave the overall alliance in an exposed position. Optimism is in short supply. Even Ambassador Mansfield, who had spoken up enthusiastically and repetitively for Pacific ties throughout the early 1980s was obliged later to remind Japanese Diet members that the 'US and Japan are partners and at the same time competitors'.[9] Only a few months earlier a sympathetic academic publication within the United States had concluded that there had been in 1987 'a new dimension of mutual animosity which was arguably the worst thus far in the postwar history of US–Japan relations'.[10]

By the late 1980s it was difficult not to sense a growing distemper in vital portions of the Washington–Tokyo partnership. This was the consequence of continuing American pressure on Japan to alter its trading and financial behaviour and an emerging view within Japan that American complaints had far less validity than in earlier years. At the crudest level it was impossible to escape frequent depiction within the American media of Japan having long existed as a 'free-rider' in avoiding an adequate sharing of the security burden within north-east Asia and the equally popular perception that the Japanese market remained less than open. At the elite level it seemed that as defence cooperation grew, the economic side of the alliance had become correspondingly more strained.

To conclude merely that both the United States and Japan are more or less equally at fault over the handling of the Pacific relationship is unsatisfactory. Readers deserve better than this, though such fence-sitting is frequently presented as more responsible than castigating only one side and permitting the other nation to escape scot-free. The historical approach outlined in this survey suggests that until recently Japan was content to follow the United States and that shifts to the present in Japan's external relations have remained cautious and incomplete. This outcome is partly through American reluctance to abandon the regional role that it eagerly adopted following the defeat of Japan in 1945 and partly through default. Japan has yet, in 1991, to shed its crysalis and adopt a foreign policy either independent of the United States or in line with much that Washington would hope might better lead to co-partnership. Certainly, Japan is a greater inter-national power than it was in the early 1970s or before Mr Nakasone assumed his lengthy premiership but in the last resort Tokyo is still a follower and an uncertain one at that. Debate within Japan on whether a larger contribution to American-led regional policies might be appropriate for the nation has not reached any definite conclusion. It is still unclear as to whether Japan wishes to aspire to either great power status or is willing to underpin its alliance with the United States along the lines that Washington has long been pressing on Japan.

It remains safer for successive Japanese prime ministers to repeat merely that 'relations with the United States are the cornerstone of Japanese foreign policy. Japan and the United States share the ideals of freedom, democracy and the market economies, and this has been a major factor underlying Japan's current peace and prosperity'. The temptation to retreat to rhetoric and to avoid the clear presentation of Japan's options is likely to persist. The divisions and uncertainties of the Japanese public perceptions of the United States and international relations in general discourage the political and bureaucratic leaders of Japan from dropping their guard. Electoral set backs to the Liberal-Democratic Party in the late 1980s left the government even less willing to confront major differences with the United States as the rapid succession of prime ministers and challenges from the opposition combined to leave many issues unresolved. The extent to which President Gorbachev's bold attempt to scale down the Cold War would reduce tensions in north-east Asia and lessen the military alliance between Tokyo and Washington was a further conundrum.

Japan remains a principal beneficiary of the post-1945 American design. The liberal international economic order may be less liberal and less ordered than a generation ago but enough remains in place for Japan to continue to gain immensely from the relatively open trading system. It can not yet be said that Japan is fully supporting the American arrangements or that the United States is yet willing to see Tokyo as much more than a contributor rather than a responsible co-partner. The dispute over an appropriate division of labour (and by implication a division of responsibilities could lead to a division of power) is only a beginning. The differences of opinion that existed until 1990 over how the United States might square its relations with its principal European allies and reckon with its own domestic criticism if it were to agree to increase Japan's national quota to the International Monetary Fund is indicative of the distance that is only slowly being traversed by Washington. Great powers and former great powers, to paraphrase John Holmes, are great snobs. Suggestions may be appearing now in some American quarters over the need for a new, political charter between the United States and Japan but the mood in Congress is hardly conducive to such enlightened thinking. To stand up for closer, co-equal links is to court unpopularity.

Concern over the ability of the United States to maintain its leadership position is now widespread within the United States and Japan. For the first time in the postwar era there has been an immense flood of publications on aspects of the Pacific alliance that inevitably reflected the precariousness seen by some over the United States' diminishing global influence. The subject of Japan and the United States is being debated with a seriousness and before a wider audience than ever before. Convincing conclusions, however, are hard to find. Beyond some rather tame generalizations on the need, stemming from American budgetary and financial restraint, to coopt Japan into a more strenuous international posture and the importance of Japan looking more to its domestic markets and providing foreign aid packages, little could be easily discerned from the exercise. It is a subject that will probably be with us throughout the 1990s. The familiar process of American submissions to Japan and then a measured response from Tokyo will continue, though more Japanese initiatives may be forthcoming in time. Beyond trade friction lies more friction; beyond present friendship is the opportunity for a deeper alliance.

The US–Japan relationship in the past decade has been dominated by economic disagreements that reflect increasing American concern at the failings of its own economy and the success of its Pacific ally. As former ambassador to Tokyo Mike Mansfield noted at West Point in the autumn of 1990, there has been a shift in American attitudes in the last generation 'from internationalism to unilateralism' that coincided with the rising prosperity of other states. It was, Mansfield maintained, 'the great irony' that [w]hen we were at our most powerful, in the first two decades after the war, we also were in our most cooperative and international mode, showing a decent respect for the opinions of others, and seeking their cooperation and support.' However, 'as others became stronger relative to us – economically, politically, and militarily – we started to try to change the world on our own, or blame others for our problems.'[11] Mansfield proposed three 'principles' that might assist in regaining the status that had been acquired in 1945. Aside from creating strength and cooperating with its allies in a 'return to internationalism', Mansfield argued that his nation 'must remain the world's economic leader'. He suggested that '[p]erhaps the single most important thing that America can do for the world – and itself – in the next decade is to get its economic act together.'[12]

The difficulties, however, of regaining portions of its former economic supremacy were formidable. It was easier for some Americans to accuse others and to hunt for scapegoats abroad. The widespread concern within the United States at the strengths of the Japanese economic and financial sectors had at its heart a sense that the United States was finding it increasingly difficult to respond to the Japanese challenge. Evidence of any slowdown in Japanese economic growth or faults in its financial markets was quickly seized upon to assure public opinion that the Pacific rival had its own share of difficulties. Media predictions that a revitalized and enlarged European Community might be the United States' chief competitor in the coming decade tended to give what may well prove to be a false sense of comfort that the threat from Japan might be lessening.

While the United States pondered how it might better engage Japan, its ally attempted to reassure Washington that the days of enormous trade imbalances might be ending and that Japan indeed had turned over a new leaf. Neither argument was more than partially true but evidence had emerged by 1990 that supported some commentaries. Japan's current account surplus, for example, did decline in the years

161

1988 and 1989 from its peak of $87.0 billion gained in 1987.[13] The Japanese economy was being transformed, albeit under outside pressure led by the United States and echoed by the EC, and the most recent criticisms from the Bush administration appeared to concentrate on relatively minor areas of complaint. Even US officials, who returned to Tokyo in January 1991 to monitor progress on the SII pact, suggested that Japan was moving 'in the right direction', though there remained uncertainty over whether 'lasting and structural change' in the current account position would be realizable.[14] The Japanese government also was now prepared gently to underline in its press briefings that much was sadly awry with the US economy; and few outsiders were likely to deny that stories of banking failures and enormous budget deficits suggest that the Japanese case had its points.

For those slightly away from the diplomatic and political disputes it was hard to disagree with Peter Peterson's remarks in November 1989 that although '[y]ou practice liberal democratic capitalism here in Japan and we practice it in the United States . . . [and] we have much in common, we are worlds apart.'[15] The Chairman of the Council on Foreign Relations suggested that 'the effort to resolve the vast systematic differences that separate us, to ameliorate our huge trade and financial imbalances, and to construct a harmonious long-term Japan–US relationship may prove just as delicate, difficult and volatile a process as the complex management of the US–Soviet relationship has been over the years.'[16] Certainly, if public opinion polls are to be believed, the mood in the United States was critical of aspects of Japan's economic behaviour before the added issue of the Gulf crisis emerged to further cloud the relationship. To the existing difficulties centred around American fears for its diminishing economic future at the hands of Japanese products and capital the middle east conflict provided yet more ammunition. Shortly after the US-led attacks against Iraq began *The Economist* noted that the chairman of Chrysler had argued for limiting not only imported Japanese cars but for restrictions on those produced domestically when American 'sacrifices may soon be called on . . . in an area of the world that supplies most of Japan's oil'.[17] The standard response of Japanese officials to charges that Tokyo was guilty of foot-dragging followed predictably with the Ministry of Foreign Affairs claiming that an open society required time in 'responding and adapting' to events abroad.[18] Neither this suggestion nor the point that bureaucratic in-fighting among Japan's career civil servants inevitably causes delays in policy formulation any longer convinces the American government.[19]

The United States government is becoming increasingly involved in

Japanese internal affairs. This recent interference, not unnaturally seen as a throwback to the occupation era by many Japanese, has to be deplored. The Japanese government, however, has found it difficult to respond with any firmness to a range of questionable demands from Washington. The persistent trade deficits have restricted any effective rebuttal from Japan, and visiting US representatives are still accorded the traditional treatment of fulsome hospitality and verbal assurances that all will be well if both sides exercise a little patience. Such Japanese tactics are badly out of date and could be revised to better answer the American charges. It ought also to be pointed out to the American government that there are serious objections to parts of the new criticism. It is surely not the function of any American ambassador, and particularly not if one is dealing with as close an ally as Japan, to address remarks to Japanese citizens on how they might better protect the consumer or reorganize entire industries. The advancement of American diplomacy is not served by the United States lecturing Japan in public on how to conduct its political and economic affairs. The tendency, of which there is already evidence, for the Japanese media and business circles to point out the faults on the American side could then become hard to resist. The problems of financial ineptitude in some American banking circles, the difficulties of restoring manufacturing industries and the issues of minorities and the disadvantaged in urban areas will hardly enhance the Japanese vision of the United States if such themes are sensationalized. Japan-bashing will inevitably lead to America-bashing; charges and counter-charges would then escalate at a dangerous pace to destabilize the alliance.

Relations between the United States and Japan are far from good and it does a disservice to the alliance to pretend otherwise. The United States administrations in the 1980s may have hoped that the trade problems associated firmly in the public's mind as the central issue in US–Japan ties might be solved in time without undue pain but this patently has not occurred and American voices are increasingly strident in their comment. Headlines such as 'It's time that Japan got some bashing' have become commonplace.[20] The mood is changing and the friends of Japan in the United States are tempted either to remain silent or to shift their ground. Widely circulated magazines could now ask in 1989 whether Japan was not a 'threat' to the United States and clearly the Japanese government was greatly concerned about the prominence and tone of such allegations. The Ministry of Foreign Affairs was obliged to answer such stories that were seen as indicative of a disturbing revisionist streak within the American media.[21] Public opinion polls, such as one that suggested that Japan's economic power posed a greater threat to the US than the military capabilities of the Soviet Union, had to be addressed seriously.[22] The Japanese governmental spokesman felt it would be more productive for the United States to regard Japan 'not as a threat but a challenge, in which the intention is not to invade territory, but to compete in the economic field for the provision of better quality goods at better prices, to the satisfaction of consumers'.[23]

Purchase of American real estate and corporations by Japanese institutions and individuals only added oil to the fire, particularly when the announcement of Sony Corporation's intention to buy up Columbia Pictures was popularly explained as Japan's invasion of Hollywood and the acquisition of 'a piece of America's soul'. Rightly or wrongly Japan's financial and economic activities within the United States appeared to be described by large sections of the American media in a different tone from purchases made by European states. Japan was popularly depicted as intent on buying up America and the conventional response by Japanese commentators that the sums involved were less than those currently invested by Britain and the Netherlands was not particularly astute, given that projections suggest that these relative levels were certain to change in the near future and with it inevitably the Japanese case. The Governor of the Bank of Japan spoke up in October 1989 of an additional problem for Japanese financial institutions in their dealings with the United States when, in conventional bureaucratic phraseology, he called for future self-restraint in providing funding for leveraged buyouts of American companies. It was a case of Japan being damned both for interfering in the US markets and for not providing large loans in other instances. Caught between the opponents of what was seen as foreign meddling and those eager to court Japanese bankers it was inevitable that Japan's financial power would be increasingly visible and subject to frequent comment in the United States. Rumours, for example, of the refusal of Japanese banks to fund the leveraged buyout of UAL were reported to be responsible for the subsequent stock market fluctuations that immediately followed on Wall Street and around the world's financial markets.[24]

The US–Japan relationship has endured for nearly four decades. It has already surpassed in length and accomplishment the record of its early twentieth-century model, the Anglo-Japanese alliance.[25] Yet US–Japan ties since San Francisco deserve better than applause merely for longevity; it is one thing for an alliance to survive, quite another for it to flourish. The Pacific relationship warrants respect for both its resilience and creativity. No partnership could have confronted the inevitable disputes and controversies surrounding allies without a considerable degree of understanding and restraint amongst its diplomats and politicians. Success might be measured in the degree of distress that the closeness of these Pacific ties engenders in both the Soviet Union and European Community.[26] It is hardly sufficient for the cynic to explain away the entire process by alleging that the United States imposed the basic framework of the relationship on a hapless Japan at the conclusion of the occupation in circumstances that left Tokyo with few options in its foreign policy. Talk (rightfully) of inequalities in the early 1950s fails to explain Japan's willingness to continue with the relationship. Equally, a less confident United States has been reluctant to press Japan too hard over its external trading behaviour out of fear of disrupting the security nexus. The relationship appears set to hold; the mould chipped at the edges but unbroken.

Qualifications, however, are in order. The US–Japan alliance has not yet been called upon during its history to confront the ultimate justification of any international pact – solidarity in the council chamber and on the battlefield. Effective, mutual response in the defence of shared values and objectives is the litmus test of the relationship. No alliance that has yet to consider this reality can be said to be complete. No amount of rhetoric from however distinguished a quarter is worth sixpence before such an event. It follows, therefore, that no conclusive verdict to the strengths or weaknesses of the alliance can be finally known until a major crisis involving the risk of bloodshed has been tackled. This unpleasant, yet presumably abiding, truth of international history must qualify one's admiration of the progress made since 1952 in the display of political and military cooperation across the Pacific. An ally is someone prepared to support one beyond the provision of currency swops and cultural exchanges. Only when lives are at stake will one discover the ultimate validity of the relationship. Only when unpopular and potentially tragic issues of war and peace are under debate will the depths of the Pacific ties become known. One hesitates to predict the outcome. All the historian owes his readers (and all, by profession, he can do) is to underline the progress made between the United States and Japan in recent years and trust that the cultural and historical differences are recognized and that 'misunderstandings' are diminishing. Caution is invariably the safest response when estimating an uncertain future even on the basis of favourable contemporary evidence. It will take a fully-fledged emergency to discern the architects' handiwork. Then we shall know soon enough. International circumstances in north-east Asia since

1952 have tended, fortunately, to make such hypotheses remote; provided the stability of the region holds, the question is unlikely to be put in such stark terms.

Japan since 1945 has been intent on redemption through hard work at home and good neighbourliness abroad, though generally within the confines of an American-led international system. Its political and economic goals and behaviour have been relatively 'clean' and clear-cut; they stand in obvious contrast to its prewar imperialism. Until the 1970s the United States both approved and frequently encouraged the Japanese state to achieve its twin objectives. Circumstances have greatly changed since the end of Japanese innocence in the early 1970s but policies set out by recent Japanese prime ministers in policy statements to the Diet and in carefully prepared statements given to overseas audiences suggest that Japan remains at heart a minimalist state. It is doing considerably more, of course, but perhaps only what is judged to be sufficient to keep Washington off its back. There appears to be little enthusiasm behind its newer commitments. A richer Japan is prepared to increase its foreign aid and military modernization schemes under American prompting but the deeper rationale for all of this appears weak. Suggestions that Japan should be assuming 'greater global strategic cooperation and help in crisis management' within the framework of the US–Japan alliance have a slightly hollow ring.[27] Neither the Japanese public nor most of its elected representatives have too much time for this kind of advice.

Evidence, for example, of the slowness of change in US–Japan relations can be seen in press briefings following Prime Minister Sato's visit to Washington in November 1967. Constant reference to issues that remain unsolved today emerged on many similar occasions, despite joint White House and Gaimusho bromides. Questions, for example, of Japan's foreign aid contributions to Asia elicited Japanese explanations 'to raise this one [then 0.65 per cent of GNP] to one percent of the Gross National Product'.[28] Expressions on the need 'to consult closely regarding trade and economic problems between the two countries with a view to finding mutually satisfactory solutions' clearly would require far more than the establishment of joint subcommittees. The entire question of what Secretary Rusk defined as 'how quickly Japan is prepared to come of age as a major league power and full partner in Asia'[29] was only first tackled in the late 1960s and it remains far from clear a generation later whether Tokyo has yet assumed 'the larger political and economic responsibilities for Asian security we now expect and need from it'. America's 'central objective' may have been 'to spur Japan to move faster – in its own interests' but that is not how successive Japanese governments invariably saw their role.[30]

To return to the issues suggested at the beginning of this survey: the continuities in the Pacific relationship are striking. The security treaty, which formed the basis for the entire alliance structure in the eyes of Washington, is still in place almost forty years after Prime Minister Yoshida signed the original pact. Born of the Cold War in north-east Asia it was modified in 1960 but thereafter has remained in force to be substantially strengthened without further alteration. The general uncertainties of international relations in Asia stand in contrast to the seemingly 'irreplaceable'[31] security arrangements between the United States and Japan. Doubts over the future of détente and concern for the cohesion of the Soviet Union are likely to counterbalance the hopes of those who looked forward to the ending of superpower rivalries in the region. There is as yet nothing anachronistic about the US–Japan security pact, though possible reductions in American military power in the Asian-Pacific area are clearly unwelcome to Tokyo and among the United States' allies in Asia. It may be that some gradual slimming will occur during the 1990s and that a corresponding diminution of US–Japan joint war games is probable as the Soviet Union also conducts fewer military exercises in the northern Pacific. For the moment, however, the security pact endures. Neither the American nor the Japanese government is likely to yet dissent from the Defence Agency's remarks in 1988 that '[t]he world military situation remains tense, complex and fluid.'[32] To lessen any shrinkage of American power in Asia, there may well be offers from the Japanese side to provide financial assistance to third parties that could have military usages.[33]

Portions of Japan's existing foreign policy, however, will have to be rethought in the next decade. Some reassessment of Japan's worth to the United States would inevitably require effort by Tokyo to contribute more to the alliance. To persuade the United States that Japan is serious about its international responsibilities will not be easy. For too long the Japanese nation has seen itself as largely an economic power and wished to distance itself from situations where it would be required to commit more than verbal assurances to the common cause. The prediction of a generation ago that Japan would be 'still falling short of leadership in Asia or the world'[34] still applies. Japan may be an economic superpower but its behaviour in international terms can be extraordinarily weak compared with its industrial and financial muscle. It remains to be seen whether the Japanese people find any discomfort in this unprecedented gap between economic strength and

167

world status. The indications in 1991 were that most citizens were unfazed by the issue and that, in the refreshingly frank comments of Vice-Minister Kuriyama, 'a national effort, including change in the consciousness of the people' would first be necessary to alter the 'flat and faceless' direction of Japanese foreign policy.[35] There is equally little evidence that the leading figures in the ruling Liberal Democratic party have much interest in devising any major alterations to Japan's general approach to the world and its alliance with the United States.

What is more likely is that incremental improvement by Japan to the Pacific relationship will continue. It will remain difficult, however, to press Tokyo to assume responsibilities that have military implications beyond Japan's own territory. The slowness of the Kaifu cabinet's reactions to the Gulf crisis is the inevitable consequence of two generations of pacifist education and national determination to consign Japan's past to (someone else's) history books. The distance from Japan's surrender in 1945 to the present is now longer than the forty years of high imperialism from the Russo-Japanese war to the humiliations of total defeat and postwar occupation. It is hard to imagine that there is about to be any backsliding; the idea of Prime Minister Kaifu leading his nation into battle is preposterous. In this respect the American occupation perhaps succeeded too well. Equally, Japan's universities have done a singularly bad job in explaining some of the more unpleasant realities of international politics to their students and persuading the public at large that peace is neither an automatic blessing nor something that has never to be defended. Japan still does not possess a coherent defence policy that is clearly enunciated by its political leaders and endorsed in turn by the electorate. War and security systems remain grubby little secrets avoided in polite company. The idea of even requiring of Japan a financial contribution to support the United States-led coalition in the Gulf war was difficult for the Japanese government to explain. Kaifu was obliged to state lamely that the 'burden has to be shared equally by the people because it is a matter of world peace'.[36] Unfortunately for the US–Japan alliance, this patently was not how the public saw the crisis. Even friends of the United States spoke frequently in private of having serious reservations over the precipitateness of President Bush's actions. Many LDP politicians and their academic advisors wished that the coalition had stayed its hand and waited longer for sanctions to bite.[37] Japan first hoped against hope that there would be no war and then was equally over-optimistic in anticipating an early end to hostilities.

Concern undoubtedly exists that American misgivings at Japan's efforts in the Gulf war will endanger the Pacific relationship. Public opinion is likely.to ask why the United States still stations its troops in Japan at a time when international tensions are being lowered. The answers received may appear confused. Remarks, such as those made by US Marine Corps Major General Henry C. Stackpole, that US forces in Japan were acting as a 'cap in the bottle' to prevent future aggression by Japan, inevitably calls into question the entire security relationship.[38] Equally, if Japan is as unthreatened, affluent and peace-loving as other Americans have come to believe, then it may appear extraordinary that 50,000 US troops have been permanently stationed in Japan since the early 1950s.[39] Both more 'burden-sharing' and greater clarification of the worth of US bases to the United States would seem to be called for in order to defuse possible antagonism. The value of Okinawa as the base for the deployment of US marines to the Persian Gulf and the fact that Yokosuka is the home port of carriers of the US Seventh Fleet deserves to be better known. The size of what is referred to in Japan as its 'sympathy budget' allocations in support of US base facilities and in allowances for Japanese personnel employed on US bases should also be explained.[40]

Greater clarity over the value of the entire US–Japan relationship is unlikely to be realized until some of the issues that hurt the alliance have been improved. There is little doubt that the 1990s will prove yet another uncomfortable decade for aspects of the partnership. It will remain hard to go beyond the disruptive trade and financial questions and tackle fresh areas cooperatively. Yet Stephen Bosworth is surely correct to maintain that it is necessary to find 'new areas of cooperation between our two countries, as a counterweight to our economic competition and to compensate for the diminishing importance of our security ties. The problems of the global environment, Third World debt, and aid to the developing world are leading candidates for joint efforts.'[41] Whether the list proposed by Bosworth is adequate enough seems in doubt and the encouragement of a larger economic and financial role by Japan in Asia and indeed beyond would appear to be a more probable way forward. The suggestion that others in the Pacific, 'especially Japan, now demand a voice in setting the regional agenda, and [that] we must pursue an approach more tailored toward compromise and consensus on the issues of trade, technology, investment, and security'[42] is undeniable. How far Japan is prepared to go in conjunction with the United States is likely to be critical in the 1990s for the well-being of the region. Tokyo's own agenda of working for the normalization of relations with North Korea and gaining the transfer of the northern territories from the Soviet Union is likely to be so important domestically and so time consuming that wider regional initiatives along American lines may have to wait.[43] Urgent issues in Japan's dealings with its immediate neighbours make it less probable that suggestions by Japanese and American sources on developing 'the broader political and economic cooperative relationship as stipulated in Article 2 of the [Security] Treaty' will be easily accomplished.[44]

If there is to be a stronger and deeper Pacific relationship it is almost certain that the impetus must come from the United States government. To wait for Japan is to court disaster. The thinkings of the past two generations are too firmly in place and the constraints of domestic politics too pressing for much to emerge out of Tokyo. Entrenched rural and service-related interests vital to the continued success of the Liberal-Democratic Party are not about to be ignored by a ruling party that presently no longer commands a majority position in the upper house of the Diet and is always subject to damaging factional disputes. It is likely that pressure from the United States will provide the best way forward. The strategy, or perhaps deliberate deception, is to tell the public that the Japanese state is obliged to give in to demands from Washington in the knowledge that to do otherwise would weaken overall US–Japan ties. Over time Japan's sectoral interests have gradually lost ground in a manner that no conservative cabinet (or opposition coalition) would countenance by itself. To explain such policy shifts as the result of arm-twisting by Washington is to gain results broadly satisfactory to both governments.

Few of these *ad hoc* improvements are sufficiently impressive to support the argument that the world is about to see a Pax Nipponica or even a fully-fledged Pax Amerinippon.[45] The United States may be in relative decline but no one state can be said to have moved near to filling its shoes. The Japanese public takes a delight in being informed of American failings but has little wish to replace the United States as the world's hegemon.[46] Much of Japan's preparedness to play a larger role is intended to placate Washington and is best seen as involuntary action designed to prevent either a major American retreat from the Asian-Pacific region or the collapse of the close economic ties by which successive US administrations have laboured to carefully graft the two nations together. Those who suggest that 'divorce between the United States and Japan is economically impossible, militarily impractical, and politically unthinkable'[47] have a fair brief for the years ahead. It would take very considerable domestic change in Japan and the United States to alter this prognosis. Only the advent of different political regimes and a transformed international economy composed of tightly guarded, exclusivist, trading and financial blocs could wreck the Pacific alliance.

Given the alternatives there is little doubt that Washington and Tokyo will stay together. Cooperation, inevitably, will be difficult on occasion and the era of automatic Japanese compliance is long gone[48] but it ought to be possible to limit the damage and retain a close friendship. Japan still needs economic and security ties to the United States that could only be broken at the expense of destabilizing Asia and leading to vast problems between Japan and its neighbours.[49] Similarly, no future American administration is likely to dissent from the remarks by Henry Kissinger and Cyrus Vance that the relationship with Japan is 'vital to both countries. What is at issue is how best to proceed, not the value of the relationship itself.'[50]

In the economic field Japan's achievements are self-evident; it is also likely that they will continue to increase. The Nomura Research Institute, one of Japan's think-tanks, has predicted that the 1990s may prove to be Japan's 'Golden Age'. With even 4 per cent annual growth rates during the decade, Nomura feel that Japan will become the world's banker, providing funds for development across the globe, and that the yen is on the verge of becoming a major international currency. Direct foreign investment by Japanese institutions is also certain to grow as more and more Japanese corporations build factories and facilities overseas and off-shore production expands. Domestic employment in such industries as steel and shipbuilding will consequently decline, though Japan's bureaucrats and businessmen are unlikely to permit any serious de-industrialization. They speak contemptuously of north American and Western European governments who have permitted the 'hollowing out' of their economies and the necessity of relying on the importation of previous locally produced industrial goods. Japan is not about to become a 'hamburger' economy.

The likely changes in the relative economic status of Japan and the United States are of deep concern to many Americans. The Nomura Research Institute suggests that by 1995, assuming 4.2 per cent real economic growth in Japan and 2.8 per cent in the USA and 2.0 per cent for the EC, Japan may account for 16 per cent of the total world GNP and Japan's per capita GNP could exceed the American level by as much as 40 per cent.[51] Already in 1988 Japan's net external assets had reached almost $300 billion in comparison with the USA's net external debt of over $530 billion. The gap between Japan's assets and America's debts will continue to grow, by 1995 it is forecast to reach $2 trillion. The United States in 1995 is reckoned to still possess a greater share of the world's wealth than Japan, but since the US population is twice that of Japan's, the per capita difference will be greatly in Japan's favour.

Japan, with perhaps net external assets of $900 billion by the turn of the century, is clearly a world-beater. It does, however, have weaknesses at home and like all of its trading rivals is vulnerable to breakdowns in international economic and financial cooperation. In any retreat to the dangerous bloc economies of the 1930s, Japan could yet come a cropper. It is for that reason that Tokyo has been shoring up its regional ties and belatedly 'discovering' the European Community. In an attempt to defeat the fears of retaliation in any future trading 'war', Japanese corporations have lately been investing heavily within the EC to gain access before the possible pulling up of the European drawbridge and the creation of 'fortress Europe' after 1992.

'From now on Japan will go out into the world and if there is a need, if there is a request from another party, we should not hesitate in meeting it'. So stated Prime Minister Kaifu Toshiki in June 1990 as his nation began to formulate new foreign policies to take account of the changing world situation. Until the beginnings of détente it had been 'politically impossible', said Kaifu, but the improvement in super power relations and the important fact that 'the reaction of other Asian nations toward Japan seems to be changing' had combined to put flesh on Japan's commitment to larger international responsibilities.[52] Yet for all this talk of new roles and heavier international burdens, the key plank of Japan's relations with the rest of the world remains its ties with the United States and here the situation is not particularly encouraging. As Prime Minister Lee Kuan Yew of Singapore noted in a satellite broadcast on continuing 'good relations between Japan and the US. If trade and investments continue between them, the rest of the Asia Pacific region will grow.'[53] All, however, was conditional on improvements in the Tokyo–Washington partnership. Lee stated categorically to the Pacific Basin Economic Council that 'Japan must resolve her trade problems with the US'.[54] Without success on this front the Asian-Pacific growth saga was doomed.

Yet the headlines and public opinion polls suggest that there is unlikely to be any solution in the medium-term to the vast number of troubling issues that divide the two nations.[55] Even friends of Japan in the United States (dubbed members of the Chrysanthemum Club by opponents) have kept their heads down in the face of angry criticism of Tokyo. The array of problems that plague the two nations is not about to go away. Even as the twelve bruising months of diplomacy behind the SII (Structural Impediments Initiative) trade talks ended in a successful agreement the US government warned, through Ambassador Michael Armacost, that Washington is certain to request further Japanese funding for the upkeep of US forces with Japan. Military cost-sharing over the 50,000 US troops may now replace the trade issue as the next sticking point. American dissatisfaction with the performance of its closest Pacific ally left little time for mutual congratulations over the 30th anniversary of the US–Japan security pact. President George Bush was quoted by Japanese wire sources as saying 'What? Thirty years?' when former Foreign Minister Abe Shintaro (the son-in-law of Premier Kishi who signed the revised pact in 1960) began a speech at the White House commemorating the event.

In the light of seemingly endless American pressure and the prospect for shifts in power realities with Asia, Japan has still to propose any radical change in its foreign policy stance. Kuriyama Takakazu, vice-minister within the Ministry of Foreign Affairs, offered one reassessment in the summer of 1990 that suggests the limits of new thinking within the Japanese establishment. Kuriyama, writing of Japan 'making active contributions to the creation of a new international order' that can transcend both the Cold War and the possible break up of the American-sponsored international economic system, was thoroughly cautious. He spoke of the necessity of trilateral cooperation (US, EC, Japan), yet appeared unclear as to whether his nation had yet seen the light. He argued:

> Today, Japan must actively participate in the international efforts to create a new international order, in order to ensure its own security and prosperity . . . Japan's foreign policy must outgrow, as soon as possible, from that of a minor power to the foreign policy of a major power.

To persuade his fellow citizens to stop retreating into dubious assertions of Japan's difference and uniqueness Kuriyama suggested that this type of riposte and 'irresponsible rule-breaking' would 'invite an international backlash'. He noted that 'the more a nation becomes a major power, the more responsibility it must bear to abide strictly by the rules'.

The difficulty of defining with any precision what type of international order Japan aspires to remains, however, apparent.[56] It wishes to conform with 'the fundamental values shared by the industrial democracies', though even this rather unexciting suggestion would require a global vision not yet readily apparent within Japanese society. Interest, for example, in the activities of environmentalist groups, the plight of Asian refugees, Amnesty International or the anti-Apartheid movement is still minimal inside Japan. For the moment the hesitancy continues and the tendency, outside the economic field, to remain a reactive power is only slowly being eroded. Public opinion professes a belief in 'internationalization' but generally sees this being realized as an economic function rather than by either Japan's 'global political relations' or through 'increasing defence commitments as a member of the western alliance.'[57] The tendency to tread water is apparent and it is hard to discern much willingness to change the economism of Japanese foreign policy.

One encouraging factor in broadening Japan's links with other societies has been its cultural diplomacy, though it is no longer possible to assume that this will provide an automatic auxiliary to strengthening US–Japan relations. Recent moves by the Japanese government to institute new cultural exchange programmes have met with considerable criticism from the American side as being less than independent.[58] Yet at the academic level American interest and scholarship on Japan in the years since the occupation began far exceeds the levels achieved in Europe or elsewhere[59] and reflects, however indirectly, some of the strengths of the Pacific relationship. Large student enrollments and faculty expansion in the field of Japanese Studies, funded in part from private and public Japanese sources must presumably have an influence on public perceptions of contemporary Japan. The claim that 'Japanese literature is coming to be taken for granted'[60] is indicative of the vast sea shift that has taken place at both elite and popular levels in awareness and appreciation of Japanese civilization.

To conclude: the two Pacific nations have to manage their relations adequately or face the consequences of deterioration and eventual disruption. Events since the occupation and San Francisco peace settlements give reasonable grounds for assuming that the worst will not happen. Adjustment, it is hoped, will take place in the 1990s to better match Japan's new wealth to its support for the United States in exchange for closer consultation by Washington and attention to Japan's views. A greater sharing, however, of major decisions will not come easily for either side, since the Japanese government has rarely proclaimed a detailed 'agenda' and restrictions on Washington's behaviour will be unwelcome. New thinking by both nations is necessary in order to beat back recent criticism of the relationship, much of which has stressed the economic dimension to the exclusion of virtually all else. Yet for all its current trials the United States–Japan partnership remains the best bet.

APPENDICES

Appendix 1: Security Treaty between the United States and Japan, September 8, 1951

Japan has this day signed a Treaty of Peace with the Allied Powers. On the coming into force of that Treaty, Japan will not have the effective means to exercise its inherent right of self-defense because it has been disarmed. There is danger to Japan in this situation because irresponsible militarism has not yet been driven from the world. Therefore, Japan desires a Security Treaty with the United States of America to come into force simultaneously with the Treaty of Peace between the United States of America and Japan. The Treaty of Peace recognizes that Japan as a sovereign nation has the right to enter into collective security arrangements, and further, the Charter of the United Nations recognizes that all nations possess an inherent right of individual and collective self-defense.

In exercise of these rights, Japan desires, as a provisional arrangement for its defense, that the United States of America should maintain armed forces of its own in and about Japan so as to deter armed attack upon Japan.

The United States of America, in the interest of peace and security, is presently willing to maintain certain of its armed forces in and about Japan, in the expectation, however, that Japan will itself increasingly assume responsibility for its own defense against direct and indirect aggression, always avoiding any armament which could be an offensive threat or serve other than to promote peace and security in accordance with the purposes and principles of the United Nations Charter.

Accordingly, the two countries have agreed as follows:

Article I. Japan grants, and the United States of America accepts the right, upon the coming into force of the Treaty of Peace and of this Treaty, to dispose United States land, air, and sea forces in and about Japan. Such forces may be utilized to contribute to the maintenance of

175

the international peace and security in the Far East and to the security of Japan against armed attack from without, including assistance given at the express request of the Japanese Government to put down large-scale internal riots and disturbances in Japan, caused through instigation or intervention by an outside Power or Powers.

Article II. During the exercise of the right referred to in Article I, Japan will not grant, without the prior consent of the United States of America, any bases or any rights, power, or authority whatsoever, in or relating to bases or the right of garrison or of maneuver, or transit of ground, air, or naval forces to any third Power.

Article III. The conditions which shall govern the disposition of armed forces of the United States of America in and about Japan shall be determined by administrative agreements between the two Governments.

Article IV. This Treaty shall expire whenever in the opinion of the Governments of the United States of America and of Japan there shall have come into force such United Nations arrangements or such alternative individual or collective security dispositions as will satisfactorily provide for the maintenance by the United Nations or otherwise of international peace and security in the Japan Area.

Article V. This Treaty shall be ratified by the United States of America and Japan and will come into force when instruments of ratification thereof have been exchanged by them at Washington.

IN WITNESS WHEREOF the undersigned plenipotentiaries have signed this Treaty.

DONE in duplicate at the city of San Francisco, in the English and Japanese languages, this eighth day of September, 1951.

Appendix 2: Treaty of Mutual Cooperation and Security between the United States and Japan, Signed at Washington, D.C., January 19, 1960

The United States of America and Japan,

Desiring to strengthen the bonds of peace and friendship traditionally existing between them, and to uphold the principles of democracy, individual liberty, and the rule of law,

Desiring further to encourage closer economic cooperation between them and to promote conditions of economic stability and well-being in their countries,

Reaffirming their faith in the purposes and principles of the Charter of the United Nations, and their desire to live in peace with all peoples and all governments,

Recognizing that they have the inherent right of individual or collective self-defense as affirmed in the Charter of the United Nations,

Considering that they have a common concern in the maintenance of international peace and security in the Far East,

Having resolved to conclude a treaty of mutual cooperation and security,

Therefore agree as follows:

Article I. The Parties undertake, as set forth in the Charter of the United Nations, to settle any international disputes in which they may be involved by peaceful means in such a manner that international peace and security and justice are not endangered and to refrain in their international relations from the threat or use of force against the territorial integrity or political independence of any state, or in any other manner inconsistent with the purposes of the United Nations.

The Parties will endeavor in concert with other peace-loving countries to strengthen the United Nations so that its mission of maintaining international peace and security may be discharged more effectively.

Article II. The Parties will contribute toward the further development of peaceful and friendly international relations by strengthening their free institutions, by bringing about a better understanding of the principles upon which these institutions are founded, and by promoting conditions of stability and well-being. They seek to eliminate conflict in their international economic policies and will encourage economic collaboration between them.

Article III. The Parties, individually and in cooperation with each other, by means of continuous and effective self-help and mutual aid will maintain and develop, subject to their constitutional provisions, their capacities to resist armed attack.

Article IV. The Parties will consult together from time to time regarding the implementation of this Treaty, and, at the request of either Party, whenever the security of Japan or international peace and security in the Far East is threatened.

Article V. Each Party recognizes that an armed attack against either Party in the territories under the administration of Japan would be dangerous to its own peace and safety and declares that it would act to meet the common danger in accordance with its constitutional provisions and processes.

Any such armed attack and all measures taken as a result thereof shall be immediately reported to the Security Council of the United Nations in accordance with the provisions of Article 51 of the Charter.

177

Such measures shall be terminated when the Security Council has taken the measures necessary to restore and maintain international peace and security.

Article VI. For the purpose of contributing to the security of Japan and the maintenance of international peace and security in the Far East, the United States of America is granted the use by its land, air, and naval forces of facilities and areas in Japan.

The use of these facilities and areas as well as the status of the United States armed forces in Japan shall be governed by a separate agreement, replacing the administrative Agreement under Article III of the Security Treaty between the United States of America and Japan, signed at Tokyo on February 28, 1952, as amended, and by such other arrangements as may be agreed upon.

Article VII. This Treaty does not affect and shall not be interpreted as affecting in any way the rights and obligations of the Parties under the Charter of the United Nations or the responsibility of the United Nations for the maintenance of international peace and security.

Article VIII. This Treaty shall be ratified by the United States of America and Japan in accordance with their respective constitutional processes and will enter into force on the date on which the instruments of ratification thereof have been exchanged by them in Tokyo.

Article IX. The Security Treaty between the United States of America and Japan signed at the city of San Francisco on September 8, 1951, shall expire upon the entering into force of this Treaty.

Article X. This Treaty shall remain in force until in the opinion of the Governments of the United States of America and Japan there shall have come into force such United Nations arrangements as will satisfactorily provide for the maintenance of international peace and security in the Japan area.

However, after the Treaty has been in force for ten years, either Party may give notice to the other Party of its intention to terminate the Treaty, in which case the Treaty shall terminate one year after such notice has been given.

IN WITNESS WHEREOF the undersigned plenipotentiaries have signed this Treaty.

DONE in duplicate at Washington in the English and Japanese languages, both equally authentic, this 19th day of January, 1960.

Appendix 3

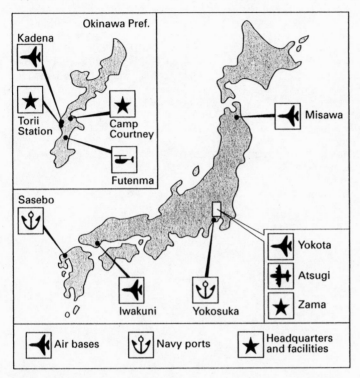

Major US Bases in Japan 1990

Service	Personnel	Major Units	Bases
Marines	24,320	1 marine expeditionary force	Okinawa, Iwakuni
Navy	7,011		Yokosuka, Sasebo
		3 attack submarines	
		1 amphibious group	
Air Force	16,013	1 air division with 120 fighter-bombers, plus transport, tanker, reconnaissance, and airborne control aircraft	Yokota, Misawa, Kadena
Army	2,048	corps HQ and support units	Zama
Total	49,422		

U.S. operating cost of U.S. forces in Japan, 1990: $4.5 Billion
Japanese spending on U.S. forces: $1.2 Billion
U.S. total cost including equipment and overhead: $9 Billion
U.S. military exports to Japan, 1990: $1 Billion
Estimated military expense Japan has saved
  since 1945 due to basing of U.S. forces in Japan: $1 Trillion
Sources: CDI, DOD, Japan, Mitsubishi Research Institute.
Chart prepared by Center for Defense Information.

Source: The Defense Monitor, vol. 19, no. 6 (1990).

Appendix 4

US Ambassadors to Japan since 1952

Name	Career or Non-Career	Appointment	Termination of Mission
Robert D. Murphy	C	18 April 1952	28 April 1953
John M. Allison	C	2 April 1953	2 February 1957
Douglas MacArthur 2nd	C	4 December 1956	12 March 1961
Edwin O. Reischauer	NC	29 March 1961	19 August 1966
U. Alexis Johnson	C	1 September 1966	15 January 1969
Armin H. Meyer	C	27 May 1969	27 March 1972
Robert Stephen Ingersoll	NC	29 February 1972	8 November 1973
James D. Hodgson	NC	20 June 1974	5 February 1977
Michael J. Mansfield	NC	22 April 1977	22 December 1988
Michael H. Armacost	C	10 March 1989	

Adapted from *United States Chiefs of Mission 1778–1982* (Washington DC, 1982)

Appendix 5

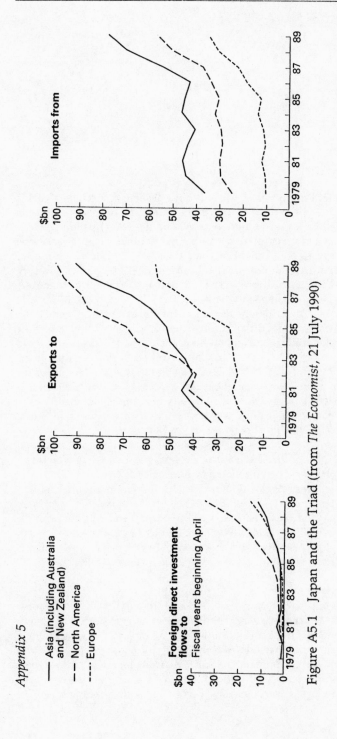

Figure A5.1   Japan and the Triad (from *The Economist*, 21 July 1990)

NOTES

Introduction

1 Professor Sodei Rinjiro's efforts in this field deserve respect, though his campaign led to the refusal by the prime minister's office to accept his petition for public release of more files relating to the occupation period.

2 To cite British examples of closure: the file entitled 'political relations between Japan and the United Kingdom' (FO271/105374) has an hundred years' embargo, several papers have been retained for a further twenty years beyond the normal thirty-year rule and the enticing document 'A Note on Mr Dulles' personality', Annex A, FJ1022/496 (FO371/92553) is unaccountably missing from the Public Record Office. On the general issue of differing American and British approaches to the release of government records see Bernard Wasserstein 'Whose History is It, Anyway?, *Times Literary Supplement*, 25 July 1986. On some current difficulties in the United States, see Warren I. Cohen's remarks on the Advisory Committee on Historical Diplomatic Documentation, *Perspectives*, May/June 1989.

3 Sansom to Hugh Borton, Director East Asia Institute, Columbia University, 30 November 1953, enclosing an outline of a proposed Japanese historical project. Sansom papers, St Antony's, Oxford.

4 Work on occupation studies can be followed in the *Japan Association of Studies of the History (JASHO) Newsletter* and the journal of the Japan Association of International Relations (*International Relations*). The basic bibliographic source remains Robert E. Ward and Frank Joseph Shulman *The Allied Occupation of Japan, 1945–1952: An Annotated Bibliography of Western-Language Materials* (Chicago, 1974). Specialists will also want to consult the two bibliographic volumes edited by Professor Asada: Sadao Asada (ed.), *Japan and the World, 1853–1952* (New York, 1989) and his *International Studies in Japan: A Bibliographic Guide* (Tokyo, 1988).

1 Roots: the occupation years

1 For examples of press coverage, see 'The Maturing of Japan' (cover story) *The Economist*, 17 August 1985, 'The Risen Sun' (cover story) *Far Eastern Economic Review*, 13 June 1985 and stories in *The New York Times*, including a controversial piece by Theodore White in its magazine section (28 July 1985) and a revealing opinion poll on American–Japanese mutual perceptions. For the results of national divisions over past and present attitudes to the Pacific war, the Allied occupation and current ties, see *The*

New York Times, CBS, Tokyo Broadcasting System poll, *The New York Times*, 6 August 1985 (p. 1). For Japanese views, see also the special number of *Japan Echo*, Summer 1985, entitled 'Split Opinion on Japan's World Role'. The JAL jumbo jet crash in Gumma prefecture on 12 August 1985 (the worst in aviation history) inevitably overshadowed reflection on the ending of the war.

2 Secretary of State Byrnes to Cabinet, 10 August 1945, quoted in John Morton Blum (ed.), *The Price of Vision: The Diary of Henry A. Wallace 1942–1946* (Boston, 1973), p. 474. Truman wrote of the Japanese in his diary for the same day that 'They wanted to keep the Emperor. We told 'em we'd tell 'em how to keep him, but we'd make the terms'. See Robert H. Ferrell (ed.), *Off The Record* (Harmondsworth, 1982), p. 61. For an account of Truman's views on Japan during the occupation era, see Buckley's essay in the forthcoming *festschrift* to Ian Nish (London, 1991). Only during the moments of greatest importance, such as the surrender period and the final moves towards gaining a peace settlement, does President Truman appear to have taken any sustained interest in Japanese affairs.

3 Statistics quoted from meeting of Joint Chiefs of Staff, 24 July 1945, in Louis Allen, *The End of the War in Asia* (London, 1976), p. 193. For a recent account of the war, see Ronald H. Spector, *Eagle against the Sun* (New York, 1985).

4 On the difficulties facing Japan, see S. Woodburn Kirby, *The War against Japan, Volume V* (London, 1969), pp. 95–9 and appendix 11. Although Japanese industry reached its peak output for ships, aircraft and munitions in only mid-1944, the decline thereafter was precipitated by Allied bombardment, bombing and blockade. Extreme shortages of petroleum had reduced the efficiency of the war economy to a hopeless level by 1945.

5 Time has not superseded Robert Butow's *Japan's Decision to Surrender* (Stanford, 1954). See also Rufus E. Miles, Jr., 'Hiroshima: The Strange Myth of a Half a Million Americans Lives Saved'. *International Security* (Fall, 1985), for recent doubts over American policy.

6 See Asada Sadao, 'Japanese Perceptions of the A-bomb Decision, 1945–1980', in Joe C. Dixon (ed.), *The American Military and the Far East* (Washington, DC, 1980). Also Buckley, 'Waiting Till Midnight: Japan's Reluctance to Surrender and its Immediate Post-War Behaviour: July–September 1945', *The Journal of Social Science* (Tokyo) (1990), ICU.

7 Eichelberger to his wife, 30 August 1945, in Eichelburger letters to Miss Em (personal file) August 1945, Eichelburger papers, Duke University.

8 The division was left unclear with the exception of Manchuria, Formosa and the Pescadores. China was to regain these territories but the fate of European possessions held presently by Japan was ignored. Roosevelt showed his communiqué first to Chiang. For British objections, see David Dilks (ed.), *The Diaries of Sir Alexander Cadogan 1938–1945* (London, 1971), pp. 577–8, and Christopher Thorne, *Allies of a Kind* (Oxford, 1978), pp. 311–12.

9 Statement released 1 December 1943. For text see SCAP Government Section, *Political Reorientation of Japan Vol. II* (Gross Pointe, Michigan, reprint, 1968), p. 411.

10 Lord Gladwyn, *Memoirs* (London, 1972), p. 117. Dismemberment of Japan was assumed by the Foreign Office post-war planners to be 'impossible'. For British thoughts on Japan, see Buckley, *Occupational Diplomacy: Britain, the United States and Japan, 1945–52* (Cambridge, 1982), chapter 1, pp. 7–26. American policies are discussed in Michael Schaller, *The U.S. Crusade in China, 1939–1945* (New York, 1979).

11 Stalin promised at the Teheran conference to enter the war against Japan once Germany had been crushed. This was indicative of a lessening of American interest in the China theatre where relations between the United States and Chiang were frequently abrasive. See Barbara Tuchman, *Sand against the Wind: Stilwell and the American Experience of China, 1911–1945* (London, 1971).

12 Potsdam Declaration, 26 July 1945.

13 Quoted in Butow, *Japan's Decision to Surrender*, p. 146. See also his discussion on the dismissive response of the government in employing the term *mokusatsu* (disregard) to rebuff the Allies.

14 Potsdam Declaration, point 6. The British government was responsible for ameliorating the terms by addressing it to the Japanese government rather than people and by referring to an occupation of 'points in Japanese territory'. Important British suggestions over the role of the Emperor were also incorporated into the surrender terms.

15 See Hatano Sumio, 'The Politics of Surrender: The Japanese Side', paper prepared for Kyoto American studies summer seminar, international affairs section, August 1986.

16 See Iokibe Makoto, 'American Policy towards Japan's "Unconditional Surrender"', in *The Japanese Journal of American Studies*, no. 1 (1981), and 'The Meaning of Unconditional Surrender', Kyoto seminar, note 15 above.

17 Authority of General MacArthur as Supreme Commander for the Allied Powers, 6 September 1945, *Political Reorientation*, Appendix A: 12.

18 For the agreement of Foreign Ministers at Moscow to establish the FEC and ACJ, see statement of 27 December 1945, *Political Reorientation*, Appendix A: 10.

19 For studies on these bodies, see G. H. Blakeslee, *The Far Eastern Commission* (Washington DC, 1953); Gordon Daniels, 'Nationalist China in the Allied Council: Policies towards Japan, 1946–1952', *Hoikkaido Law Review* (November 1976), and the work edited by Alan Rix on the diaries of Macmahon Ball. Also E. E. Ward, *Land Reform in Japan 1946–1950, the Allied Role* (Tokyo, 1990).

20 This was largely the result of Australian proposals by E. E. Ward.

21 See Spector, *Eagle Against the Sun*, pp. xiv–v. Spector, while noting 'his undoubted qualities of leadership', sees MacArthur as 'unsuited by temperament, character, and judgement for the positions of high command which he occupied throughout the war'.

22 *The Gallup Poll*, vol. I, 1935–1948 (New York, 1972). See surveys in 'most admired person' for 17 June 1946 and 9 March 1947. The material is fascinating, yet did not prevent him from failing in the 1948 Republican presidential primaries. Even MacArthur's staunchest admirers might have had reservations if they had heard him boast that 'he had been actively

associated with the Far East for fifty years and had been out in this area for about 25 years . . . probably no white man was more thoroughly familiar with the area and its problems than he'. MacArthur's remarks to Ambassador at Large Jessup, Tokyo, 8 January 1950.

23 For a highly detailed biography of MacArthur, see the trilogy by D. Clayton James, *The Years of MacArthur*. The occupation years are covered in vol. 3, *Triumph and Disaster, 1945–1964* (Boston, 1985). William Manchester's *American Caesar* (London, 1979) has a lighter touch but only one chapter on the years in Japan. Michael Schaller has also written on MacArthur. See his *The American Occupation of Japan: The Origins of the Cold War in Asia* (New York, 1985).

24 Ferrell (ed.), *Off The Record*, diary entry for 17 June 1945, p. 47. Truman thought then that MacArthur should have been ordered by Roosevelt to surrender to the Japanese rather than by Wainwright. He termed MacArthur as 'a play actor and a bunco man.'

25 Ferrell (ed.), *Off The Record*, diary entry for 10 August 1945, p. 60. There is very little in the Truman presidential papers that deals with MacArthur. For an important overview of the occupation, see John Dower, 'Occupied Japan and the Cold War in Asia', in Michael J. Lacey (ed.), *The Truman Presidency* (Cambridge, 1989).

26 Basic Initial Post-Surrender Directive to SCAP for the Occupation and Control of Japan, approved by State-War-Navy Coordinating Committee and sent to MacArthur through the JCS. On the related issue of planning, see E. H. F. Svensson, *The Military Occupation of Japan: The First Years of Planning, Policy Formulation and Reforms*, unpublished PhD/University of Denver, 1966; also Marlene Mayo, 'American Wartime Planning for Occupied Japan', in Robert Wolfe (ed.), *Americans as Proconsuls: United States Military Government in Germany and Japan, 1944–1952* (Carbondale, IL, 1984).

27 See comments by General Frank Sackton in Thomas W. Burkman (ed.), *The Occupation of Japan: The International Context* (Norfolk, VA, 1984), pp. 22–5. Sackton suggested that MacArthur was personally involved, while still in Manila, in the debate over the appropriate policies to be applied in Japan, but it remains the case that the planners in Washington alone had had the time and resources to map out much that later bore fruit in Japan.

28 *Off The Record*, diary entry for 25 July 1945. Truman wrote that '[e]ven if the Japs are savage, ruthless, merciless and fanatic, we as the leader of the world for the common welfare cannot drop this terrible bomb on the old capital or the new.' Much of downtown Tokyo was already rubble by August 1945. See Gordon Daniels, 'The Great Tokyo Air Raid, 9–10 March 1945', in W. G. Beasley (ed.), *Modern Japan: Aspects of History, Literature and Society* (Tokyo, 1976).

29 See Iokibe Makoto interview with Hugh Borton, Asahi Television documentary 'Top Secret: Wartime Planning for Occupied Japan', April 1985. Also Hugh Borton, *American Presurrender Planning for Postwar Japan* (New York, 1967).

30 Gallup poll findings published 29 June 1945 (on the Emperor), 22 August (treatment of Japan), 26 August (atom bomb), in *The Gallup Poll*, pp. 512, 521–2.

31 For texts of the Imperial Rescripts of 14 August and 2 September, see Butow, *Japan's Decision to Surrender*, pp. 248–9.

32 Both Australia and New Zealand advised against retaining the Emperor, whom the New Zealand department of external affairs termed the 'capstone' of 'that whole structure of feudalism'. India was willing to turn the other cheek and the British Foreign Office argued that 'the Emperor is the greatest asset we hold in the control of Japan. It was not the atomic bomb which caused the Japanese to surrender; it was the Emperor's rescript ordering them to do so'. See also the wide-ranging essays by Robert Ward on treatment of the Emperor and Sakamoto Yoshikazu on 'The International Context of the Occupation of Japan', in Robert E. Ward and Sakamoto Yoshikazu (eds.), *Democratizing Japan* (Honolulu, 1987). The work is subtitled the 'Allied' occupation.

33 The extent to which contemporary Japanese public opinion has come to terms with the changes instituted by the occupation is discussed by Takeda Cho in 'The Dual Image of the Emperor', *Japan Times*, 29 April 1986. The recent extended period of the late Emperor's final illness, death and the accession of his son was rarely used to clarify Japanese thinking on either Japan's past or its Imperial institution. Intimidation by ultra-nationalists was effective in stifling debate.

34 Statement by MacArthur, 17 September 1945, *Foreign Relations of the United States, 1945, Vol. VI* (Washington, DC, 1969), pp. 715–16.

35 Truman, as quoted by Acting Secretary of State Dean Acheson, 17 September 1945, *Foreign Relations of the United States, 1945, Vol. VI* (Washington, DC, 1969), p. 717. MacArthur's reply – following a reprimand from General Marshall – begins without the slightest suggestion of penitence.

36 Shigemitsu–Sutherland meeting, 4 September 1945, A–1.0.0.2–1 (General Correspondence), Japanese Diplomatic Record Office, Tokyo.

37 Theodore McNelly in *The Occupation of Japan: The Proceedings of a Seminar on the Occupation of Japan and its Legacy to the Postwar World* (Norfolk, VA, 1976), p. 5.

38 Author's interview with Sakomizu Hisatsune, Chief Cabinet Secretary to the Suzuki government, 26 January 1977. Sakomizu suggested that Suzuki thought US military rule probable, but remained confident that the Japanese bureaucracy and police would obey orders.

39 See Watanabe Takeshi, 'Observations on the Occupation', *JASHO Newsletter*, December 1985, also Amakawa Akira, 'Occupation by "Indirect Control": The Case of Japan', paper presented to the Hoover Institution Conference on Patterns of US Occupation Policies.

40 See Iriye Akira, 'Wartime Japanese Planning for Post–War Asia', in Ian Nish (ed.), *Anglo–Japanese Alienation, 1919–1952* (Cambridge, 1982).

41 George Atcheson Jr. to President Truman, 5 November 1945, *Foreign Relations of the United States 1945 Vol. VI*, pp. 825–6.

42 Atcheson, writing in this context of employing Konoye to rewrite the Japanese Constitution. *Ibid*, p. 827.

43 On postsurrender events in Korea, see Bruce Cumings' two volumes on *The Origins of the Korean War* (Princeton, 1981 and 1990). For Okinawa, see Watanabe Akio, *The Okinawa Problem* (Melbourne, 1970).

44 Hans Baerwald, *The Purge of Japanese Leaders under the Occupation* (Westport, Conn., reprint, 1977), p. 83. See also Baerwald, 'Reminiscences of a Mis-Spent Youth: Tokyo 1946–1949', in Ian Nish (ed.), *Aspects of the Allied Occupation of Japan* (London, 1986).

45 The Governor of the Bank of Japan in the mid- and late-1980s entered the Ministry of Finance in 1935. The Japanese press was quick to note the bureaucratic links behind members of the newly formed second Ohira cabinet in November 1979 that stretched back to Japan's control of North China in 1939.

46 Statistics quoted in Ralph Braibanti, 'The MacArthur Shogunate in Allied Guise', in Robert Wolfe (ed.), *Americans as Proconsuls: United States Military Government in Germany and Japan, 1944–1952* (Carbondale Il., 1984).

47 William Sebald to author, 9 September 1976.

48 Charles Kades to author, 6 September 1985. For a spirited account of the bureaucratic background within SCAP GHQ, see Theodore Cohen *Remaking Japan* (New York, 1987). For a more critical picture on SCAP and US figures, see Howard B. Schonberger *Aftermath of War: Americans and the Remaking of Japan, 1945–1952* (Kent, Ohio, 1989).

49 Michael Schaller, 'MacArthur's Japan: The View from Washington', *Diplomatic History*, winter, 1986.

50 For the text of the Constitution and a discussion by American and Japanese scholars on some of the issues surrounding it, see Dan Fenno Henderson (ed.), *The Constitution of Japan* (Seattle, 1968).

51 The phrase is misleading if MacArthur's instructions to his staff are to be regarded as the sole criteria. He spoke only of retaining the Emperor, wanted Japan to renounce war and prohibit any defence establishment, ordered that feudalism be abolished, and thought that the budget ought to be modelled on the British system. Kades' notes of conversation with MacArthur, 3 February 1946.

52 D. Rees-Williams MP, 437 HC debs, 5s, col 1910, 16 May 1947.

53 Yoshida to MacArthur, 9 April 1951, GS(B)–01746 (GHQ/SCAP Record Group 331) copy in Diet Library. Comment by Frank Rizzo, chief of Government Section, to the commander-in-chief General Ridgway, was concerned (rightly) that foreign governments would see any later shifts by the United States as indicative of the impermanence of the SCAP reforms.

54 Marshall Green to Max Bishop on 'views of Mr Kades', 15 February 1949, 849.00/2–1549 State Department files. On Yoshida, see John Dower, *Empire and Aftermath* (Cambridge, Mass., 1979), and Kosaka Masataka, *Saisho Yoshida Shigeru* (Tokyo, 1968). Portions of Yoshida's autobiography have been translated, see Yoshida Shigeru, *The Yoshida Memoirs* (London, 1961). From 1939–1945 Yoshida had no official position and was imprisoned in the spring of 1945 for his defeatism.

55 On land reform, see Ronald Dore, *Land Reform in Japan* (London, 1959). See also Fukutake Tadashi, *Japanese Rural Society*, trans R. P. Dore (London, 1972). On education, see Nishi Toshio, *Unconditional Democracy* (Stanford, 1982) and Mark T. Orr, 'The Reformers: Japanese Education during the Allied Occupation', *Research Bulletin of Education Reform*, Nagoya University, February 1986.

56 See Eleanor Hadley, *Anti-Trust in Japan* (Princeton, NJ, 1970), and Yamamura Kozo, *Economic Policy in Postwar Japan* (Berkeley, 1967).

57 Marshall Green to Max Bishop on 'views of Mr Kades', note 54 above.

58 For a valuable discussion on the Dodge line, see contributions by Dick Nanto, Orville McDiarmid and Howard Schonberger in Lawrence H. Redford (ed.), *The Occupation of Japan: Economic Policy and Reform* (Norfolk, VA, 1980).

59 See *Fortune* magazine, April, June and October 1949. Neither side gave any ground in the debate over Japan's economic position.

60 Over the role of economic bureaucracy see Chalmers Johnson, *MITI and the Japanese Miracle* (Stanford, 1982), and Okita Saburo *Japan's Challenging Years* (Canberra, 1983). Portions of the Foreign Ministry's holdings can be seen in Eto Jun (ed.), *Senryo shiroku* (Tokyo, 1981–2).

61 Yoshida statement to MacArthur, 15 July 1949, Folder 1: Japanese Diet Proceedings, 1948–50, Box 88, Record Group 5, MacArthur Memorial.

62 Suzuki Tadakatsu to author, 22 April 1977. The Eichelberger papers testify to Suzuki's ability to impress himself upon the Eighth Army's staff.

63 Sebald noted in early 1949 that the remarkable improvement in Yoshida's standing with the public when compared with the previous election in 1947 and attributed it 'quite clearly' to 'Mr Yoshida's display of independence'. This 'overwhelming endorsement' was a smack in the face for those in SCAP who had 'long entertained a dislike of Prime Minister Yoshida Shigeru and the Democratic Liberal Party for their allegedly reactionary ideology'. Sebald to State Department, 21 February 1949, 894.002–2149, Decimal Files.

2 Peace: the San Francisco settlements

1 For an overview, see Nagai Yonosuke and Akira Iriye (eds.), *The Origins of the Cold War in Asia* (Tokyo, 1977). For Japanese versions, see Nishimura Kumao, *Nihon gaikoshi, vol. 27: San Furanshisuko heiwa joyaku* (Tokyo, 1971), and Igarashi Takeshi, *Tainichi kowa to reisen* (Tokyo, 1986).

2 In *The American Occupation of Japan* (Oxford, 1985), Schaller claims that '[i]n defiance of MacArthur, the State and Defense departments halted many basic Occupation reforms in pursuit of economic recovery and political stability' (preface p. ix). This seems somewhat doubtful since most reforms were already in place (hence MacArthur's plea for ending the entire exercise in 1947) and the austerity measures that were to follow did little to make the Japanese enamoured of the US. It was later American mobilization for the Korean war that led to much of the Japanese economic recovery; no wonder Korean procurement orders were popularly seen as a new providential kamikaze.

3 Quoted in Buckley, 'Joining the Club: The Japanese Question and Anglo-Japanese Peace Diplomacy, 1950–51', *Modern Asian Studies*, April 1985.

4 See Uchiyama Toshiro, 'The US Occupation Policy for Japan: Deconcentration Controversy and the origins of the "Reverse Course"', IUJ, Centre for Japan–US Relations, student working paper No 1. Uchiyama's comments on Army Secretary Royall's San Francisco speech of January 1948 are an antidote to some recent accounts of the 'reverse course'. See Uchiyama,

'US Occupation Policy', pp. 136–140, and Schaller, *American Occupation*, for assessments of Royall's remarks.

5 No Chinese regime was likely to go easy on Japan. Chiang Kai-shek set an example of reconciliation that had few followers within the ranks of the KMT. The attitude of the PRC was to be tougher still. Soviet strategists were merciless, though largely ineffective.

6 India may be an exception to this generalization. Certainly Justice Pal's verdicts at the IMTFE and limited reparations claims suggest tolerance.

7 See James E. Auer, *The Postwar Rearmament of Japanese Maritime Forces, 1945–71* (New York, 1973).

8 *New York Times*, 3 March 1950. The paper noted that the text of Eichelberger's New York address had been released by the Department of Defense and that the retired general had made what was 'construed as the first pleas for a Japanese army from an authoritative source'.

9 UK embassy Washington to FO, 26 January 1950, FJ1021/16 (FO371/83828).

10 Allison to Butterworth 7-12-49, FW 740.00119 Control (Japan)/11–2949 (RG 59 Box 3827), State Department files, National Archives.

11 Hugh Borton had completed a draft peace treaty as early as February 1947. It was the assessment of these proposals that spurred MacArthur to make his 17 March speech. See the unpublished paper by Hugh Borton, then chief of the Division of Japanese Affairs. 'Special Official Mission to Japan and Korea, Spring 1947'. Borton noted that MacArthur had wanted Japan to attend the proposed peace conference and SCAP to be chairman. Borton wrote of MacArthur: 'I concluded that diplomacy and international affairs were not his forte'.

12 *New York Times*, 19 May 1950.

13 Failure of the United States to live up to its promises embarrassed Acheson at successive meetings with Bevin. Acheson had to apologize for this inability to provide detailed peace proposals, but British sources acknowledge that '[t]he Americans were the masters of Japan ... they could therefore make the peace'. UK record of Bevin-Acheson meeting (London), 10 April 1950, Bevin papers (FO800/449).

14 Stewart Alsop was less optimistic. See his 'Matter of Fact' column, 22 May, entitled 'Dangerous Deadlock', *New York Herald Tribune*, 22 May 1950. On Japanese reactions, see *New York Times*, 20 May 1950.

15 Ronald W. Pruessen *John Foster Dulles: The Road To Power* (New York, 1982), p. 448.

16 *Ibid.*, p. 454.

17 Truman statement of 14 September, reported in *New York Times*, 15 September 1950.

18 Dulles to Esler Dening, 23 September 1950, FJ1021/128(FO371/83833). Dening's influence within the Foreign Office was to lead to his appointment as the first postwar British ambassador to Tokyo.

19 By June 1950 MacArthur could write that 'despite Japan's constitutional renunciation of war its right to self defense in case of predatory attack is implicit and inalienable. In such a situation Japan must muster all of its available human and material resources in support of the security forces committed to its defense.' MacArthur memorandum on 'Concept Governing

Security in Post-War Japan', 23 June 1950, MacArthur Memorial Archives, RG 5, SCAP peace treaty file, Box 88.

20 On the tangled question of the US policy towards the PRC, see: Nancy Tucker, *Patterns in the Dust* (New York, 1983); Dorothy Borg and Waldo Heinrichs (eds.), *Uncertain Years* (New York, 1980); and Robert M. Blum, *Drawing the Line* (New York, 1982).

21 Sebald's comment on Diet resolution of 28 November 1948 in report to State Department, 9 December 1948, 740.0011 PW (Peace)/12-948, RG 59, Box 3593.

22 Dulles memorandum, 6 July 1950, Dulles papers, Box 49, MacArthur file, Princeton.

23 First meeting, Council on Foreign Relations study group report on Japanese Peace Treaty Problems 23 October 1950. Borton was the secretary of a group that included Kades, Dooman, Draper, Allison and Reischauer.

24 *Ibid.*

25 For a discussion of the Socialist party's approach, see Allan B. Cole, George O. Totten and Cecil H.Uyehara, *Socialist Parties in Postwar Japan* (New Haven), pp. 32-6, 42-8; also the Peace Issues Discussion Group's report 'On Peace – 1950', reprinted in *Peace Research in Japan, 1976* (Tokyo, 1977). The 1950 document was drafted by Maruyama Masao.

26 On the history of the ideological twists, see Arthur Stockwin, *The Japanese Socialist Party and Neutralism* (Melbourne, 1968).

27 Japan had hoped for an agreement corresponding to the newly devised NATO model.

28 It worried George Kennan too.

29 See Narasimha Murthy *India and Japan: Dimensions of their Relations* (New Delhi, 1986), pp. 274, 414-15.

30 Robert Fearey 'Summary of Negotiations Leading up to the Conclusion of the Treaty of Peace with Japan', 18 September 1951, in Thomas W. Burkman (ed.), *The Occupation of Japan: The International Context* (Norfolk, Va., 1984), p. 295.

31 Truman to Arthur Krock (unsent), 11 September 19652, in Robert H. Ferrell (ed.), *Off the Record* (Harmondsworth, 1980), p. 270.

32 See Marie D. Strazar 'Japanese Efforts to Influence a Peace Settlement, 1945-1951', in Burkman (ed.), *Occupation of Japan*.

33 In addition, Dulles, Eden and Dening all possessed short tempers. It is a wonder that there ever was a treaty.

34 See Kosaka Masataka, *Saisho Yoshida Shigeru* (Tokyo, 1968).

35 Sansom interview with MacArthur, 17 January 1951, FJ1019/3(FO371/92521). Sansom's scepticism over Japan had existed since he first began considering Japan's long-term future during the war. See, for example, his article, 'Can Japan Be Reformed?' *Far Eastern Survey*, 2 November 1949.

36 Sansom interview, *ibid.*

37 Acheson executive session Senate Foreign Relations Committee, 10 January 1950, in *The Senate Foreign Relations Committee's Historical Series, vol. viii, Reviews of the World Situation: 1949-1950* (New York, 1979), p. 135.

38 See extracts from the sixth and final meeting of the Study Group on

Japanese Peace Treaty problems (25 May 1951) in M. A. Guhin, *John Foster Dulles: A Statesman and His Times* (New York, 1972), appendix A.

39 See Buckley, 'Joining the Club: The Japanese Question and Anglo-American Peace Diplomacy, 1950–1951', *Modern Asian Studies* (April 1985).

40 Yoshitsu concludes his findings on this saga by calling it 'a most curious ending to a most curious succession of events'. Yoshitsu *op. cit.* p. 83. On the British repercussions, see Buckley, *Occupation Diplomacy*, pp. 176–7, and David Carlton, *Anthony Eden* (London, 1985), pp. 303–4. See also Reinhard Drifte, *The Security Factor in Japan's Foreign Policy, 1945–1952* (Sussex, 1983), pp. 126–31.

41 Reischauer, 19 October 1949, 740.0011 PW (peace)/10–1949, State Dept. records, National Archives.

42 Stanley S. Carpenter, American vice-consul Kobe, on 'US Army Morale in Kobe', 16 June 1949. 740.0019 Control (J)/6–1649 (RG 59, Box 3826), State Dept. records, National Archives. The same report spoke of high VD rates, drug peddling and blackmarketeering that made Kobe 'the number one trouble spot in Japan'. The US Army had yet to be desegregated in this period.

43 A message from the commander-in-chief on 'The Japanese Peace and Security Treaties', GHQ publication, September 1951. The code of conduct advised that soldiers would become guests in Japan and that they ought to 'get acquainted with Japan and the Japanese people' and 'respect the Japanese way of life. Their culture was already old when Columbus was born.'

44 Max Bishop to Butterworth and Allison, 7 February 1949, FW 740.0019 Control (Japan)/2–1649 (RG 59, Box 3825), State Dept. records. Allison minuted enthusiastically on Bishop's report that the US army be reduced to purely garrison duties: 'this is the best piece yet on the occupation'.

3 Inequality: the 1950s

1 John Dower's important book *War without Mercy* (New York, 1986) touches on some of the factors behind this transformation. It may be that additional ones, such as American benevolence over food supplies, rapid rotation back to the United States of those who had served in the Pacific fighting, the fact that with the major exception of Okinawa it had not been necessary to engage in combat on the Japanese homeland and the retention of a modified role for the Emperor could also be cited. Perhaps, too, the propaganda war made less impact than Dower attempts to show. The hatreds he graphically portrays in the media might be contrasted with letters from combatants. It is difficult to imagine that race really determined the fighting. The Nazi–Soviet campaigns on the Eastern front were as bestial as the Pacific fighting.

2 MacArthur was reported by the publisher and editor William R. Mathews as having said 'Japan is no longer a first-rate power. She is not even a third-rate power. Bad leadership brought her to her present humble position.' Mathews to Dulles, Boxes 49, MacArthur file, Dulles papers. A thorough analysis of MacArthur's concept of occupied Japan remains to be written. Idolatry and irreverence stand variously in the way.

3 National Intelligence Estimate, 29 May 1952, *FRUS*, 1952-54, vol. XIV, p. 1264.
4 *Ibid.*, p. 1265.
5 *The Manchester Guardian*, quoted in *Japan News*, 22 March 1952.
6 John Allison, report on tour of South East Asia, September - November 1952, copy to F. S. Tomlinson, Foreign Office, F10345/15(FO371/99218).
7 General Ridgway to the Department of the Army, 9 April 1952, *FRUS, 1950-54, Vol. XIV*, p. 1236.
8 *Ibid.* Ridgway recommended to his government that a public statement be issued to ally doubts once the security pact had come into effect. He also argued for American encouragement and assistance over Japan's future entry into the United Nations and alignment between Japanese and South Korean military units.
9 Allison report, note 6 above.
10 Makato Momoi, 'Basic Trends in Japanese Security Policies' in Robert A. Scalapino (ed.), *The Foreign Policy of Modern Japan* (Berkeley, 1977), p. 344. The suggestion that tanks were called 'special purpose vehicles' is denied by Inoki Masamichi. See his letter to the *New Statesman*, 16 September 1978.
11 For an early example of this thesis, see Martin Weinstein, *Japan's Postwar Defense Policy, 1947-1968* (New York, 1971).
12 *Japan News*, 11 January 1951. Even that staunchest of anti-Communists and determined rabble-rouser Akao Bin had difficulty in speaking up in support of permitting US bases in Japan.
13 See, for example, Dening's comment that 'the American Forces take their own line regardless of Japanese susceptibilities'. Dening to W. D. Allen (FO), 10 January 1956, FJ10345/2(FO371/121042).
14 'The Japanese Peace and Security Treaties', (SCAP, GHQ, Tokyo 1951) The 'code of conduct' enjoined GIs to 'respect the Japanese way of life. Their culture was already old when Columbus was born. When you're driving through Japanese villages, remember that their main street is very like American community centres - the New England village green, or the mid-Western county-house square. Don't speed through, scattering dust in all directions, as well as the inhabitants'.
15 The British embassy in Tokyo reported on Yoshida's Diet performance after the Ikeda-Robertson meetings that 'the [Yoshida] Government in short seem to have abdicated any claim to leadership on this issue and to be content to be borne along by a tide which seems near to overwhelming them'. A. S. Halford to John Pilcher, 4 November 1953, FJ1192/100(FO371/10594).
16 Dening, 'Annual Report for 1954', FJ1011/1(FO371/115220).
17 George Murakami, *Asahi Evening News*, 3 August 1987.
18 See Kosaka Masataka's *Saisho Yoshida Shigeru* (Tokyo, 1968) for a rebuttal of earlier attacks.
19 Yoshida may have played up the past when talking to British figures in order to regain their confidence. Thanks to the obduracy of British governments in the 1950s, his attempts to invoke the 1930s got nowhere with Eden or the Foreign Office.

20 *Asahi Shimbun* statistics on House of Representatives ratification vote, quoted in Igarashi, 'Peace-Making and Party Politics: The Formation of the Domestic Foreign-Policy System in Postwar Japan'.

21 *Asahi Shimbun* public opinion surveys 12, 13, 14 September 1951, enclosed in George Clutton's despatch to the Foreign Office, 28 September 1951, FJ1022/1432(FO371/92600). The lack of interest among Japanese respondees is a humbling commentary for politicians, diplomats and historians alike. When asked 'what impressed you the most at the San Francisco peace conference?' the largest group to reply said 'no particular impression' and again when asked 'what do you think are the serious post-treaty problems of Japan?' the biggest response was 'don't know'.

22 Kenneth Younger's report on his meeting with Yoshida, 3 September 1951, FJ1022/1334(FO371/92594). Younger was the *de facto* head of the British delegation since Secretary Morrison was on holiday in Norway at the start of the conference.

23 Andrei Gromyko, 4 September 1951, quoted in Rodger Swearingen, *The Soviet Union and Postwar Japan* (Stanford, 1978), p. 78. On the Soviet position from 1945 to 1956, see R. K. Jain, *Japan's Postwar Peace Settlements* (Atlantic Highlands, N.J.), chapter 3, pp. 40–54; also John Stephan on Soviet policy before San Francisco in his chapter included in Hosoya Chihiro (ed.), *Japan and Postwar Diplomacy in the Asian-Pacific Region* (IUJ, Niigata, 1984).

24 Reparations to south-east Asian nations were not completed until July 1976. The subject was both politically controversial in Asia and immensely complicated.

25 On the creation of the National Police Reserve, see John Welfield, 'Japanese Rearmament, 1945–1955', in Hosoya Chihiro (ed.), *Japan and Postwar Diplomacy in the Asian-Pacific Region*.

26 John Welfield, *The Postwar International Order and the Origins of the Japanese–American Security Treaty* (Canberra, 1982), pp. 55.

27 Japanese documents on the Dulles-Yoshida talks of February 1951 have not been released. The *Tokyo Shimbun* is regarded by experts as having published an authentic version in May 1977. See comments by Hosoya Chihiro in his article 'Japan's Response to US Policy on the Japanese Peace Treaty: The Dulles–Yoshida Talks of January–February 1951', *Hitotsubashi Journal of Law and Politics*, December 1981.

28 Memorandum by Acting Director of the Office of Northeast Asian Affairs on Allison's remarks to Department of Defense, 18 February 1954, *FRUS, 1952–1954, Vol. XIV*, p. 1609.

29 Eisenhower was speaking within the context of reorganizing the administration of Okinawa. He said that such issues 'would become urgent only when our forces were removed from Japan and Okinawa became the more important base'. Memorandum of NSC meeting. 17 February 1954, *FRUS Vol. XIV, 1952–1954*, p. 1608. This was, of course, a view that MacArthur had strenuously supported during most of the occupation. British diplomats in Tokyo thought that 'if the Japanese continue their present tactics and anti-American feeling increases, there may come a time when they will be tempted to enforce the threat'. Dening, Foreign Office, 5 August 1953, FJ1013/16(FO 371/105362).

30 See Dower, *War without Mercy*, pp. 389–95.
31 Ashida comments to Yoshida during Lower House budget debate, *Tokyo Evening News*, 31 July 1953. Ashida was in tears when he spoke of the confusion surrounding the role and morale of the National Safety Force personnel. Yoshida continued to insist that the US–Japan security pact would remain the basic tenet for Japan's defence.
32 Roger Makins report on Dulles' conversation to Foreign Office, 11 August 1953, FJ1081/32(FO371/105377).
33 Auer, *Postwar Rearmament*. The four advances, according to Auer, for rebuilding Japan's navy were: (i) the transfer of US naval vessels to Japan in January 1953, (ii) the legislation of 1 July 1954 that created the Defense Agency Establishment Law and the Self-Defence Forces law, (iii) the May 1957 Basic National Defence Policy statement on methods to be employed to prevent aggression (both direct and indirect) and, 'once invaded, to repel it', and (iv) the approval in June 1957 of the first long-range defence programme.
34 Statistics contained in Douglas H. Mendel, Jr., *The Japanese People and Foreign Policy* (Westport, CT, 1971), p. 88.
35 Churchill to Chiefs of Staff, 21 April 1953, FJ1192/22(FO371/105391).
36 For a detailed study of the road to the 1957 Australia–Japan Commerce Agreement, see Alan Rix, *Coming to Terms: The Politics of Australia's Trade with Japan 1945–57* (Sydney, 1986).
37 Quote in Osamu Ishii, 'United States Policy toward Japan in 1952–1954', *Kyoto American Studies Summer Seminar Specialists Conference 1986* (Kyoto, 1986), p. 114. See also R. Ferrell (ed.) *The Diary of James C. Hagerty* (Bloomington, Ind, 1983) pp. 70 and 111
38 Roger Dingman 'Alliance in Crisis: The Lucky Dragon Incident and Japanese–American Relations, 1954–1955', in Warren I. Cohen and Akira Iriye (eds.), *The Great Powers in East Asia: 1953–1960* (New York, 1990).
39 US embassy Tokyo to State Dept., 12 April 1954, *FRUS, 1952–54, Vol. XIV, part 2*, cited in footnote p. 1633. The Eisenhower administration was also having its share of troubles with the Atomic Energy Commission and what is now referred to as the scientific community.
40 John M. Allison, *Ambassador from the Prairie* (Tokyo, 1975), p. 263. Allison in retirement regretted that he had not made a speedier apology to the Japanese government. He spoke initially only of his 'concern' and was repeatedly chastised by the Japanese press for this slight.
41 Thomas R. Havens, *Fire Across the Sea: The Vietnam War and Japan, 1965–1975* (Princeton, NJ, 1987), p. 9. A multi-million signature drive demonstrated that virtually any Japanese would be prepared to put his or her name to a petition opposing nuclear weapons. The campaign began as a non-partisan affair among housewives in one of Tokyo's most affluent suburbs.
42 *FRUS, 1952–1954, Vol. XIV*, p. 1643.
43 *Ibid.*, p. 1644.
44 A study of Dulles' attitudes towards Japan is still awaited. His vision of Japan appears to have been a contradictory one of a nation capable of great international responsibilities but simultaneously hampered by the fact that 'Japan was a desperately poor country and it should not be pressed too

194

hard to reestablish a large military force until its economy had grown more healthy'.

45 Undated memorandum quoted in Dower, *War without Mercy*, p. 473.

46 *Ibid.*, p. 471.

47 *Asahi Shimbun*, interview, 7 January 1954.

48 See minutes from British officials following receipt of translation of the USSR-Japan joint declaration 31 October 1956. FJ10388/65(FO371/121041).

49 Two rival assessments are those of Donald C. Hellmann, *Japanese Domestic Politics and Foreign Policy: The Peace Agreement with the Soviet Union* (Berkeley, 1969), and Hiroshi Kimura, *Diplomatic Normalization between Japan and the USSR (1956): Background, Process and Assessment*, Paper presented to the conference on American East Asian relations in the Eisenhower era, Bellagio, Italy, September 1987.

50 *Department of State Bulletin*, 24 September 1956. See also Dulles' comments at press conference of 2 October at which he said that, although it was primarily a Japanese responsibility, any settlement should not 'infringe upon our rights under the Japanese peace treaty'. *New York Times*, 3 October 1956.

51 Professor Kimura distinguishes between the 'London' and 'Adenauer' formulae for tackling the USSR by Japan. The first approach – named after the venue for the earlier talks which assumed that the Soviet Union would be amenable to territorial discussions – was later replaced by a weaker diplomacy that downplayed the islands issue. The provisional fisheries deal was dependent on some diplomatic exchange later; prior to this Tokyo had wanted to talk about fish after a peace treaty.

52 The immediate American diplomatic response was to predict that the Soviet Union would now increase its subversive activities, propaganda outlets and espionage rings in Japan. It needs to be recalled that the USSR already had an established mission in Tokyo through its role in the Allied occupation.

53 Hellmann's opinion that 'the Soviet held the diplomatic initiative from the outset' thanks to the divisions inside the conservatives' camp is almost certainly correct but, despite the chaos of rival political shifts interfering continually with policy, it remained the case that much was accomplished. Some later premiers have been sufficiently assertive also to bypass the LDP's constraints.

54 Quoted in Kimura, *Diplomatic Normalization*.

55 Dulles to Eisenhower, 1 December 1954, *FRUS, 1952–1854, Vol. XIV*, p. 1793. Dulles also noted that though the US held that the Habomais were not part of the Kuriles, it was unfortunate that the 'MacArthur line' had left them within the Soviet occupation zone.

56 William Sebald's remarks as reported by Arthur de la Mare to the Foreign Office, 31 October 1956, FJ10338/66(FO371/121041). Sebald said resignedly that the 'Russians were there and if they remained there much longer they would acquire a sort of prescriptive right by virtue of possession'. He felt 'there was probably nothing doing'.

57 Etorofu and Kunashiri's future should logically have been based on whether they were part of the Kurile island chain or not. If they were found to be so, then the Japanese case falls apart.

58 The *People's Daily*, 21 October 1956. The Soviet press noted that the US feared a Japanese deal with the USSR because this might well presage similar plans for the PRC. *Izvestia*, 2 September 1956.

59 For a very useful discussion of People's diplomacy, see Chae-Jin Lee, *Japan Faces China* (Baltimore, 1976), pp. 64–82.

60 *Ibid.*, p. 9. Only 54.1 per cent knew that Japan did not have diplomatic relations. The same percentage gathered that Beijing was not a member of the United Nations, while 80 per cent were aware that the PRC had exploded nuclear weapons.

61 See Qing Semei, 'The Eisenhower Administration and Changes in Western Embargo Policy against China, 1954–1958', in Cohen and Iriye op. cit.

62 Chalmers Johnson, 'The Patterns of Japanese Relations with China, 1952–1982' *Pacific Affairs*, autumn 1986. On the Japanese embargo cooperation with the USA, see Yoko Yasuhara, 'Japan, Communist China, and Export Controls in Asia, 1948–52', *Diplomatic History*, winter 1986.

63 Johnson, 'Patterns of Japanese Relations'.

64 Eisenhower to Cabinet, 6 August 1954, cited in Qing Semei, 'Eisenhower Administration'. The president was acting in response to warnings from Tokyo over the deteriorating state of the Japanese economy and its balance of payments difficulties. He claimed to see this switch over permitting fewer restrictions on Sino-Japanese trade as a means whereby the USSR and the PRC might be split, since it would divide Beijing from economic linkage to Moscow. (A similar argument had frequently been put to the American government by Britain and invariably rejected.)

65 For statistics on the meagre level of Sino–Japanese trade 1954–1971, see table in Peter G. Mueller and Douglas A. Ross, *China and Japan – Emerging Global Powers* (New York, 1975), p. 41. Until 1964, Japan ran an annual trade deficit with the PRC.

4 Crisis: revision of the security treaty

1 'Japanese Public Opinion. Mid-1956', forwarded by Dulles to Eisenhower, Japan 1953–56 (1), Dwight D. Eisenhower Presidential Papers (Anne Whitman File), International Series, Box No. 38.

2 *Ibid.* (underlined in original). The report noted (in an analysis where, after the first sentence, the word Britain could frequently have been substituted for Japan) '[M]illions of Japanese, as soldiers of pre-1945 colonizers, have had personal experience in China. The Japanese believe they know China and the Chinese well. There is a common notion that "Communist China" is almost a contradiction in terms; that the Chinese can never be "Communist" in the sense that this term is applied by Japanese to the Russians, for example. Even professional Japanese diplomats believe that Peiping can be split from Moscow by peaceful means'.

3 'State Department Interest and Participation in Matters Concerning Japanese Rearmament', (top secret) security information, 7 April 1952, Lot File 55D 282, RG 59, National Archives, Washington, DC.

4 John Allison, 17 December 1952 on review of Far Eastern Programs NSC 135, *ibid.* (note 3).

5 Minute by Bureau of Far Eastern Affairs, State Department, on 'Budget

Bureau action on Fiscal Year 1954, Mutual Security Program for the Far East', 18 December 1952, Lot File 55D 282, RG 59.

6 For contemporary press comment, see Gordon Walker 'The Japanese Road to Rearmament', *Christian Science Monitor*, 28 July 1958, and 'Japan Climbs Back to Sun from War's Shadow', *ibid*, 23 June 1958. See also Dower, *Empire and Aftermath*, op. cit. for a critical account of early moves to rearm. For an alternative view for the position as of 1960, see *US Army Area Handbook for Japan* (Washington DC, 1964), pp. 802–15.

7 *Izvestia*, quoted in *Japan Times*, 18 January 1958.

8 *Manchester Guardian*, 17 May 1958 and *Soviet News*, 20 June 1958.

9 *Soviet News*, 23 May 1958.

10 Chinese press attention to Japan–US military ties and Kishi's domestic difficulties appears more concentrated than the USSR's. See *Hsinhua* reports 19 November, 23 November and 5 December 1958.

11 For texts of the NBC broadcasts by Cecil Brown and Diet responses, see *Japan Times* 17 October 1958.

12 *Ibid*.

13 Top secret Security Information 'Department of State Draft Analysis of Japanese Attitudes', 27 May 1952, lot file 55D282, RG 59.

14 *Ibid*.

15 *Ibid*. The report also noted 'the difference between Japanese and American intellectual traditions' and the clash over opposing social value systems. National stereotypes were, however, occasionally similar with regard to third parties. Two months prior to the Psychological Strategy Board's survey on exchange took place in Washington between Ambassador Araki Eikichi and Secretary of Defense Lovett. When Lovett stated that 'the North Koreans are a particularly primitive and barbaric type of people', Araki quickly agreed, 'indicating that all Koreans are the same. However, the North Koreans are particularly difficult.' Memorandum by Charles A. Sullivan on Lovett–Araki meeting, 20 August 1952, *FRUS, 1952–1954, Vol. XIV*, p. 1315.

16 'Dept. of State Draft Analysis of Japanese Attitudes'.

17 Ambassador Allison to Lieutenant General Carter B. Magruder, Chief of Staff, HQ, Far East Command, Tokyo, 28 September 1954, 611.94/10–1254, Box 2865, RG 59. Magruder had been military advisor to the Dulles mission that paved the way to the San Francisco peace conference, while Allison had been its senior State Dept. Representative.

18 See Buckley, *Europe in the Pacific: The EC and Contemporary Asian–Pacific Relations* (IUJ, Niigata, 1986).

19 'A Preliminary Reappraisal of United States Policy With Respect to Japan', 25 October 1954, 611.94/10–2554, Box 2865, RG 59.

20 *Ibid*.

21 The US embassy complained that lack of internal security gave 'the communists and their apparatus of neutralists, pacifists, innocents, and dupes a remarkable opportunity for agitation, propaganda, and economic disruption. They have used this opportunity fully, and there has been since 1949 a steady seepage in internal political influence away from the conservatives toward an immature and unstable left.' Similar complaints

were voiced in two reports of 19 May 1954. See 'Recommended Attitude of the US toward Yoshida' and 'Recommended US Policy toward Japan', 611.94/6–754, Box 2872, RG–59.

22 USPOLAD, Tokyo, 'Japanese Reaction to the Conclusion of the Administrative Agreement', 14 March 1952, 611.94/3–1452, Box 2868, RG–59.

23 *Ibid.*

24 USPOLAD, Tokyo, 10 April 1952, 611.94/4–952, Box 2868, RG–59.

25 Underlined in original. Ambassador Murphy to State Dept., 9 May 1952, 611.94/5–952, Box 2868, RG–59, recounting a most detailed picture of sensational Japanese media attacks on US military behaviour. Murphy was sensitive to concern that in the event of Soviet–American conflict in east Asia it might be Japan that would become the battlefield with Japan experiencing devastation once again. John Allison wrote to the Pentagon after receipt of Murphy's cable to urge that 'continued indoctrination of United State forces and their dependents in Japan as to the properties [sic] and values of Japanese society' be maintained.

26 Bradley and Collins quoted at Dept. of State–Joint Chiefs of Staff meeting, Washington, 2 April 1952, *FRUS, 1952–54, Vol. XIV, p. 1227*. The talks concerned the future of Okinawa and US military and diplomatic eagerness to stay put.

27 Sebald, 2 April 1952, *FRUS, 1952–1954, Vol. XIV*, p. 1226. For Sebald's later views on Okinawa, see William J. Sebald and C. Nelson Spinks, *'Japan: Prospects, Options and Opportunities'* (Washington, DC, 1967), p. 89.

28 Allison to State Dept., 21 September 1956, 611.94/9–2156 Box 2578, RG–59; the despatch was described as 'a combined Embassy product'. Marshall Green's comments on the above from the Bureau of Far Eastern Affairs were reported in 611.94/10–1256, *ibid*. He argued that postwar US–Japan relations had worked on a four-year cycle and that now was the moment to once again prevent 'souring' by improving the military links.

29 *Ibid.*

30 *Ibid.*

31 *Ibid.*

32 *Ibid.*

33 *Ibid.*

34 *Ibid.*

35 *Ibid.*

36 The American embassy in London cabled that United Press reports quoted Dulles as having told Foreign Minister Shigemitsu of this and that the latter was 'stunned'.

37 Memorandum of conversation between Minister Kuraishi Tadao and Robert Murphy, Deputy Under Secretary, State Dept., 5 July 1956, 611.94/ 7–556, Box 2578, *ibid*.

38 Department of State, Office of Intelligence Research, *The Growing Role of Domestic Politics in the Formulation of Japan's Foreign Policy*, No. 7289, 5 July 1956, and *Recent and Prospective Foreign Relations of Japan (1956–1961)* No. 7331, 12 September 1956, (with FO comments) copies in FJ1022/5 and FJ1022/7 (FO371/121036).

39 *Recent and Prospective Foreign Relations of Japan (1956–1961)*, *ibid*.

40 George R. Packard, *Protest in Tokyo* (Princeton, 1966).
41 Saburo Okita, *Japan in the World Economy* (Tokyo, 1975), pp. 103–18. Okita headed the Economic Planning Agency's Over-all Planning Bureau in 1960 when the Ikeda cabinet adopted the national income doubling plan. See also Okita's *Japan's Challenging Years* (Canberra, 1983), pp. 78–80.
42 On the revival of the Japanese economy, the choice of Japanese and English-language material is embarrassingly large when compared with the publications on postwar political and diplomatic affairs.
43 Douglas H. Mendel, *The Japanese People and Foreign Policy* (Westport, CT 1971), p. 49, reporting on the author's interview with Ambassador MacArthur in December 1957.
44 On the rapid growth era from San Francisco to the first oil shock, see Takafusa Nakamura, *Economic Development of Modern Japan* (Tokyo, 1985).
45 Dulles to Minister of State Kenneth Younger, 5 June 1951, cited in Buckley, 'Joining the Club: The Japanese Question and Anglo–American Peace Diplomacy, 1949–1951, *Modern Asian Studies*, April 1985. The latest documents released on Kishi suggest that MacArthur ordered his Legal Section to consider indicting nineteen Japanese Class A suspects on lesser crimes to speed up hearings. *Japan Times*, 28 Dec 1987.
46 See Packard, *Protest in Tokyo*, pp. 47–54, for an account of Kishi's career.
47 Progress Report (top secret) on Japan (NSC 5516/1), to Walter Robertson, Assistant Secretary for Far Eastern Affairs, 12 June 1956, 611.94/6–1256, *ibid*. The issues dividing the US and Japan centred on 'the Bonin islanders, war criminals, territorial issues, the tendency to establish new relations with the USSR and Communist China, Pacific fisheries, security arrangements, Japanese trade, and Asian development'.
48 MacArthur to State Dept., reporting Japanese text of 'analysis of causes impeding smooth cooperation between Japan and US', 10 April 1957, 611.94/4–1057, Box 2578, RG–59.
49 MacArthur to State Dept., *ibid*. The ambassador cabled that 'I shall be glad [to] hear views US Government of these and any other points which it may like [to] take up', which suggests that his earlier briefings may have been less than complete.
50 *Ibid*.
51 *Ibid*. (punctuation added). The Japanese text added that these public fears 'may stem largely from misunderstandings and misapprehensions' but hoped that joint studies might contribute to the removal of what clearly were grave concerns.
52 *Ibid*.
53 MacArthur to Washington, 13 April 1957, 611.94/4–1357, Box 2578, RG–57.
54 *Ibid*. MacArthur cited as an example the differences in Japanese press handling of British and Soviet nuclear test programmes.
55 Dulles to MacArthur, 18 April 1957, 611.94/4–1857, *ibid*.
56 For MacArthur's reply see his cable of 19 April, 611.94/4–1957, *ibid*.
57 MacArthur to Dulles, 17 April 1957, 611.94/4–1757, *ibid*.
58 Dulles to MacArthur, 8 May 1957, 611.94/5–857, *ibid*.
59 *Ibid*.
60 *Ibid*.

61 *Ibid.*

62 Fukuda statement to MacArthur during a breakfast meeting on US–Japanese relations, 22 April 1957. Fukuda stressed Japanese sensitivities that war 'must be avoided no matter how high the cost' and spoke of US–Japan ties in two phases: pre-Constitutional change and after, with domestic economic growth in the former and 'positive' Pacific cooperation later.

63 MacArthur–Kishi conversation, 16 May 1957, 611.94/5–16557, *ibid.*

64 *Ibid.*

65 'Follow-Up Actions, Kishi Visit 1957', 8 July 1957, 611.94/7–527, *ibid.*

66 MacArthur to Under Secretary, 17 September 1957 (underlined in the original).

67 *Ibid.*

68 Dulles to Eisenhower, memorandum on Kishi's official visit to the United States, 12 June 1957, Box 31, Japan 1957–59 (4) Eisenhower Library.

69 *Ibid.*

70 Operations Coordinating Board Report on Japan (NSC 5516/1), 23 July 1958, Eisenhower papers White House Series, OSANSA (NSC Policy Paper Subseries), Box 15.

71 *Ibid.*

72 *Ibid.*

73 Dulles to Ichimada, Washington, 26 September 1957, 611.94/9–2657, *ibid.* It was a bizarre meeting with Ichimada worrying about a Soviet economic offensive in south east Asia resulting from superpower disarmament agreements. The US generally poured cold water on Tokyo's attempts in the 1950s to encourage economic development in the region.

74 MacArthur to State Dept., 13 October 1959, 611.94/10–1359, Box 2580, RG–59.

75 MacArthur to Dulles, 5 June 1958, seen by Eisenhower, copy in Box 30, Japan 1957–59(2) file, Eisenhower Library.

76 *Ibid.*

77 *Ibid.* Macarthur wanted Japan to defend the home islands, the Ryukyus and Bonins.

78 Operations Coordinating Board Report on Japan (NSC 5516/1) 8 April 1959, White House series OSANSA (NSC policy paper subseries), Box 15.

79 Eisenhower-Kishi meeting, 19 January 1960, Box 31, Japan 1960 (4) file.

80 MacArthur to State Dept., 13 October 1959, note 74 above.

81 See John Baylis, *Anglo–American Defence Relations 1939–1984* (London, 1984), and Lewis J. Edinger, *West German Politics* (New York, 1985) for accounts of how the United States handled two of its European allies in the security area. Anglo-American ties have probably been at their closest in the defence field.

82 MacArthur to State Dept., 13 October 1959, note 74 above.

83 MacArthur to Robertson, 4 May 1959, 611.94/5–459, Box 2580, RG–59.

84 See Packard, *Protest in Tokyo*, pp. 70–81 for an account of the in-fighting.

85 Hiroshi Fujimoto (ed.), *Fifty Years of Light and Dark* (Tokyo, 1975), p. 301.

86 *Japan Times*, 8 December 1958, cited in Packard, *Protest in Tokyo*, footnote p. 73.

87 'The conservatives lost only 0.2% of the popular vote they had received in 1958' in the 1960 elections following the June crisis and actually gained 2

seats, while the Socialists lost 21. Nathaniel B. Thayer, *How the Conservatives Rule Japan* (Princeton, 1969), p. 118 and Fujimoto, *Fifty Years*, p. 308.

88 For the ideological background to the history of a divided party, see Arthur Stockwin, *The Japanese Socialist Party and Neutralism* (Melbourne, 1968), particularly chapters 8 and 9. The fact that the JSP had moved considerably to the left by 1960 resulted in Nishio Suehiro pulling his faction out to form the small Democratic Socialist Party.

89 The Japan Communist Party would disagree; it felt that the JSP's concentration on attacking Kishi overlooked the American presence in Japan.

90 The Supreme Court ruled that the US forces aided Japan, since it alone did not possess sufficient power to defend itself and had, therefore, to rely on 'the peace-loving peoples of the world' for military assistance.

91 For text of the new security treaty, see appendix 2, pp. 176–8.

92 Constitutional and political difficulties on the Japanese side prevented this.

93 Eisenhower–Kishi Joint Communiqué 19, Japan 1960, text in Packard, *Protest in Tokyo*, appendix E.

94 The issue of what constituted 'prior consultation' was important since this would determine Japan's rights over the 'major changes' in deployment of US personnel and either equipment that Washington accepted as requiring Japan's consent. The opposition wanted this changed to 'prior agreement'. Much criticism was also attached to the ten-year term of the treaty; many felt this to be far too long.

95 For an overview of events in 1960 and after, see Frank Langdon, *Japan's Foreign Policy* (Vancouver, BC, 1973), particularly pp. 7–21 and 191–207.

96 For the Joint Declaration, see Packard, *Protest in Tokyo*, Appendix F. The press, in a volte face following the escalation of violence, now appealed for calm and for the LDP and opposition parties to cooperate 'to protect parliamentary democracy'.

97 Eisenhower to MacArthur, 22 June 1960, Japan Far East trip-cancelled (2) (folder 3) Box 32, International Series, Eisenhower Library.

98 MacArthur to Eisenhower via General Goodpaster, 10 June 1960, Japan Far East trip-cancelled (4) (folder 3) Box 32, International Series, Eisenhower Library.

99 *Ibid.*

100 *Ibid.*

101 *Ibid.*

102 See review by Tsunekawa Makoto of Douglas Mendel's *The Japanese People and Foreign Policy* in *Japan Quarterly*, July–September 1962.

103 Fringe rightists were responsible for attacking Kishi, Asanuma and Kawakami Jotaro, advisor to the JSP and former chairman.

104 Weinstein maintains that the LDP party has 'succeeded brilliantly' over its defense diplomacy, *Japan's Postwar Defense Policy*, p. 103.

105 Unlike NATO.

106 Weinstein admits that successors to Kishi 'have never explained the essential of this [defense] policy to the Japanese people or gained their support for it' (*Japan's Postwar Defense Policy*). If true, this would be a

damning remark by an author sympathetic to Japan's postwar remilitarization. See also Tadashi Azuga's analysis, Hitotsubashi Journal of Law &
Politics, Feb. 1985.

5 Readjustment: the 1960s

1 A generation later this is still true, though more surprising today.
2 Edwin O. Reischauer, 'The Broken Dialogue with Japan', Foreign Affairs
(October 1960). He admitted later (in his autobiography, My Life Between
Japan and America (Tokyo, 1986)) that it was less a case of broken dialogue
than no dialogue at all. Ambassador MacArthur had reason to feel
aggrieved at this statement.
3 Reischauer, My Life, p. 165.
4 Comments by Shirai Kensaku in the Australian Bicentennial Symposium
describing present Japan–Australia relations as comparable to the dis-
tortions that existed 'about twenty years ago' in US–Japan ties, Asahi
Evening News, 26 January 1988. In the 1960s the US distorted its picture by
reducing the size of its partner and the smaller power responded by
enlarging its vision of the USA. For a study of American perception of
postwar Japan, see Sheila K. Johnson, The Japanese Through American Eyes
(Tokyo, 1989).
5 Statistical information on the progress of the Japanese economy during the
1950s can be found in Edward F. Denison and William K. Chung, How
Japan's Economy Grew So Fast (Washington, DC, 1976). For a contemporary
analysis, see Okita Saburo's remarks in the same issue of Foreign Affairs
(October 1960) as Reischauer's criticisms of American policies towards
Japan. Okita, 'Japans' Economic Prospects', cites 'availability of an abundant supply of labour' as the first of his explanations for Japan's postwar
growth. It was a highly reassuring report for American readers that
suggested no major problems were in the offing, thanks to 'the free
economic system, based upon private initiative'.
6 Reischauer, My Life, p. 181. He said of Sato Eisaku – the brother and
successor to Ikeda – that he was 'a very jovial, friendly person, but I felt he
lacked the backbone of Ikeda'.
7 See, for example, remarks by Hans Baerwald on Ohira in Baerwald's Party
Politics in Japan (London, 1986), p. ix.
8 JSP Chairman Eda Saburo had attempted to rethink his party's policies, but
he was defeated in May 1965 by Sasaki Kozo. Reischauer had avoided
meeting Eda in order not to embarrass him.
9 For statement of JSP platform adopted at its 22nd national convention, 28
November 1962, see The Japan Annual of International Affairs 1962 (Tokyo,
1962), pp. 191–6. The complexities of JSP's ideological debate are discussed
in Stockwin.
10 On Professor Sakisaka, a party theoretician who advocated a campaign of
mass action, see his obituary in Japan Times, 23 January 1985.
11 For details of the test ban treaty negotiations see S. R. Ashton, In Search of
Détente (Basingstoke, 1989). The treaty of August 1963 was seen by both
China and France as evidence of global bipolarity that needed to be ended
as soon as possible.

12 Chinese government statement on test ban treaty 31 July 1963, *Peking Review*, 2 August 1963, quoted in Alan Lawrence, *China's Foreign Relations Since 1949* (London, 1975), p. 84. Beijing said that Kennedy's actions were 'diametrically opposed to the wishes of the peace-loving peoples of the world' and warned that the US had gained military superiority from the partial test-ban arrangements. For Mao Tse-tung's views expressed at Moscow in 1957, see 'We Must Not Fear Nuclear War' in Stuart Schram (ed.), *The Political Thought of Mao Tse-tung* (Harmondsworth, 1969), pp. 408–9.

13 The extent to which political neutralism can be maintained while adopting both very clear views on the behaviour of the United States in Asia and sympathy towards the PRC is for others to explain.

14 Reischauer, *My Life*, p. 194.

15 For the text of the payments agreement, see Ohira Zengo, 'Settlement of the USA's Postwar Assistance to Japan', in *The Japan Annual of International Affairs 1962*, pp. 144–7. For accounts of how GARIO (Government and Relief in Occupied Areas) funds were used and later calculations devised over Japanese repayment, see comments on Japanese trade in *The Occupation of Japan: Economic Policy and Reform*, pp. 270–316.

16 *The Japan Annual of International Affairs 1962*, p. 188.

17 Reischauer, *My Life*, p. 247.

18 Saeki Kiichi and Wakaizumi Kai, 'The Problems of Japan's Security', in Alastair Buchan (ed.), *China and the Peace of Asia* (New York, 1965), p. 217.

19 For the text of the 20 May 1957 decision, see Saeki and Wakaizumi, 'Problems', p. 221.

20 For American military comments on the evolution of the SDF in the 1960s, see *US Army Area Handbook for Japan* (Washington, DC, 1964) and James E. Auer, *The Postwar Rearmament of Japanese Maritime Forces, 1945–71* (New York, 1973).

21 'Most of our people entertain little fear of Communist China', observed Saeki and Wakizumi, and added that Japan could understand China better than the West thanks, in part, to intellectual respect and the view that 'China is not so difficult a country to deal with' ('Problems', p. 226).

22 Schram (ed.), *The Political Thought of Mao Tse-tung*, p. 413, statement of 12 January 1964.

23 *Ibid.*, message of 28 November 1964 to the Congolese people (Leopold-ville), p. 384.

24 For tabular information of both the first and second defence programmes of the Maritime Self-Defence Forces, see Auer, *Postwar Rearmament*, p. 156 (table 10.1) and p. 158 (table 10.2).

25 Aichi Kiichi, *Foreign Affairs* (October, 1969). US Ambassador Meyer would dedicate his memoirs of this period to Aichi.

26 Auer, *Postwar Rearmament*, p. 168.

27 See statistical evidence in Shiratori Rei, 'Image of the Major Parties in Japan, the LDP and the JSP', in Hosoya Chihiro and Ori Kan (eds.), *Japan Institute of International Affairs Annual Review, vol. 4, 1965–68* (Tokyo, 1969). Shiratori notes that '[w]hat workers look for from the JSP today is not an ideological and abstract discussion of foreign affairs but a substantial and

material improvement of their daily life'. The failure of both the LDP and JSP to formulate foreign policies in accord with any majority thinking should be noted.

28 The term is employed by Hidaka Rokuro in his work *The Price of Affluence* (Tokyo, 1984). The work traces, in chapter 4, the value changes of the postwar years in reaction to earlier statism. For the shifts in voter thinking on security questions during the 1960s, see Royama Michio, 'The Domestic Factors Affecting Japanese Foreign Policy: Problems of the Year 1970' in Hosoya and Ori.

29 See Okita Saburo, *Japan's Challenging Years*, pp. 78–9. The three objectives of the Ikeda plan ('Kokumin shotoku baizo keikaku') have been defined as '(1) Maximum growth (2) improvement of living standards (3) Full employment'. See Kosai Yutaka and Ogino Yoshitaro, *The Contemporary Japanese Economy* (London, 1984), p. 122.

30 International comparisons are discussed in Edward F. Denison and William K. Chung, *How Japan's Economy Grew So Fast* (Washington, DC, 1976). During the 1960s, Japan's GNP overtook that of Italy, France, Britain and West Germany. The prospect of eventually outrunning the United States then began to be discussed as Japan's economic confidence grew.

31 See Baerwald, *Party Politics in Japan*, chapter one, 'The Political Party System, 1955–1985', for factors behind the success of the LDP. Statistics on the relative party strengths of the LDP and the opposition can be found on pp. 42–3. The LDP was unchallenged until the 1976 election that followed in the wake of the Lockheed scandal.

32 *Ibid.*, p. 131. Fukuda Takeo's remarks in 1963 were an attack on Ikeda's style of parliamentary accommodation with the opposition parties.

33 Draft statement by National Security Planning Board on US Policy toward Japan, 20 May 1960, for NSC meeting 2 June 1960, NEC 6008, Eisenhower papers, White House series OSANSA (NSC policy paper subseries), Box 28.

34 *Ibid.*

35 *Ibid.*

36 *Ibid.*

37 See memorandum for the president on Civil Aviation Negotiations with Japan, 16 June 1965, NSF country file (Japan), Japan cables vol. 3 9/64–10/65, Box 250, Johnson Library.

38 US–Japan relations are reviewed in *The Administrative History of the Department of State*, vol. 1, chapter 7 (East Asia), Johnson Library.

39 In September 1967 Dean Rusk was still urging Johnson at a forthcoming meeting with Foreign Minister Miki to '[s]pell out the heavy burden we now shoulder for both the security and economic development of Asia'. Rusk memorandum for the president, 4 September 1967, confidential file CO 141, Johnson Library.

40 Sooner or later a presidential visit to Tokyo would have become essential if only for consideration of American prestige and the need to erase the 1960 fiasco.

41 President Johnson used Walt Rostow to organize departmental objectives in preparation for Sato's meetings at the White House.

42 MITI Minister Fukuda at third meeting of joint US–Japan Committee on Trade and Economic Affairs, Tokyo, 27 January 1964, Japan memos vol. 1 11/63–4/64, NSF country file (Japan) Box 250, Johnson Library.

43 *Ibid*.

44 Secretary Hodges, *ibid*.

45 *The Administrative History of the State Department*.

46 The US deficit in its balance of payments with Japan had reached $906 million by 1967.

47 The State Department writers noted that 'Japan's hesitancy to open its doors to US economic competition' hurt US ceramic tiles manufacturers, steel makers and car exporters. Somewhat charitably the same authors suggested that restrictive Japanese economic behaviour in the late 1960s could be seen as 'rooted in historical Japanese concern over foreign influence.' See *The Administrative History of the State Department*.

48 'The Future of Japan', State Dept policy outline, 26 June 1964, Japan cables, vol. 2 5/64–11/64, NSF country file (Japan), Box 250, Johnson Library.

49 *Ibid*.

50 George Ball to Secretary of State, 12 July 1961. Ball passed on Ikeda's point that there might be 'regression in US foreign economic policy. As Ikeda talks in Washington indicated, while Japanese growth phenomenal, the greater the growth the greater their need for markets.'

51 It is doubtful if Japanese governmental thinking had made a similar shift.

52 Unfortunately the European states tended to be defensive in their treatment of Japan and the invoking of article 35 of GATT in 1955 was a bitter blow to Japan. See Endymion Wilkinson, *Japan versus the West* (Harmondsworth, 1990), p. 168. Japan's entry into the OECD did not end the import restrictions of early postwar years.

53 *The Administrative History of the State Department*.

54 *Ibid*.

55 Walt Rostow to Johnson on 'Talks with the Japanese', 11 September 1967, Appointment File (diary backup) 9/13/67–9/21/67, Box 76, Johnson Library.

56 *Ibid*.

57 *Ibid*.

6 Shocks: economic and diplomatic reorientation

1 Henry Kissinger, *White House Years* (Boston, 1979), p. 335.

2 For an overview of the fighting, see Spector, *Eagle against the Sun*, pp. 532–40.

3 *US Army Area Handbook for Japan* (Washington, DC, 1964), p. 520. Japan agreed to turn their administration over to the United States for an indefinite period.

4 *Ibid*.

5 For a succinct description of Okinawan grievances, see the contribution by Robert K. Saka and Sakihara Mitsugu in the *Kodansha Encyclopedia of Japan* (Tokyo, 1983), vol. 6, pp. 88–91. See also Akio Watanabe, *The Okinawa Problem* (Melbourne, 197?).

6 I. M. Destler *et al.*, *Managing an Alliance* (Washington, Dc, 1976), p. 24.

7 Edwin O. Reischauer interview, John F. Kennedy Oral History Programme, JF Kennedy Library.

8 *Ibid.*

9 *Ibid.*

10 *Ibid.*

11 Data in Douglas H. Mendel, Jr., 'Japanese Views of Sato's Foreign Policy: The Credibility Gap', *Asian Survey*, July 1967.

12 Johnson replaced Reischauer in the autumn of 1966 and was in post until January 1969. He was succeeded by another career officer, Armin Meyer.

13 Thomas R. H. Havens, *Fire Across the Sea: The Vietnam War and Japan* (Princeton, NJ, 1987), p. 179. See also the chapter by John Welfield in *An Empire in Eclipse*, entitled 'Domestic Politics, Foreign Policy and the Reversion of Okinawa, 1960–1972'. He concludes that for Japan the reversion was not 'entirely without redeeming features'. On the extension of the security treaty, see Omori Shigeo, 'June 1970', *Japan Quarterly* (October 1970).

14 National Security Council meeting, 30 August 1967, NSC file, NSC mtgs file, Box 2, vol. 4, Tab 56, Johnson Library.

15 LBJ Appointments file (diary backup) 29 March 1967, Box 59. Also present and doing most of the talking was Representative Matsunaga. Johnson promised more economic aid to Okinawa and said of those Okinawans who were anti-American that 'this was true in many places and was just something we have to live with'.

16 W. W. Rostow to LBJ, 11 September 1967, President's appointment file (diary backup), Box 76. It was hoped that Japan would increase its purchases of US military equipment, provide more funding for the Asian Development Bank and a 'significant increase in Japanese economic assistance to South Vietnam, including enlarged private investment in such areas as small and medium industry'.

17 Secretary Robert McNamara to Johnson, 30 August 1967. *Ibid.*

18 Messages to Johnson, March 1966 from numerous Japanese sources, LBJ General CO 141, Japan, Box 48. For a detailed account of Japanese attitudes towards Vietnam see Thomas R. H. Havens, *Fire Across The Sea* (Princeton, 1987). There was to be no lasting damage to US–Japan relations from the Vietnam War and the parallels with the 1960 Ampo crisis should not be overstressed.

19 Johnson–Sato joint communiqué, 15 November 1967, LBJ Appointments file (diary backup), Box 82.

20 Press questions at background briefing on Johnson–Sato joint communiqué, *ibid.*

21 Talking points, Dean Rusk to Johnson, 13 November 1967, *ibid.*

22 *Ibid.*

23 *Ibid.*

24 McGeorge Bundy to the President, 'through' Walt Rostow, 23 May 1966, NS File subject file, LBJ Library, Box 51, National Security file. Bundy was then president of the Ford Foundation.

25 *Ibid.*

26 Kissinger, *White House Years*, p. 327.

27 *Ibid.*

28 *Ibid.* This should not be taken to imply that the claimed unity was total. The JCS were certainly in no hurry to surrender US rights to store nuclear weapons on the islands. On both American military and civilian thinking over reversion, see also the detailed study by Frederick L. Shiels, *America, Okinawa, and Japan: Case Studies for Foreign Policy Theory* (Washington, DC, 1990).

29 James H. Buck, 'Japan's Defense Options for the 1970's', *Asian Survey* (October 1970).

30 *Ibid.*

31 Destler and his collaborators argue that the Okinawa 'agreement on nuclear-free, home-level reversion was directed explicitly toward meeting broad Japanese domestic concerns' and note how several of the officials involved in the talks had earlier been involved in the security revision question. This, they maintain, 'reinforced their determination to avoid a replay of the 1960 crisis, and their already established personal relationships limited the range of potential misperception as the Okinawa talks proceeded'. Destler *et al.*, *Managing an Alliance*, p. 173.

32 Kissinger, *White House Years* p. 331. The private talks were held at the initiative of Sato, who neglected to inform his foreign minister Aichi Kiichi of their existence. Welfield, *Empire in Eclipse*, p. 245.

33 Kissinger, *White House Years*, p. 334. Former ambassador MacArthur said in 1990 that the Japanese government knew in 1960 that port calls by US ships carrying nuclear weapons would not be subject to prior consultation with Tokyo. He stated that Foreign Minister Fujiyama understood that the introduction of nuclear weapons only applied to their storage on Japanese territory. See *Japan Times*, 17 June 1990.

34 Kissinger, *White House Years*, p. 334.

35 Roger Morris, *Uncertain Greatness* (London, 1977), p. 105.

36 Armin H. Meyer, *Assignment: Tokyo* (Indianapolis, 1974), pp. 269–70. The issue was handled largely by the White House and Congress with the US embassy in the wings.

37 See, in particular, I. M. Destler, Hideo Sato and Haruhiro Fukui, *The Textile Wrangle: Conflict in Japanese–American Relations 1969–71* (Ithaca, NY, 1979).

38 Meyer, *Assignment: Tokyo*, p. 299.

39 See, for example, I. M. Destler and Hideo Sato (eds.), *Coping with US-Japanese Economic Conflicts* (Lexington, MA, 1982) and Stephen D. Cohen *Uneasy Partnership: Competition and Conflict in US–Japanese Trade Relations* (Cambridge, MA, 1985). The literature is now vast.

40 For the domestic political background to Nixon's textile diplomacy, see Destler, Sato and Fukui, *The Textile Wrangle*, chapter 3, 'From Campaign to Confrontation' (July 1968 – May 1969).

41 For US arguments and Japanese counter-claims over textiles in the autumn of 1969, see Destler, Sato and Fukui, *The Textile Wrangle*, pp. 109–10.

42 *Asahi Shimbun*, 26 June 1970, quoted in Destler, Sato and Fukui, *The Textile Wrangle*, p. 206. Others were less happy. The Japanese ambassador to Washington Shimoda Takeso resigned once the Miyazawa-Stans talks failed.

43 Sato Eisaku, farewell address to the Diet 17 June 1972, *In Quest of Peace and Freedom*, p. 216.

44 *Ibid.*, p. 217.

45 *Ibid.*

46 Roger Morris *Uncertain Greatness: Henry Kissinger and American Foreign Policy* (London, 1977), p. 105. Morris criticizes Kissinger for being 'an unquestioning accomplice in the original fiasco with the Japanese because he understood the trade issue no better than Nixon'.

47 Nixon in *Sunday Times*, 25 June 1989.

48 See, for example, Destler *et al.*, *The Textile Wrangle*, pp. 242–50. Peter Flanigan may have come close to gaining a settlement in his talks with Ambassador Ushiba in December 1970, although any US agreement would have been rather less than the textile industry had expected.

49 'I have no doubt that Sato was sincere in his pledges. He was far too intelligent to attempt such clumsy evasions, far too honorable to resort to tricks with a country that he genuinely liked and toward a President he respected. We had demanded too much of him; he promised more than he should have, and he was deeply embarrassed by his inability to deliver'. Kissinger, *White House Years*, p. 339. Wilbur Mills, chairman of the House Ways and Means committee, and Donald Kendall, chairman of Pepsi-Cola, both tried to solve the issue. For Kissinger's account of his efforts, see *White House Years*, pp. 335–40.

50 Peterson's doubts about the affair were firmly expressed in a speech to the Foreign Correspondents' Club of Japan nearly twenty years later.

51 Tanaka's role is examined in depth in Destler's work. See in particular, pp. 304–11.

52 Ratification of the arrangements of the reversion of Okinawa by the US Senate, rather than by presidential directed executive agreement, was widely seen as a deliberate threat to remind Tokyo of the consequences of failing to solve the textile issue.

53 Destler, *et al.*, *The Textile Wrangle*, p. 317.

54 Destler and Sato, *Coping with US-Japanese Economic Conflicts*, p. 271.

55 Meyer, *Assignment: Tokyo*, p. 112. Nixon's speech was televised the previous afternoon Pacific daylight time.

56 Kissinger, *White House Years*, p. 761. Meyer describes this rebuff to Japan as 'Asakai's nightmare'; referring to the earlier dread of Ambassador Asakai 'that he would wake up one morning and read in *The Washington Post* that the United States had recognized Peking and was negotiating diplomatic relations'. Meyer, *Assignment Tokyo*, p. 113. It is difficult to imagine the robust Asakai ever losing his sleep over even such a sensitive national issue.

57 Roger Morris, *Uncertain Greatness* (London, 1977), p. 204.

58 Contained in Nixon's 15 July 1971 remarks, for text, see Kissinger, *Memoirs*, vol. 1, pp. 759–60.

59 For Ambassador Meyer's analysis of Japanese views towards the PRC see *Assignment Tokyo*, pp. 115–18. On the LDP factional positions see Welfield, *An Empire in Eclipse*.

60 For careful analyses of the entire China question, see Wolf Mendl, *Issues in*

Japan's China Policy (London, 1978), and Chae-Jin Lee *Japan Faces China* (Baltimore, 1976).

61 Richard Nixon, *Memoirs*, vol. 2 (New York, 1978), p. 36.

62 *Ibid.*, p. 47. The joint communiqué was, as Kissinger put it, 'an extended statement of differences', particularly with regard to Taiwan.

63 Foreign Minister Ohira, *Asahi Shimbun* for 8 July 1972, cited in Chae-Jin Lee's *Japan Faces China*, p. 112.

64 For the text of the joint statement, see Chae-Jin Lee, *Japan faces China*, pp. 210–12.

65 Masayoshi Ohira, *Brush Strokes* (Tokyo, 1979), p. 100.

66 Ohira, *Brush Strokes*, p. 110.

67 The issue is debated by Welfield. See *An Empire in Eclipse* chapter 11, 'Japan, the United States and China, 1970–1972'.

68 See Foreign Minister Chen Yi's statement 29 September 1965, Alan Lawrence, *China's Foreign Relations since 1949* (London 1975), p. 149. In the summer of 1971 Chou En-lai insisted that Japan would in due course acquire nuclear weaponry; by 1973 he was reportedly in favour of the US–Japan Security Pact as a balancing factor against the Soviet Union.

69 *Ibid.*

70 Susan Hattis Rolef, 'The Changing Circumstances of Japan's Foreign Policy', *Asian Survey* (November 1976). Former Taiwanese and Japanese diplomats remained in place after ties were broken to man the new unofficial liaison offices. For discussion on the economic dimension of normalization, see Chae-Jin Lee, chapter 4, 'The Politics of Economic Cooperation'.

71 Meyer held that the Nixon shock was useful ammunition for anti-American groups within Japan and 'a few Japanese officials who found the president's surprise action a convenient scapegoat for other troubles besetting Japan' (*Assignment Tokyo*, p. 137).

72 The changes in US–Japan ties during this period are discussed in Ralph N. Clough's *East Asia and US Security* (Washington, DC, 1975), chapter six, 'Maintaining the Alliance with Japan'.

73 Kissinger, *White House Years*, p. 1052.

74 Meyer, *Assignment Tokyo*, p. 149.

75 *Izvestiia*, 13 May 1973, quoted in Rodger Swearingen *The Soviet Union and Postwar Japan* (Stanford, 1978), p. 201.

76 Kissinger suggests that the wording of this anti-hegemony clause was of American origin.

77 Gerald R. Ford, *A Time to Heal* (New York, 1980), pp. 204–5. Ford's memoirs make no further mention of US–Japan relations.

78 Ford and Secretary of State Kissinger felt that Tanaka would not be in office much longer. He resigned in December to be succeeded by Miki Takeo.

79 Edwin Reischauer's introduction to Priscilla Clapp and Morton H. Halperin (eds.), *United States-Japanese Relations: The 1970s* (Cambridge, MA, 1974), p. 2.

80 *Ibid.*, p. 4. For recent discussion of Japan's handling of the intricate normalization process with the PRC and the more recent past, see Jiang Wenran's review article, 'Understanding China's Relations with Japan and

the United States', *The Journal of International Studies* (Sophia University, Tokyo), January 1991.

81 Ohira, *Brush Strokes*, p. 117.

82 *Ibid*.

83 Priscilla Clapp, 'US Domestic Politics and Relations with Japan', in Clapp and Halperin (eds.), *United States–Japanese Relations: The 1970s*, p. 57.

84 President Carter established close personal ties with Ohira. Carter later acknowledged on Japanese television that the only other foreign leader with whom he had a similar rapport was Anwar Sadat of Egypt. Carter on NHK television, 15 June 1990. Brief attention to US–Japan relations can be found in Gaddis Smith's *Morality, Reason, and Power: American Diplomacy in the Carter Years* (New York, 1986) and in the memoirs of Carter's National Security Adviser Zbigniew Brzezinski's *Power and Principle* (New York, 1985 edn). That both works should have such similar titles may say something about the aspirations of the Carter presidency.

85 Quoted in Gaddis Smith, *Morality, Reason and Power*, p. 108. Smith also notes that Japan's per capita defense budget in 1980 was merely $82 compared to the US per capita equivalent of $550. For additional comment by Brown, see his article 'The United States and Japan: High Tech is Foreign Policy', *SAIS Review* (summer-fall, 1989). Brown argues that the 'challenge to the United States is to join Japan in managing the likely future evolution of Japan in the international system.'

7 Troubles: defence and trade issues today

1 Gerald L. Curtis, preface to *The United States and Japan: Issues for the 1980s* (East Asia Institute, Columbia University, 1980), pp. 5–6.

2 The phrase became the hallmark of Ambassador Mike Mansfield, who used it repeatedly during his long years at the American embassy in Tokyo.

3 See, for example, comments by Michael Armacost, Mansfield's successor, calling for 'a Japanese physical presence in the Gulf' and stressing that growing costs and risks for the United States in the area meant that 'it is only natural that we will continue to look to our friends for additional help – both financial and political'. *Japan Times*, 11 December 1990.

4 Robert S. Ingersoll in *The View from the Embassy* (Japan Society Forum, New York, 1981), p. 3.

5 *Ibid*. Ingersoll had co-chaired a bilateral panel with Ushiba Nobuhiko that had made a host of recommendations for improving trade relations.

6 Mike Mansfield, 'A Shared Destiny', *Journal of Japanese Trade & Industry*, no. 5 (1988). He noted that '[d]espite the overlay of emotionalism that has sometimes marred the relationship, we can proudly point to many concrete examples of bilateral and multilateral cooperation and achievement across a broad range of issues'.

7 Undersecretary of State Lawrence Eagleburger, 10 June 1981, *State Department Bulletin*, August 1981, cited in Fareed Zakaria, 'The Reagan Strategy of Containment', *Political Science Quarterly*, Fall 1990.

8 George W. Ball, 'Reflections on a Heavy Year', *Foreign Affairs*, vol. 59, no. 3 (1981).

9 Andrew Nagorski 'East Asia in 1980', *Foreign Affairs*, vol. 59, no. 3 (1981).

10 *Ibid.*

11 Perhaps a similar point might be made for Reagan's general achievements in foreign policy. His successes in countering the Soviet Union may be too easily ascribed to the internal weaknesses of the USSR, the policies of Gorbachev and the pressure for change from within Eastern Europe. See Zakaria, 'Reagan Strategy', for a discussion on Reagan's record.

12 Congressman Elwood Hillis statement before the Subcommittee on Economic Goals and Intergovernmental Policy of the Joint Economic Committee Congress, 25 October 1983, (Washington, DC, 1984), p. 13. Hillis had introduced the concurrent resolution the previous month that argued for continuing restraint since 'the original expectations for the restraint program did not materialize, causing it to be less effective in increasing United States production and jobs'. The resolution stated that 'auto trade represented $54,000,000,000 or one-third of the total United States bilateral trade deficit with Japan over the past five years'.

13 'Measures Concerning the Export of Passenger Cars to the United States', MITI statement of 1 May 1981, reproduced in Subcommittee hearings, *Subcommittee on Economic Goals*, pp. 40–1. For objections later by Reagan's budget director to this form of disguised protectionism, see David A. Stockman *The Triumph of Politics* (New York, 1987), pp. 168–72.

14 See Martin E. Weinstein, 'Japan's Defense Policy and the May 1981 Summit', *Journal of Northeast Asian Studies*, March 1982, for an extended analysis of Suzuki's behaviour.

15 Joint communiqué, 8 May 1981, excerpts in Defence Agency white paper *Defense of Japan, 1983* (Tokyo, 1983), p. 299.

16 Weinstein, 'Japan's Defense Policy'.

17 Joint communiqué, note 15, p. 300.

18 *Asahi Shimbun*, 24 July 1982, translated in the *Asahi Evening News*, 26 July 1982.

19 *Ibid.* For the text of the Mid-term Defence Program Estimate for FY 1983–87 see *Defense of Japan, 1983*, pp. 286–90.

20 See J. W. M. Chapman, R. Drifte and I. T. M. Gow, *Japan's Quest for Comprehensive Security* (London, 1983). Prime Minister Ohira had begun this new thinking.

21 Nakasone, 27 November 1982, quoted in *Journal of Japanese Trade and Industry*, no. 5 (1988).

22 For a characteristic self-assessment, see Nakasone's remarks in the *Harvard Business Review* (March-April 1989).

23 Hugh Cortazzi, 'A Former British Ambassador Speaks Out', *Japan Quarterly*, April–June 1986. Mr Nakasone's own insistence on employing English impressed his supporters but made life more difficult for the diplomats.

24 Gallup polls conducted between 1972 and 1987 suggest that US perceptions of Japan as a 'threatening' economic power grew during the 1980s. See *Asahi Evening News*, graph, 6 April 1987.

25 Japanese Foreign Ministry spokesman on Mansfield's conversation with Nakasone, *Asahi Evening News*, 26 July 1985, quoted in Buckley, 'Japan–Bashing and Japanese Stonewalling: Japan, the United States and the

Politics of International Trade, January–July 1985', *Bulletin of the Graduate School of International Affairs, International University of Japan*, December 1985.

26 *The Japan Times*, 11 April 1985, reprinted from the *Los Angeles Times*.

27 George Shultz, *Six Steps to Prosperity* (Tokyo, 1985). He suggested that 'the more meaningful measure of Japan's external balance is not our bilateral imbalance but Japan's overall trade surplus, estimated at 44,000 million dollars in 1984'.

28 *Ibid.*

29 *Ibid.* For the details of Nakasone's programme and the disappointing reaction of the Japanese public to his campaign to buy foreign goods, see Buckley, 'Japan–Bashing and Japanese Stonewalling'.

30 Harada Akira during panel discussion on 'What is "Fair Trade"?' in December 1985, International University of Japan seminar proceedings, published in *Constructing a New Japan–US Relationship* (Niigata, 1986).

31 *Ibid.*

32 Miyazawa referred to his visit to Washington with Prime Minister Ikeda in 1961 where President Kennedy agreed to support Japan's application to full OECD membership in return for trade liberalization measures. *ibid.*

33 *Ibid*, recalling the months before Pearl Harbor he hoped that Japan and the US could this time 'evade such a collision course'. The analogy with 1941 was a popular one in 1985.

34 Leslie Fielding, 4 June 1985, in *EC Flash*, June 1985, EC Delegation, Tokyo.

35 *Ibid.*

36 The length, however, of Nakasone's reign stands in contrast to the short periods in office of all his main rivals: Tanaka, Miki, Fukuda, Ohira and Suzuki. Nathaniel Thayer accurately predicted Nakasone's long tenure in late 1982.

37 On Nakasone's general performance, see William Horsley and Roger Buckley, *Nippon, New Superpower: Japan since 1945* (London, 1990), pp. 171–201. See also S. Javed Maswood, *Japanese Defence* (Singapore, 1990).

38 Nakasone interview, *Harvard Business Review*, March–April 1989, p. 85.

39 *Ibid.*

40 See, however, commentary that under 'Prime Minister Nakasone Japan has begun to play a more energetic role in respect of security, foreign policy and foreign aid' in International Institute for Strategic Studies, *Strategic Survey 1986–1987* (London, 1987), p. 160.

41 Statement by Chief Cabinet Secretary Gotoda, 30 December 1986.

42 The report turgidly advocated the expansion of 'domestic demand effectively so as to produce multiplier effects on economic growth and stimulate individual consumption, with a view toward restructuring the export-dependent economy of Japan into a more vigorous economy led by domestic demand.'

43 For changes in the composition of Japan's imports within the Japanese economy, see *The Japan Foundation Newsletter*, vol. 17, nos. 5–6, p. 7. Nakasone's alternative method of explaining Japan's predicament was to suggest that his nation was in a similar position to the mahjong player who kept on winning and by doing so ran the risk of destroying the game.

44 Prime ministerial speech at the opening of 103rd session of the Diet, *Japan Times*, 16 October 1985.

45 For discussion of the American view of Japan's economic behaviour in the decade, see Edward J. Lincoln, *Japan's Unequal Trade* (Washington, DC, 1990).

46 Ezra Vogel, 'New Attitudes for a New Era', in *US–Japan Relations: New Attitudes for a New Era* (Cambridge, MA, 1985).

47 Controversy surrounded Nakasone's statements on defence in January 1983 when his translator spoke loosely of the premier's purported wish to see Japan as once more an 'unsinkable aircraft carrier' and his careless talk of the problems that faced American society through its multiracial character.

48 An early example of what became a deluge of anti-Japanism was Marvin J. Wolf's *The Japanese Conspiracy* (London, 1983). It was subtitled *The Plot to Dominate Industry Worldwide – and How to Deal with It*.

49 Cited in Peter Hannaford, 'Why the Japanese Listen to Reagan', *The Washington Times*, 31 October 1989. Hannaford, a former Reagan aide, suggested that Reagan's visit to Japan in April 1978 was crucial in influencing the future direction of his thinking on Japan.

50 On the record of the Reagan administration, see Lincoln, *Japan's Unequal Trade*, chapter 6. The MOSS talks concerned access for the four categories of telecommunications, electronics, pharmaceuticals and forestry. The question of automobile parts was later added to the discussions.

51 Bush statement reported in *Asahi Evening News*, 29 June 1990.

52 Commentary on SII, *ibid*.

53 Opening statement by the Japan–US Working Group on SII cited in *Japan Times*, 30 June 1990. Among the specific measures to be taken by the Japanese government were a reduction in the current account surplus by encouraging imports, the promotion of social overhead capital, higher penalties for bid-rigging, and the arming of the Fair Trade Commission with formal powers.

54 Government statement read by Chief Cabinet Secretary Sakamoto Misoji, *Asahi Evening News*, 29 June 1990.

55 *Ibid*. Consumer groups had little clout in contemporary Japan.

56 As one anonymous senior official of the Ministry of Foreign Affairs' North American bureau remarked: 'Washington must have regarded the Gulf crisis as a test case of this new partnership and is apparently dissatisfied that Japan has not tried to play the role of a global partner.' Quoted in *Japan Times*, 3 January 1991.

57 Kaifu statement at the opening of the 119th session of the Diet, *Japan Times*, 13 October 1990.

58 Newspaper editorials and public opinion polls indicated that there was little enthusiasm for risking Japanese lives in a region where Japan had long claimed to be no more than an observer. The importance of the Gulf region as a supplier of oil to Japan would suggest that this argument had severe limitations; some American politicians certainly held that Japan's refusal to take an active role could lead to American troops fighting to protect Japan's energy resources.

59 Ozawa statement at LDP seminar quoted in *Japan Times*, 9 November 1990.

60 Both legal advisors to the Foreign Ministry and the cabinet's Legislation Bureau appeared to doubt that the premier was correct. See comment in *Mainichi Daily News*, 20 October 1990.

61 Japan had reserve oil stocks equivalent to 142 days of consumption as of 30 November 1990. Crude oil imports from the middle east represented 73.6 per cent of Japan's total crude imports in the same month. Statistics in *Asahi Evening News*, 15 January 1991.

62 Prime Minister Kaifu's speech to the opening of the 119th extraordinary session of the Diet, 12 October 1990.

63 If SDF forces had been sent to the Gulf (in any capacity) the SDF law would have had to have been revised to permit peace-keeping activities abroad. The government's plan of gaining a UN Peace Cooperation Law, employing SDF members in non-combatant roles under the prime minister's supervision, was withdrawn after clear evidence that the nation was highly sceptical of any such deployment.

64 The calculations behind the naming of the proposed bill were pointed out by Ms Sheila Smith in her address at International House of Japan, 17 January 1991. For a critical assessment see Odawara Atsushi 'The Kaifu Bungle', *The Japan Quarterly* (January–March 1991).

65 The *Asahi Shimbun* termed the programme a 'Flawed Defense Plan'. Editorial of 21 December 1990, translated in *Asahi Evening News* of the same day. Intransigence by the Soviet Union over the northern territories undoubtedly left the Japanese unconvinced that the Asian region was about to enter a post-Cold War phase. President Gorbachev was scheduled to visit Tokyo in April 1991 to discuss a range of issues, but Japanese public opinion was skeptical of the prospects for substantial improvement in Soviet–Japanese relations.

66 Foreign Aid (termed Overseas Development Assistance by Japan) has been one means of easing Japan back into the international arena. It has been the subject of considerable research. See, for example, Alan Rix, *Japan's Economic Aid: Policy-Making and Politics* (New York, 1980), and Robert M. Orr, Jr., *The Emergence of Japan's Foreign Aid Power* (New York, 1990).

8 Future: relations to the twenty-first century

1 Dulles' address before the Governors' Conference, Gatlinburg, Tènn., 1 October 1951, Box 53, Dulles correspondence, Princeton.

2 Ian Nish employs the phrase when defining the Anglo-Japanese alliance. No study has yet appeared that examines the importance of the US embassy in handling American–Japanese ties.

3 Only 150 letters reached the White House. See Eisenhower, Int. Series, Box 32, Japan Far East Trip cancelled (2) (folder 3), Eisenhower Library.

4 MacArthur to Eisenhower after cancellation announced, *ibid*. The president's message was a sensitive, one-sentence cable: 'I think I have some faint understanding of what you have just been through.'

5 Ridgway to JCS, 14 September 1951, FW611.94/9–2951, State Dept. paper, National Archives.

6 Sebald to State Dept., 29 September 1951, 611.94/9–2951 on the 'ugly questions' concerning US–Japan relations in the 'critical years which lie ahead'. Sebald wanted to prohibit dependents in order to prevent 'vestiges of "colonialism"'.

7 Dulles memorandum to Secretary of State on his conversation with Truman, 3 October 1951, 611.94/10–351.

8 See, for example, the cover of *Time* magazine for 13 April 1987, where Uncle Sam is rolling up his sleeves to do battle with a crouching sumo wrestler to the accompaniment of the headline 'Trade Wars: The US Gets Tough with Japan'.

9 Ambassador Mansfield's remarks as reported in *Asahi Evening News*, 6 April 1988.

10 *The United States and Japan in 1988: A Time of Transition*, SAIS (Washington, DC, 1988), pp. 78–9.

11 Mike Mansfield's acceptance speech for 1990 Sylvanus Thayer award, *Pointer View*, 5 October 1990.

12 *Ibid*. Mansfield, in looking to the future, claimed that 'we Americans must recognize that we are not a "European" country, or "North American" or a "Pacific" country. Our interests lie everywhere.' Secretary Forrestal made the same point in defining the mission of the US Navy in the immediate postwar period.

13 Yoko Sazanami, 'Perspectives on the Declining Current Account Surplus', *Japan Review of International Affairs* (Fall/Winter 1990), p. 166. The trade surplus dropped again in 1990 to $52.4 billion according to Japanese sources and the trade imbalance with the United States was reduced to $38.03 billion. However, US officials in Tokyo for trade talks called the gap 'staggeringly large' and felt that future improvements were unlikely. See *Asahi Evening News*, 23 January 1991.

14 Assistant Secretary Charles Dallara of the US Treasury, quoted by Reuters, in *Asahi Evening News*, 14 January 1991. Dallara warned that 'time is not on their side' and that 'fundamental and systematic change in the Japanese economy' was still the American goal.

15 Peter Peterson, 'Towards a "Win-Win" Solution to Trans-Pacific Capital Flows', Tokyo, 8 November 1989.

16 *Ibid*. Peterson offered as some consolation the fact that the two Pacific powers are 'today linked by closer ties and a deeper infrastructure of economic and human relationships than any time in our histories'.

17 Lee Iacocca, quoted in *The Economist*, 19 January 1991.

18 Correspondence from Chiba Kazuo, *The Economist*, 2 February 1991.

19 The argument features in much of the literature on postwar policy affairs. See, for example, Chikara Higashi, *Japanese Trade Policy Formulation* (New York, 1983). Higashi's book contains forewords from both Nakasone, then premier, and Watanabe Michio, former minister of finance.

20 Headline to article by columnist Richard Reeves, *Philadelphia Inquirer*, 10 August 1989.

21 Ambassador Armacost also commented unfavourably on the revisionists. For one of a number of critiques of the so-called revisionist 'school', see George Packard, 'Name-calling Could Lead to Worse', *Japan Times*, 13

October 1989, reprinted from *The Washington Post*. The names of Chalmers Johnson, Clyde Prestowitz, James Fallows and Karel van Wolferen are frequently cited as being revisionist, though they have little in common.

22 See, for example, the New York Times/CBS News poll, reprinted in *Asahi Evening News*, 7 February 1990. Commenting on the less friendly American perception of Japan, Professor Gerald Curtis noted 'a real erosion in the popular mood about Japan'. Some Japanese polls were also disturbing.

23 Foreign Ministry spokesman Watanabe Taizo quoted in *Japan Times*, 5 October 1989.

24 *Japan Times*, 19 October 1989. Western journalists wondered aloud whether the Ministry of Finance had coordinated a national strategy through suggesting the Japanese institutions take note of their government's concepts.

25 See Ian H. Nish, *The Anglo–Japanese Alliance* (London, 1966), and *Alliance in Decline* (London, 1972).

26 One recent example is Reuters report on a new, annual exchange of views between the EC and Japan inaugurated only in 1987. It noted that 'no American was present yet the shadow of the United States stalked the conference tables'. See Eric Hall (Reuters), 'EC–Japan Relationship: Tokyo–Washington Bonds Hard to Crack', *Asahi Evening News*, 17 September 1987.

27 Introduction by Ronald Morse to Morse (ed.), *US–Japan Relations: An Agenda for the Future* (Lanham, MD, 1989), p. xii.

28 Background briefing by William P. Bundy, assistant secretary of State for east Asian affairs, 15 November 1967, PM Sato of Japan's visit, LBJ Appointments File (Diary Backup), Box 82, LBJ Library.

29 Rusk memorandum for the president, forwarded by Rostow, 13 November 1967, *ibid*.

30 Rusk, *ibid*.

31 *Defense of Japan, 1983* (Tokyo, 1983), p. 81. Translation from the Japanese Defence Agency's white paper for 1983.

32 *Bilingual Summary of Defense of Japan* (Tokyo, 1988), p. 11.

33 The outcome of US–Filipino base negotiations is not yet known but some Japanese bureaucrats have mentioned privately that their government might consider paying some of the costs involved in maintaining an American presence in the Philippines.

34 Ian Nish, 'The Reemergence of Japan', in F. S. Northedge (ed.), *The Foreign Policies of the Powers* (London, 1974), p. 317.

35 Kuriyama Takakazu, 'New Directions for Japanese Foreign Policy in the Changing World of the 1990s', Tokyo, 1990. Kuriyama was vice-minister of foreign affairs. He doubted if the public had yet appreciated that the changed circumstances of affluence required a greater contribution to global affairs by his country.

36 Kaifu text in *Japan Times*, 23 January 1991. The government announcement that it would contribute 9 billion dollars to the coalition's funds was made at this time.

37 See Urban Lehner, *International Herald Tribune*, 17 January 1991.

38 *The Washington Post*, 27 March 1990. His remarks were disowned by the Pentagon but the damage had been done. One unnamed Japanese SDF general was quoted as saying 'Oh I see, US forces in Japan will resume their original role of the occupation forces of 45 years ago'. *Aera* magazine, reprinted in translation, *Asahi Evening News*, 20 May 1990.

39 During the entire length of the occupation proper, perhaps one million Americans were in Japan. What influence, if any, returning US personnel have had on US policies towards Japan is unclear.

40 The Japanese government has budgeted Yen168 billion ($1.1 billion) for fiscal 1991 in the latest of an annual appropriation that began in 1987.

41 Stephen Bosworth, 'US Is Asia's Security Blanket', *Asian Wall Street Journal*, 25 September 1989.

42 *Ibid*. Bosworth notes that as Asia becomes more democratic the tasks in the near-term of American diplomacy become harder. He insists that the United States alone, however, can assume responsibility for regional leadership, for organizing a regional consensus on key issues such as trade and security'.

43 For Mr Kaifu's thinkings on the prospects for Pacific Rim cooperation, see *Daily Yomiuri*, 20 May 1990. Suspicions of a joint US–Japanese dominance of the region are certain to delay action between ASEAN states and the advanced industrialized powers of the Pacific Basin.

44 Kuriyama, 'New Directions'.

45 Possible changes are discussed in Takashi Inoguchi's 'Four Japanese Scenarios for the Future', *International Affairs* (winter 1988/89). See also Donald Hellmann's contribution in John H. Makin and Donald C. Hellman (eds.), *Sharing World Leadership? A New Era for America and Japan* (Washington DC, 1989). Note too the caution of Kenneth B. Pyle's 'Japan, the World and the Twenty-First Century', in Takashi Inoguchi and Daniel I. Okimoto (eds.), *The Political Economy of Japan*, vol. 2. (Stanford, 1988).

46 Of course this works both ways. Best-sellers in Japan, whether Ishihara Shintaro's work (*The Japan That Can Say No* (New York, 1991)) or the translation of Paul Kennedy's *The Rise and Fall of the Great Power* (New York, 1989), should be balanced by the surge of criticism in the United States of Japan. For example, Bill Emmott's predictions on Japan's economic decline are eagerly sought after in the West.

47 Ellen L. Frost, *For Richer, For Poorer* (Tokyo, 1988), p. 163.

48 Perhaps the early 1970s provides as good a marker as any of the shift in Japanese foreign policy. In this I am echoing the views of Professor Sato Hideo among others. For discussion of later examples of Japanese initiative, see Ronald A. Morse, 'Japan's Search for an Independent Foreign Policy: An American Perspective', *Journal of Northeast Asian Studies*, summer 1984 and Michael Yoshitsu, *Caught in the Middle East: Japan's Diplomacy in Transition* (Lexington, MA, 1984).

49 For an analysis of Japan's predicament, see 'Asia's Emerging Standard-Bearer' in *The Economist*, 21 July 1990.

50 Henry Kissinger and Cyrus Vance, 'Bipartisan Objectives for American Foreign Policy', *Foreign Affairs*, (summer, 1988). The authors called for 'a

national strategy' and for 'the dialogue with Japan [to] be lifted to a more comprehensive level.'

51 Nomura Research Institute, *Nomura Medium-Term Economic Outlook For Japan and the World (1989)* (Tokyo, 1989). Purchasing power parity comparisons reduce the relative strengths of the Japanese economy.

52 South-east Asian states, led by Singapore, appear now to be encouraging some cautious moves towards a Japanese security presence in the region under United Nations' auspices. See *The International Herald Tribune*, 8 March 1991.

53 Lee Kuan Yew, 20 May 1990, Plenary Session, (satellite session), Pacific Basin Economic Council General Meeting, Tokyo.

54 *Ibid.* On Lee Kuan Yew's anxieties over the possible disruption of the US–Japan alliance and the subsequence 'expansion of Japanese power' in Asia, see *The International Herald Tribune*, 28 May 1990.

55 Those who complain that the United States and the EC risk making too many policy suggestions to Japan have a strong case. The temptation might be better resisted and more attention paid to the faults of Western societies. Harold Brown's plea that 'the United States needs a consistent overall policy covering its military, political, and economic relations with Japan' is eminently sensible, though organizing this would be difficult given the fragmentation of power within the American system of government and the differing priorities of the private sector. At the very least, regular meetings of heads of government need to be instituted and deserve to alternate between Washington and Tokyo, if the United States wishes to demonstrate that a new era is at hand.

56 There remains a danger of critics ignoring the financial role already being undertaken by Japan. The IMF noted in the spring of 1990, following Japan's rise to second-equal status on the IMF board, that 'it might not be desirable for Japan to eliminate its external surplus over the next few years, especially through actions that would reduce national saving.' With the vast reconstruction programmes being prepared for the Gulf region, in addition to the problems of Eastern Europe and south-east Asia, the financial power of Japan hardly needs being underlined. The likely increase in the United States' financial liabilities during the 1990s further strengthens the world's reliance on Japan as the major global creditor nation.

57 *Public Opinion Survey on Diplomacy*, Prime Minister's Office (Tokyo, April 1989).

58 See Steve Weisman in *The New York Times*, reprinted in *Asahi Evening News*, 9 March 1991. Some of these doubts have been reinforced by the reception of Pat Choate's book *Agents of Influence*, in which he suggests that lobbyists have had access to American officials in order to develop substantial 'Japanese penetration of the American political system.'

59 For surveys, see Marius Jansen, 'Japanese Studies in the United States', *The Japan Foundation Newsletter*, October, 1988, and Grant Goodman, 'The Development of Asian Studies in the United States: A Perspective of Four Generations and Four Decades', *Asian Studies Programs for Japanese Universities*, vol. 1 (Sophia University Tokyo, 1990).

60 Edward Seidensticker, 'Japanese Literature in the United States' in *The Voice of the Writer 1984* (47th PEN Congress, Tokyo, 1986), p. 178.

SELECTED BIBLIOGRAPHY

The following books should prove useful for those wishing to learn a little more on postwar US–Japan relations. More extensive bibliographies can be found, for example, in William R. Nester's *The Foundation of Japanese Power: Continuities, Changes, Challenges* (Basingstoke, 1990) and by combing the notes of Takashi Inoguchi and Daniel I. Okimoto's edited work, *The Political Economy of Japan: Volume 2, The Changing International Context*, (Stanford, 1988).

Most of the following basic texts are available in paperback and provide their own clues as to additional reading. The only Japanese works listed here are those that have been translated into English. For a comprehensive listing of both English and Japanese materials (books, journals, reference sources, and databases) see The International House of Japan Library's *A Guide to Reference Books for Japanese Studies* (Tokyo, 1989).

Auer, James E., *The Postwar Rearmament of Japanese Maritime Forces, 1945–1971* (New York, 1973).

Beasley, W. S., *The Rise of Modern Japan* (Tokyo, 1990).

Bergsten, C. Fred and Cline, William R., *The United States–Japan Economic Problem* (Washington, DC, 1985).

Buckley, Roger, *Occupation Diplomacy: Britain, the United States and Japan, 1945–1952* (Cambridge, 1982).

Burkman, Thomas W. (ed.), *The Occupation of Japan: The International Context* (Norfolk, VA, 1984).

Butow, Robert J. C., *Japan's Decision to Surrender* (Stanford, 1954).

Castle, Emery N. and Kenzo Hemmi (eds.), *US-Japanese Agricultural Trade Relations* (Washington, DC, 1982).

Chapman, J. W. M., Drifte, R. and Gow, I. T. M., *Japan's Quest for Comprehensive Security* (London, 1983).

Cohen, Stephen D., *Uneasy Partnership: Competition and Conflict in US–Japanese Trade Relations* (Cambridge, MA, 1985).

Collins, John M., *US–Soviet Military Balance 1980–1985* (Washington, DC, 1985).

Destler, I. M. *et al.*, *Managing an Alliance: The Politics of US–Japanese Relations* (Washington, DC, 1976).

Destler, I. M. Fukui Haruhiro and Sato Hideo, *The Textile Wrangle* (Ithaca, 1979).

Dower, John C., *Empire and Aftermath: Yoshida Shigeru and the Japanese Experience, 1878–1954* (Cambridge, MA, 1979).

Dunn, F. S., *Peace-making and the Settlement with Japan* (Princeton, 1963).

Foreign Relations of the United States, series on Japan and east Asia (Washington, DC, ongoing).

Frost, Ellen L., *For Richer, For Poorer: The New US–Japan Relationship* (Tokyo, 1988).

Gilpin, Robert, *The Political Economy of International Relations* (Princeton, 1987).

Havens, Thomas, R. H., *Fire across the Sea: The Vietnam War and Japan, 1965–1975* (Princeton, NJ, 1987).

Hellmann, Donald C., *Japan and East Asia: The New International Order* (London, 1972).

Higashi Chikara, *Japanese Trade Policy Formulation* (New York, 1983).

Holland, Harrison M., *Managing Diplomacy: The United States and Japan* (Stanford, 1984).

Horsley, William and Buckley, Roger, *Nippon, New Superpower: Japan since 1945* (London, 1990).

Inoguchi Takashi and Okimoto, Daniel I., *The Political Economy of Japan: Volume 2, The Changing International Context* (Stanford, 1988).

James, D. Clayton, *The Years of MacArthur: Triumph and Disaster, 1945–1964* (Boston, 1985).

Japan, Defence Agency, *Defence of Japan*, annual publication (Tokyo, ongoing).

Japan, Ministry of Foreign Affairs, annual, *Diplomatic Bluebook* (Tokyo, ongoing).

Japan, Ministry of International Trade and Industry, *White Paper on International Trade* (Tokyo, ongoing).

Johnson, Chalmers, *MITI and the Japanese Miracle* (Stanford, 1982).

Kissinger, Henry, *White House Years*, (Boston, 1979).

Kosaka Masataka, *A History of Postwar Japan* (Tokyo, 1972).

Kodansha Encyclopedia of Japan (9 vols, Tokyo, 1983; supplement, 1986, Tokyo).

Lacey, Michael J. (ed.), *The Truman Presidency* (Cambridge, 1989).

Langdon, F. C., *Japan's Foreign Policy* (Vancouver, 1973).

Lee, Chae-Jin, *Japan faces China* (Baltimore, 1976).

Lincoln, Edward J., *Japan: Facing Economic Maturity* (Washington, DC, 1988).

Lincoln, Edward J., *Japan's Unequal Trade* (Washington, DC, 1990).

Livinston, Jon, Moore, Joe and Oldfather, Felicia, *The Japan Reader: vol. 2: Postwar Japan* (Harmondsworth, 1976).

Maekawa Haruo *et al.*, *The Report of the Advisory Group on Economic Structural Adjustment for International Harmony* (Tokyo, 1986).

Makin, John H. and Hellmann, Donald C. (eds.), *Sharing World Leadership?: A New Era for America & Japan* (Washington DC, 1989).

Mendl, Wolf, *Issues in Japan's China Policy* (London, 1978).

Ohkawa Kazushi and Rosovsky, Henry, *Japanese Economic Growth* (Stanford, 1973).

Packard, George R., *Protest in Tokyo* (Princeton, NJ, 1966).

Patrick, Hugh and Rosovky, Henry (eds.), *Asia's New Giant* (Washington, DC, 1976).

Prestowitz, Clyde, *Trading Places* (New York, 1988).

Pruessen, Ronald W., *John Foster Dulles: The Road to Power* (New York, 1982).

Reischauer, Edwin O., *My Life between Japan and America* (Tokyo, 1986).

Scalapino, Robert A. (ed.), *The Foreign Policy of Modern Japan* (Berkeley, 1977).

Stockwin, J. A. A., *The Japanese Socialist Party and Neutralism* (Melbourne, 1968).

Swearingen, Roger, *The Soviet Union and Postwar Japan* (Stanford, 1978).

Tsurutani Taketsugu, *Japanese Policy and East Asian Security* (New York, 1981).

United States Embassy, Tokyo, *Daily Summary of Japanese Press* (ongoing).

Weinstein, Martin E., *Japan's Postwar Defense Policy, 1947–1968* (New York, 1971).

Welfield, John, *An Empire in Eclipse* (London, 1988).

Wolferen, Karel van, *The Enigma of Japanese Power* (London, 1989).

Yamamura Kozo and Yasuba Yasukichi, *The Political Economy of Japan: Volume 1, The Domestic Transformation* (Stanford, 1987).

Yoshida Shigeru, *The Yoshida Memoirs* (London, 1961).

Yoshitsu Michael, *Japan and the San Francisco Peace Settlement* (New York, 1982).

Zengage, Thomas R. and C. Tait Ratcliffe, *The Japanese Century* (Hong Kong, 1988).

INDEX